Funn
Abou

Funny Thing About Murder

Modes of Humor in Crime Fiction and Films

DAVID GEHERIN

McFarland & Company, Inc., Publishers

Jefferson, North Carolina

LIBRARY OF CONGRESS CATALOGUING-IN-PUBLICATION DATA

Names: Geherin, David, 1943– author.
Title: Funny thing about murder : modes of humor in crime fiction
  and films / David Geherin.
Description: Jefferson, North Carolina : McFarland & Company, Inc.,
  Publishers, 2017 | Includes bibliographical references and index.
Identifiers: LCCN 2017036638 | ISBN 9781476669113
  (softcover : acid free paper) ∞
Subjects: LCSH: Detective and mystery stories, American—History
  and criticism. | Wit and humor in motion pictures. | Humor in
  literature. | Detective and mystery films—History and criticism. |
  American fiction—20th century—History and criticism.
Classification: LCC PS374.D4 G393 2017 | DDC 809.3/87209358—dc23
LC record available at https://lccn.loc.gov/2017036638

BRITISH LIBRARY CATALOGUING DATA ARE AVAILABLE

ISBN 978-1-4766-6911-3 (print)
ISBN 978-1-4766-2978-0 (ebook)

On the cover: Paul Newman as Henry Gondorff aka Shaw in
The Sting, 1973 (Universal Pictures/Photofest); typewriter © 2017 iStock

Printed in the United States of America

McFarland & Company, Inc., Publishers
  Box 611, Jefferson, North Carolina 28640
  www.mcfarlandpub.com

For Diane

Table of Contents

Preface

You could say I began writing this book in 1980. That was the year I published an essay in *The Armchair Detective* entitled, "Comic Capers and Comic Eyes: Humor and Contemporary Mystery Fiction." Since then I have written seven books on various aspects of crime and mystery fiction, none specifically focused on the subject of humor. However, many of the authors I have written about did employ humor in their work, which I touched on but did not explore in any great detail. Writing this book has given me the opportunity to take a more systematic, in-depth look at the subject of humor in crime fiction and to expand its scope to include comic crime films as well.

This book is not an all-inclusive catalog of every humorous crime novel or film. It is intended to be an introduction to the subject that focuses on those writers and filmmakers most effective at combining crime and comedy. The examples range from artists who are primarily humorists to those whose aim is to produce serious works yet know how useful humor can be in achieving their ends. If I've failed to include one of your favorites, I hope this book might introduce you to some unfamiliar writers and films that you can add to a list of new favorites.

In the chapters that follow I will describe how each author and filmmaker uses humor, identify comic influences on their style, and assess the function it serves in their works. The best way of illustrating humor, however, is through example, and I will allow that humor to speak for itself by providing a generous sampling from each film and each author's body of work.

Admittedly, many readers of mystery novels are purists who, like some fans of magic, don't necessarily want to be distracted by humor. But just as there are those who enjoy the way Penn and Teller artfully combine

1

magic and humor, many fans of crime novels and movies welcome a laugh or two. My hope is that every reader of this book will find something that will make them laugh (or at least smile a little).

A brief note about organization: authors in the section on crime fiction are discussed in chronological order, based upon the date of publication of their initial comic crime novel. The comic crime films are divided into four separate categories, each one arranged in chronological order.

Introduction

Crime certainly isn't funny, but crime fiction and films often are. As Raymond Chandler once observed, "It is not funny that a man should be killed, but it is sometimes funny that he should be killed for so little" (*Simple* 20). Humor in a crime novel or movie can add a new element without necessarily diminishing the seriousness of the work. Shakespeare fully understood the value of giving his audience some comic relief even in his darkest tragedies; for example, he pauses amidst the bloody violence in *Macbeth* to insert a humorous scene with a drunken porter that offers the audience a welcome emotional break from the intensity of the previous action.

The comic and the serious are not necessarily mutually exclusive. Humor can be a very effective way of addressing a serious subject, as for example Richard Pryor's classic standup comedy routine about nearly dying after setting himself on fire while freebasing cocaine. The Netflix series *Orange Is the New Black*, which is set in a woman's prison, was nominated for a Golden Globe Award as Outstanding Comedy Series in 2014; the following year it was nominated as Outstanding Drama Series. Which is it, a comedy or a serious drama? The answer is both.

Edgar Allan Poe not only invented the detective story, he was one of the first to use humor for effect in a murder tale. His 1846 story "The Cask of Amontillado" is narrated by a man named Montresor who carefully plans and carries out the cold-blooded murder of a rival ironically named Fortunato. He tricks Fortunato into joining him in the catacombs beneath his palazzo where he intends to wall him up alive in a niche in the stone wall. Along the way, Montresor can't help joking at his victim's expense. He joins Fortunato in a toast to long life, knowing just how short the man's life will actually be. He also responds to Fortunato's question

3

about whether he's a member of the society of Masons by jokingly producing a trowel he has hidden in his clothes which he will shortly use to entomb him. The dark humor only intensifies the chilling nature of the story.

What makes us laugh? Some theorists on humor make a distinction between laughter and amusement. Laughter is a physical response, what Jonathan Miller describes as a "respiratory convulsion" (Durant 6) like sneezing which can be triggered by something that isn't at all funny (e.g., by tickling). One of the most dramatic incidents of this phenomenon occurred in Tanganyika (now Tanzania) Africa in 1962 when three girls at a mission boarding school in Kangera began laughing. The giggling spread so quickly and lasted so long that the school had to be shut down. Over the next several months, the giggling spread to fourteen more schools in the country and eventually involved a thousand people before subsiding. The laughter wasn't triggered by anything funny but by mass hysteria likely brought on by stress. Amusement, on the other hand, is more a state of mind, and laughter can be seen as its byproduct.

General Observations on Laughter and Humor

Laughter can take many forms, ranging from a spontaneous belly laugh at something silly to a knowing smile at a witty remark to an apologetic gasp at something that isn't supposed to be funny, but is: e.g., a body being stuffed into a wood chipper with only a foot in a bloody sock still visible in the film *Fargo.*

Humor is subjective. Not everyone finds *The Three Stooges* a laugh riot. Imagine a group of people listening to a joke. The response to the punch line might range from a blank stare to a smile, from a giggle to a guffaw. The joke is the same, but not everyone shares the same sense of humor. And yet almost everyone finds something funny.

It's important to note here that actions or words are in themselves not funny. As Henri Bergson noted, "events must at some point intersect with human consciousness to become comic" (Stott 8). Like the tree that falls in a forest but makes no sound unless a listener is present, comedy requires a receiver in order to produce a laugh. A funny movie or a standup routine without an audience or a book without a reader cannot produce laughter. Humor requires an audience that is at least minimally receptive to it.

One doesn't have to laugh out loud to find something funny, just as one doesn't have to shed tears to find something tragic. A person sitting in a theater viewing a comic movie may easily find him or herself laughing out loud along with everyone else. That same person sitting alone in a chair reading a comic novel may remain silent, even though he or she may be fully enjoying the humor internally.

Humor is remarkably flexible; it all depends on how it is used and the purpose it is designed to serve. As Noel Carroll observed in his valuable book on the subject, "Intrinsically humor is neither virtuous nor vicious, neither liberating nor oppressive, neither rigid nor flexible." He goes on to say that humor "can serve any cause—good or evil, constructive or destructive, conservative or radical" (156). Humor can be loving, as in affectionate banter between couples, or hateful, as in racist jokes. It can divide us or remind us that although the human condition may be absurd, we're all in the same boat.

Why We Laugh

At the outset it is important to note that this book doesn't aim to propose any theory of comedy. Doing such a thing isn't an easy task; as E. B. White once famously warned, "Humor can be dissected, as a frog can, but the thing dies in the process" (xvii). "Trying to define humor," cartoonist Saul Steinberg added, "is one of the definitions of humor" (191). How can one propose an all-inclusive theory that attempts to explain how laughter can be produced both by something fully expected (e.g., Lucy pulling the football away when Charlie Brown attempts to kick it after she has once again assured him she won't) and something completely unexpected (e.g., the punch line to most jokes)? Nevertheless, beginning as far back as Plato and Aristotle, philosophers, psychologists, anthropologists, sociologists and literary theorists, among them such influential thinkers as Arthur Schopenhauer, Henri Bergson, Sigmund Freud, and Arthur Koestler, have bravely attempted to formulate a theory that explains why we laugh.

These theories can be boiled down to three main ones:

(1) *The Superiority Theory.* We laugh when we feel superior to others. Proponents of this theory include Plato, Aristotle, and Thomas Hobbes, who in 1651 put it this way: "Laughter is nothing else but sudden glory arising from some sudden conception of some eminency in ourselves, by comparison with the infirmity of others" (Morreall *Philosophy* 20).

(2) *The Relief Theory.* Proponents of this theory, notably Herbert Spencer and Sigmund Freud, argue that laughter serves as a social or psychological release of emotional energy; in other words, jokes are a kind of safety valve that allows one to address feelings about taboo issues that would otherwise have to be suppressed.

(3) *The Incongruity Theory.* This theory, first proposed by Francis Hutcheson in *Thoughts on Laughter* (1725) and later expanded by Arthur Schopenhauer, is the one most widely accepted today. Its main point is that the key to comic amusement, in the words of Noel Carroll, "is a deviation from some presupposed norm—that is to say, an anomaly or an incongruity relative to some framework governing the ways in which we think the world is or should be. Sometimes this idea is stated in terms of a subversion of expectation" (17). John Morreall, author of several essential contemporary books on humor, cites the simple example of a bowling ball in a refrigerator. There's nothing funny about either of them separately, but brought together in a surprising and unexpected way is likely to produce a smile.

We know that everyone laughs; it is a cultural universal. But what purpose does laughter serve? Peter L. Berger argues that simple everyday humor offers "a brief, refreshing vacation from the seriousness of existence" (136) that makes it "easier to get though the day and to manage the minor irritations" (100). Paul Lewis contends that humor serves purposes "that reflect the diversity of human experience: the humor of the classroom and the comedy club, the locker room and the bedroom, the cancer ward and the haunted house" (156). Noted British actor, director, humanist and physician Jonathan Miller suggested that laughter can benefit our mental health:

> It has something to do with the exercise of some sort of perception which enables us to see things for the first time, to reconsider our categories and therefore to be a little bit more flexible and versatile when we come to dealing with the world in future.... The more we laugh the more we see the point of things, the better we are, the cleverer we are at considering what the world is like. [We use] the experience of humour as sabbatical leave from the binding categories that we use as rules of thumb to allow us to conduct our way around the world. This is why humour plays such an important part in our social arrangements [Palmer 57–58].

It may even help maintain our physical health. Laughter, as the old saying goes, is the best medicine. Norman Cousins, longtime editor of the *Saturday Review,* claimed in his bestselling book, *Anatomy of an Illness as Perceived by the Patient* (1979), that watching (and laughing at) a steady diet of Marx Brothers films helped cure a debilitating case of ankylosing spondylitis he suffered from.

Laughter can be a coping mechanism that helps us face our problems. "With a sense of humor," John Morreall argues, "we ride out the storm, not by deceiving ourselves that everything is going great, but by keeping our cool and our sense of perspective" (*Humor* 32). On the other hand, a person without a sense of humor, as Henry Ward Beecher once wrote, "is like a wagon without springs. It's jolted by every pebble on the road" (Weems 81). Amos Walker, Loren D. Estleman's hard-boiled private eye, states it much more bluntly: "Sometimes a sense of humor is what's left after everything else is gone.... Sometimes it's the only thing keeping you from spraying your brains all over the ceiling" *(Midnight* 224).

The focus in this book will mainly be on comedy in practice: i.e., How writers, using only language, and filmmakers, using both language and visual action, make us laugh. And why they do it. Humor is not an essential component of a crime or mystery novel or film. The reasons for using it vary: some authors use humor sparingly for a limited purpose (like Shakespeare's use of comic relief); others have such a natural comic sensibility that it is simply the way they view the world.

The mere presence of humor in a work that isn't intended primarily as a comedy can enhance its appeal to an audience. Brad Parks, author of a series of humorous novels about investigative reporter Carter Ross, puts it this way:

> To me, a book should be like a good friend. I don't want a book that's brooding and serious all the time anymore than I'd want a friend who is that way. I appreciate friends who can be serious and silly, who can make me think and make me laugh, who can tell a good story and tell a good joke. Above all, I like books (and friends) who are fun. So I guess I try to be mindful of that when I'm writing. There's a balance, of course. I guess my general rule is that, every so often, I try to throw in a scene that— while it marginally bumps the plot forward—is mostly just there for comic relief. I mean, we read these books for fun, right? [Forbus].

Craig Johnson, whose crime novels are narrated by Wyoming sheriff Walt Longmire, knows that a sense of humor can help a person in a tough job like law enforcement get through the day. But he also knows there's another good reason to give a first-person narrator a healthy sense of humor: "Would you want to spend three hundred pages in the head of a dullard?" he asks ("Penguin" *Another* 3).

Writers and filmmakers who use humor often do so simply because it pleases them. Rex Stout once confessed, "If I'm not having fun writing a book no one's going to have any fun reading it" (Baring-Gould vii). Quentin Tarantino, famous for mixing violence and humor in his films, confesses: "I love it. I think it's like a Reese's Cup, two great tastes that taste great together" (Bauer 112).

Humor may also serve purposes beyond entertainment. It can provide insight into the characters who use it, as for example it does in the case of Philip Marlowe. It has the capacity to reduce anxiety and release tension, both for the reader and in some cases for the character using it. Cops, for example, are known for developing their own kind of dark humor as a way of coping with the sometimes dangerous or chilling things their work exposes them to. Humor can also be an effective weapon in exposing mankind's evil or foolishness. Satirists know that ridiculing a person or a behavior can be both funny and thought-provoking at the same time.

This is not to suggest that a crime novel or film without humor can't be entertaining. Writers make a variety of creative choices, and many of them decide not to include any humor at all. This does not necessarily imply that they lack a sense of humor. Donald E. Westlake, author of a series of hilarious comic capers featuring the jinxed John Dortmunder, also wrote (under the name of Richard Stark) a series of deadly serious crime novels about a professional thief named Parker. Christopher Fowler, himself an author of a very funny series of crime novels, agrees that humor and tragedy go together very well in crime fiction, but does warn that, "comedy will get you delisted from awards ceremonies." People, he says, tend to "take you more seriously when you don't get laughs" ("Funny").

A case can be made that the mere presence of humor in a crime novel or film enhances rather than detracts from its realism. Ordinary day-to-day life is filled with funny moments. Joel Coen, for example, cites the following as an example of why he and his brother Ethan inject humor into even their darkest films: "It seems to us, that it's present in life. Look at those people who recently blew up the World Trade Center. They'd rented a van to prepare the explosion, and, once the job was finished, they returned to the rental agency to reclaim their deposit. The absurdity of that is, in itself, terribly funny" (Luhr 118). Booker Prize–winning comic novelist Howard Jacobson insists that humor is such an integral part of daily life that literature ought to reflect this: "Show me a novel that's not comic," he says, "and I'll show you a novel that's not doing its job" ("Howard").

It is also true that realism is not necessarily the aim of every crime writer. Edmund Crispin, for example, wrote humorous mysteries that reflected his belief that, "crime stories in general and detective stories in particular should be essentially imaginative and artificial in order to make their best effect" (Pedersen 256). But whether they are primarily humorists who use elements of the crime genre in the service of their humor, or authors whose aim is to produce serious realistic fiction, all can agree that humor has its place and entertaining the reader is a worthy goal.

Humor is not limited to any one kind of crime novel or film. It can be found in classic whodunits that feature professional, semi-professional, or amateur detectives, as well as in hard-boiled private-eye stories, police procedurals, and the like. Criminal activities are often funny. Sherlock Holmes's nemesis Professor Moriarty may be a criminal mastermind, but for every genius like him, there's an army of bumbling crooks waiting in the wings. Crime capers that go awry have more comic potential than police investigations that lead to the arrest of the wrong man. There's also the additional fact that criminals are often misfits and outsiders whose attitudes (and language) can be colorfully portrayed.

Types of Humor

Laughter can arise from language, action, character, or any combination of the three. In a visual medium like film, action alone can be the primary source of humor. Silent film comedians like Charlie Chaplin and Buster Keaton and creators of animated cartoons have ably demonstrated that humor can be entirely wordless. In a literary text, however, language and character usually bear the burden of providing the laughs.

Verbal

Verbal humor can arise from a single word, a colorful phrase, a lengthy conversation, or an extended description. Simple wordplay like a pun can trigger a laugh by exploiting the meaning or sound of a single word ("Santa's elves are just a bunch of subordinate Clauses"). The alliterative repetition of the sound of multiple words can also be humorous, as in a tongue-twister like "Peter Piper picked a peck of pickled peppers."

Some forms of verbal humor, like jokes or wisecracks, aim at producing an immediate laugh. Other types, like puns or irony, may take a moment or more for the joke to sink in. In the case of Jonathan Swift's classic "A Modest Proposal," for example, which suggests that the Irish can solve their hunger problem by eating their children, some readers take the words literally and fail to get the ironic humor. A character may say things that are not intended to be funny but are by confusing similarly sounding words—"Michelangelo painted the famous Sixteenth Chapel"—which is known as a malapropism. Sometimes a character says things he thinks are funny but aren't, making him the butt of the joke, like the character of David Brent as played by Ricky Gervais in the British and Steve Carrell in the American versions of *The Office*.

There are two main categories of language usage in a novel: spoken words exchanged between characters (i.e., dialogue) and those heard only by the reader. In dialogue, humor takes many forms, such as conversations between characters and wisecracks that, especially in crime fiction, come from the mouth of the main protagonist. For example, when a prospective client tells Philip Marlowe, "I don't think I'd care to employ a detective that uses liquor in any form, I don't even approve of tobacco," Marlowe fires back, "Would it be all right if I peeled an orange?" (*Little* 3). Or when a cop threatens Robert B. Parker's Spenser by telling him, "You're working my side of the street, and if you get in my way I'll kick your ass right into the gutter," he parries with, "Can I feel your muscle?" (*Godwulf* 27).

In each case the wisecrack is intended to be funny, but it also serves the purpose of deflecting what was said. Equally important, it also helps to reveal the character of the wisecracker, for as Dennis Porter observed, "He who makes wisecracks is a wise guy. That is to say, someone who is no respecter of authority, wealth, power, social standing, or institutions. A wise guy talks too much, asks too many questions, and answers back when an effort is made to put him in his place" (166).

A distinction can be made between spoken remarks that are meant by the speaker to be funny, like wisecracks, and those that are funny though not intended to be so by their speaker. Elmore Leonard is a master of this kind of humor. He creates characters whose words reveal the way they think, though the speaker is usually unaware that those words may also be funny. Violence against women isn't a laughing matter, but utter ignorance can be. For example, after learning that a woman in the U.S. is beaten or physically abused every eighteen seconds, a character in Leonard's *Bandits* says in all seriousness and without humorous intent, "You wouldn't think that many women get out of line, would you?" (120).

Spoken dialogue is found in virtually every novel, but there are also words that come from the narrator but are heard only by the reader. There are two basic types of narration: first-person (spoken to the reader by a character in the novel) and third-person (spoken to the reader by an anonymous voice). Third-person narration is often called omniscient because it can freely enter the thoughts of each and every character and can roam from past to present and even into the future. By contrast, first-person narration is limited to the perspective of the character in the novel who is telling the story and is delivered in the specific language of that one character as opposed to an anonymous voice.

First-person narration is an especially effective method of telling a story, for it in fact actually tells *two* stories: it is both an account of the action of the novel and of the person describing the action. While third-person narrative is often detached, seemingly objective, just a recording device, first-person narration is totally subjective, and in the telling it can become a revealing self-portrait, a deliberate act of self-presentation on the part of the narrator. Timothy Hallinan, author of three crime series, two dark and serious narrated in third-person, one humorous and narrated in first-person, notes that the "root of the difference in my books is the voice. I can't think of any single aspect of writing that changes the way a story is presented more than the voice in which it's told" (DeSilva). It is the voice of the first-person narrator that is often the main source of humor in a novel that is otherwise about very serious business.

It's important to distinguish here between author and narrator. Huck Finn was created by Mark Twain, but the voice we hear in the novel is not Twain's: it's the voice of a fourteen-year-old Missouri boy that gives the novel its distinctive flavor.

Wisecracks and smarty-pants comebacks are public utterances designed to be heard by other characters and aim at making an impression on that audience. But the bulk of first-person narrative is private, heard only by the reader, and these words can create a distinctly different impression. A character who is tight-lipped and laconic in public may be trying to hide his or her true self, but in the privacy of first-person narrative may reveal much more than the public utterances do. Here is where we can hear colorful commentary and witty similes that are never heard by the other characters in the novel. Here the narrator can let his or her hair down, so to speak, revealing a more thoughtful, sensitive, intelligent side that it may be in his or her best interest to keep hidden from the outside world. It is here where a whole different sort of humor may be expressed.

A word about similes. A simile is simply a figure of speech in which two unlike things are directly compared using "like" or "as." Poets are particularly fond of similes as a way of expressing meaning in a fresh way. For example, in the line, "My love is like a red, red rose," Robert Burns finds an apt way of comparing his beloved to a beautiful flower. A comic simile is one that derives its humor from an incongruous comparison. A classic example is Philip Marlowe's description of Moose Malloy as looking "as inconspicuous as a tarantula on a slice of angel food" (*Farewell* 4). Such a comparison is funny because of the unusual connection between unlikely objects. At the same time, it also sheds light on the inventive mind that would think of such a connection in the first place. In this case, humor serves a dual purpose; it amuses the reader while at the same time exposes aspects of the narrator's personality.

Marlowe

There is a form of third-person narration called *free indirect discourse* that combines the intimacy of first-person narration with the omniscience of third-person. The third-person narrator directly enters into the mind of a character and allows the reader to hear an uncensored account of what that character is thinking. The words are not spoken directly to the reader as they are in first-person but are simply overheard by the reader. This is another effective method of revealing aspects of a character's personality that might otherwise be hidden. It can also be a rich source of humor. For example, Ben Rehder's Blanco County mysteries feature a colorful and opinionated redneck named Red O'Brien. Here we get to listen in on his private thoughts about a local gangster named Sal Mameli:

> Hell, everybody knew that your average Eye-talian American was nothing but a street thug. From what Red could tell, watching cable TV shows, the wops who made it into the mafia were just the ones with the biggest balls, the ones willing to take the biggest chances. But none of them—whether they were in the mob or not—could be trusted. Oh, sure, you had a few exceptions to the rule. Real Italian heroes, like Sylvester Stallone and Arnold Schwarzenegger. But Sal Mameli wasn't sophisticated like those guys [*Bone* 213].

Action-Based

In a film, action is presented visually, leaving the viewer free to make a judgment based on what he or she sees. In a novel, action must be presented through language, and once again, as with similes, the words a narrator employs to describe what is happening can provoke laughter while at the same time revealing that narrator's comic sensibility. For example, action can be described in a simple just-the-facts-ma'am-fashion like this:

"She shot me in the arm."

But a first-person narrator who chooses to describe it another way, as Colin Bateman's jokester narrator Dan Starkey does, reveals as much about himself as the mere fact of his being shot:

> She pulled the trigger. There was a bang and something bit into my arm. Putting two and two together is my business. I thought it reasonable to assume that I'd just been shot. I thought about it while I was spun around. I settled on my conclusion as I dropped to my knees [*Shooting* 207].

Character-Driven

Characters are presented to the reader through both action and language. How they act, how they talk, and how others talk about them all help to reveal their personality. First-person narrators with a sense of humor, like Philip Marlowe, Spenser, Kinsey Millhone, etc., are often a reliable source of wit and humor as they describe the characters they interact with. Their descriptions can be humorous even if the person they are describing is not funny. Anonymous third-person narrators can also adopt a comic voice in describing action and characters from a perspective outside that of any of those in the novel.

The actions, eccentricities, habits, quirky attitudes, etc., of a character are all potential sources of humor. Inspector Clouseau's clumsiness, Martha Grimes's Detective Alfred Wiggins's comic hypochondria, Christopher Fowler's Arthur Bryant's facility for infecting every electronic appliance he touches are just three examples of behavior that becomes a running joke in the works in which these characters are featured.

One especially popular use of a character for comic purposes is the role he or she plays as the main character's sidekick. Faithful companions have been important characters in literature ever since Enkidu joined up with Gilgamesh in the ancient Mesopotamian epic, considered the earliest surviving work of literature. Don Quixote and Sancho Panza, the Lone Ranger and Tonto, Batman and Robin are only three of the most famous pairings. Classic comedy teams like Bud Abbott and Lou Costello, Bob Hope and Bing Crosby, Dean Martin and Jerry Lewis, Edgar Bergen and Charlie McCarthy, among many others, illustrate the comic possibilities in the pairing of a straight man with a jokester sidekick. In crime fiction, both traditions are often found together, with the sidekick serving as an essential aide to the hero while also playing a distinctive comic role.

Sidekicks perform a variety of functions. Nero Wolfe's Archie Goodwin does the footwork for his boss Nero Wolfe, who is unwilling or unable to do it himself. Spenser's friend Hawk does the morally dirty work Spenser himself prefers not to do. Dr. Watson records Sherlock Holmes's adventures, ensuring his fame. But in each case, the sidekick also plays a comic role.

Much of the humor in both the Sherlock Holmes and Nero Wolfe stories arises from the living arrangements of the main characters, who reside together under the same roof. Their Odd-Couple partnership eventually takes on many of the qualities of a long-standing marriage, with the two of them bickering like couples whose petty jealousies and resentments occasionally flare up. The creators of the popular BBC *Sherlock* films have great fun with this aspect of the Holmes-Watson relationship. At one point Holmes asks Watson if he heard him when he asked him to punch him in the face. Watson replies, "I always hear 'punch me in the face' when you're speaking." When Archie Goodwin gives a succinct answer to a question his boss asks, Wolfe praises him by saying, "That's why I put up with you; you could have answered with fifty words and you did it with one." To which Archie retorts, "I've often wondered. Now tell me why I put up with you" (*Homicide* 76).

The relationship between Spenser and his black sidekick Hawk is different but no less fruitful for comic purposes. Their barbed comic banter is the kind that is only possible between longtime friends who share affection and a deep mutual respect that allows them to play around with racial stereotypes. When Spenser spots his friend at the airport dressed in a three-piece suit and a lavender tie, wearing a white straw hat with a matching lavender band tipped forward over his face, he jokingly says to him, "Excuse me, Mr. Fetchit, I've seen all your movies and was wondering if you'd care to join me for a bite of watermelon." Hawk fires back, "Y'all can call me Stepin, bawse" (*Judas* 75). Later, when Spenser tries to tell him how to do his job, Hawk retorts, "Yowsah, boss, y'all awful kind to hep ol Hawk lak yew do." "Why don't you can that Aunt Jemima crap," Spenser parries. "You're about as down-home darkie as Truman Capote" (*Judas* 81).

Because they usually feature a large and diverse cast of characters, police procedurals are another rich source of humor. Most police departments feature at least one character who provides comic relief, either because of incompetence or some other reason. The decidedly serious Martin Beck novels by Maj Sjöwall and Per Wahlöö include a pair of klutzy Keystone Kops named Karl Kristiansson and Kurt Kvant whose bumbling efforts provide laughs. Andrea Camilleri's Salvo Montalbano procedurals feature a department receptionist whose linguistic ineptitude is routinely played for laughs. Joseph Wambaugh's Hollywood Division series features a pair of cops nicknamed Flotsam and Jetsam who speak in a comic surfer language all their own.

Characters can also be put in comic situations. For example, Sue Grafton's Kinsey Millhone makes the mistake of hiding in a bathroom shower when the owner of the home she's searching unexpectedly returns. She has to endure the embarrassment of helplessly listening as the woman enters the bathroom to use the toilet, praying that she doesn't decide to take a dump. Andrea Camilleri puts his short-tempered Inspector Montalbano into a frustrating situation—he tries to open a padlock by attacking it with a hacksaw, a chisel, a hammer, even a pistol—and then describes him slowly boiling over until he erupts "like Donald Duck," and starts "kicking and punching the door, screaming like a madman" (*Excursion* 235).

The master of comic frustration is Donald E. Westlake whose John Dortmunder is like a modern-day Job beset by an avalanche of misfortune. Dortmunder didn't set out to be a bungling burglar. The humor in the novels arises out of the misfortunes that bedevil him. Frustration is never funny to the individual suffering from it. On the other hand, it can be hilarious to those who observe it.

Pastiche and Parody

Comic imitation can be simply entertaining or it can have a critical edge to it. Sometime it is both. An impressionist who does impersonations of famous people may only wish to entertain, say by imagining John Wayne as a Little League coach or Jack Nicholson as a driving instructor. But impressions done on *Saturday Night Live* usually serve an entirely different purpose. Just ask Donald Trump.

The same is true of comic imitation in crime fiction. The private-eye hero was born in the 1920s, mainly in the stories by Dashiell Hammett that appeared in the pages of *Black Mask* magazine. In 1933, Raymond Chandler published his first story in the same magazine on his way to taking the emerging detective hero in a new direction with the creation of Philip Marlowe. Another pulp writer, Robert Leslie Bellem, adopted a different approach. Rather than adding something new to the emerging figure of the private eye, he simply borrowed a few basic features and squeezed all the comedy out of them he could. This is especially true in the case of the tough-guy narration that had become an easily identifiable convention: he found colorfully inventive ways of talking tough ("cork it before I lump you up, sister"), employing similes ("dead as a Hitler promise," "deader than George Washington's cherry tree"), and describing the female anatomy (he was a virtuoso in finding new ways of describing female breasts: "mounded yumps," "creamy bon-bons," "perky pretty-pretties"). Bellem wasn't spoofing the genre; he was simply finding comic ways of mimicking its conventions.

Often, however, comic imitation is more critical. The comic imitation of a familiar work, style, convention, even an entire genre, for the purpose of poking fun at that which is being imitated is called a parody or spoof. It is a counterpart of caricature in visual art where a famous person's recognizable physical feature (e.g., Richard Nixon's furrowed brow or Donald Trump's distinctive hair) is exaggerated for comic effect. Parody has a long history. One of the earliest examples is the *Batrachomyomachia*, a 5th Century BCE parody in the style of Homer's *Iliad* which recounts in heroic fashion a battle between frogs and mice. One of the very first novels in English, Samuel Richardson's *Pamela,* which appeared in 1740, was parodied just one year later by Henry Fielding in *Shamela.*

Parody is sometimes confused with pastiche, which is more a faithful imitation of a work or style. Where parody mocks, pastiche aims at paying homage to what it imitates. There are, for example, numerous pastiches of famous detectives like Philip Marlowe and Sherlock Holmes. Robert B. Parker and Benjamin Black have both written "new" Philip Marlowe novels in Chandler's style, and following Parker's death, Ace Atkins has continued the Spenser series by closely mimicking Parker's style. Because parody depends upon familiarity with whatever is being parodied, once any individual work, style, or genre becomes well known, it also becomes a ripe target. Writers with prose styles as distinctive as Ernest Hemingway's, for example, are an obvious and all-too-easy target for parodists.

Crime fiction offers plenty of opportunities for parody. The tough-talking, wisecracking style of early hard-boiled detective writers like Dashiell Hammett and Raymond Chandler has often been imitated. Hammett's *The Maltese Falcon* has inspired several film parodies, most notably Neil Simon's *The Cheap Detective (1978)* starring Peter Falk, which spoofs both Hammett's novel and actor Humphrey Bogart, who famously portrayed Sam Spade in the classic film version of the novel in 1941.

Philip Marlowe's colorful narrative style and wisecracking manner have also been spoofed. One of the most famous examples is humorist S. J. Perelman's 1944 *New Yorker* piece, "Farewell, My Lovely Appetizer," a knowing nod both to Chandler's *Farewell, My Lovely* as well as to the entire tough-guy genre. Perelman perfectly mimics the world-weary style of the private-eye narrator. For example, his private eye Mike Noonan is attracted to his secretary's ears, especially "the way they were joined to her head. There was something complete about them; you knew they were there for keeps. When you're a private eye, you want things to stay put" (191). And like his fellow private eyes, Noonan doesn't give up once he's on the scent. He tries to phone a guy he knows named Little Farvel, but "it took a while to get the dope I wanted because the connection was bad and Little Farvel had been dead two years, but we Noonans don't let go easily" (195).

Between 1978 and 1983, Ross H. Spencer published five wacky novels featuring a Chicago private eye named Chance Purdue that specifically parodied the terse, laconic narrative style that Hammett and others used in their hard-boiled tales. Spencer's novels, narrated in first-person by Purdue, consist entirely of one-sentence paragraphs which take the terse style to its ridiculous extreme. Here's a sample:

I said I drove clear from Belmont and Kimball.
Brandy said how far is that?
I said eight miles.
I said in the rain.
Brandy said gosh that's not far.
I said in the rain?
Brandy said even in the rain.
I said in Chicago?
Brandy said Purdue eight miles is eight miles.
I said not in Chicago.
I said not in the rain.
I said people have starved to death driving eight miles in Chicago in the rain.
I said others have gone insane.
I said there have been numerous suicides.
Brandy said Purdue knock it off [*Reggis* 87].

Unlike Bellem, Spencer isn't so much creating his own style as aping a familiar one by reducing its clipped rhythms to what Earl F. Bargainnier calls "the level of the Dick-and-Jane reading texts of elementary school" (68).

Ron Goulart's "The Peppermint-Striped Goodbye" is a very funny parody of the distinctive similes that Ross Macdonald (one of whose novels is titled *The Zebra-Striped Hearse*) characteristically employed that often involved extended literary allusions. Here Goulart squeezes four similes into a single sentence.

Spent time is somewhat like the bird in that poem by Coleridge and we carry it around our neck like a gift necktie that we have to wear to please the giver, who gave it to us like somebody passing out the second-rate wine now that the guests, who sit around like numbed patients in some sort of cosmic dentist's waiting room, are too unsober to know or care [284].

He also includes a simile that spoofs the lengths to which an author will go to include one even when it isn't needed: "He fell over onto the stale chocolate cake, making the silent falling sound that a giant tree does when it topples alone in a distant wood" (285).

It's no surprise that Sherlock Holmes, the world's most famous detective, is the most parodied character in all of crime fiction. In 1892, only five years after Holmes's debut, he was parodied by Robert Barr in "The Adventures of Sherlaw Kombs." One year later, Rudolph Chambers Lehmann published a parody entitled "The Adventures of Picklock Holes." Among the cleverest of all are the thirty-two stories Robert L. Fish wrote between 1959 and 1981 about the adventures of Schlock Homes of 221B Bagel Street, most of which were later collected in two volumes: *The Incredible Schlock Homes* (1965) and *The Memoirs of Schlock Homes* (1974).

The humor in them comes from the inventive twists on the original characters' names (John Watney, Criscroft Homes, Professor Marty, Inspector Balustrade, Irene Addled), elaborate puns (English villages with names like Elbow Twisting and Herts and Yulebe, Surrey), clever wordplay (Homes is especially fond of religious music like the "Suite Sistine" by the Beadles), and cases with names like "The Adventure of the Perforated Ulster" (about a postage stamp), "The Adventure of the Steamed Clans" (about feuding Scottish families), "The Adventure of the Purloined Litter" (about stolen kittens), and "The Sound of the Basketballs."

But the biggest laughs come from Homes's obtuseness. For example, in "The Adventure of the Big Plunger," a noted financier jumps to his death one October day in 1929 holding a mysterious piece of paper in his hand. Homes struggles for days to figure out the meaning of the letters and numbers on the paper before concluding they are a coded message about the financier's declining health. Homes reasons that the man killed himself rather than submit to the inevitable wasting away of his life. When Watney later shows him a newspaper story about the stock market crash, Homes is relieved: "There is one consolation" he tells Watney. "At least poor Lord Fynch-fframis was spared the added pain of seeing his life savings swept away in the holocaust" (*Memoirs* 29).

In "The Disappearance of Whistler's Mother," Homes agrees to assist famed French detective C. Septembre Duping (a stand-in for Poe's C. Auguste Dupin) in the search for Whistler's famous painting which has disappeared from the Louvre. Homes, however, overlooks the obvious and instead mistakenly deduces that Whistler's missing mother is an elderly wine-stewardess who has stolen expensive cognac from a nightclub she worked at called The Louver. He is happy to receive the news that thanks to his efforts the woman has been returned to the Louvre, but dismayed to learn she has subsequently been hung.

In *Case for Three Detectives* (1936), Leo Bruce affectionately spoofs three of the most famous fictional detectives of the time. The murder of a woman in a locked room in her country house brings to the scene Lord Simon Plimsoll (Dorothy L. Sayers's Lord Peter Wimsey), M. Amer Picon (Agatha Christie's Hercule Poirot) and Monsignor Smith (G. K. Chesterton's Father Brown). Bruce effectively captures the distinctive personalities and speech mannerisms of all three who spend the bulk of the novel chasing down clues. In the end, each proudly issues his convoluted theory of the crime before revealing the identity of the killer. Each, however, is dead wrong. If only they had listened to local Sheriff Beef, whose repeated claim, "I know who dune it," is ignored by all.

Fans of mystery pastiches and parodies will also enjoy two collections of comic imitations of popular crime writers. In *The Anagram Detectives* (1979), Norma Schier offers up clever pastiches of such famous fictional detectives as Hoskell Chomers (Sherlock Holmes), Pierre Choulot (Hercule Poirot), Owen Foler (Nero Wolfe), and a most unusual case, Mooch Sheckls (Robert L. Fish's Schlock Homes), which is a pastiche of a pastiche. Jon L. Breen's *Hair of the Sleuthhound* (1982) affectionately spoofs such other giants in the genre as Ed McBain, Ellery Queen, John D. MacDonald, Dashiell Hammett, and John Dickson Carr, among others.

Satire

Like parody, satire uses humor for more than simple entertainment. It employs such comic techniques as ridicule, exaggeration, and irony as a way of criticizing evil, human folly, and the like. Satire is usually divided into two types named after famous Roman practitioners of the art: Horatian (after Horace) is gentle and playful; Juvenalian (after Juvenal) is angry and forceful. Both types, however, share the same aim of exposing what the satirist determines demands correction.

Sometimes a writer makes a satiric jab only in passing when the opportunity presents itself. For example, whenever a crime novel is set in Hollywood, it's hard to resist the temptation to aim a few satiric shots at the movie industry. Joseph Wambaugh's *The Glitter Dome* is about an investigation into the murder of a Hollywood producer, which gives him an opportunity to use the producer's over-the-top funeral to poke fun at Hollywood's pretense and phoniness. Later in the novel, the cops investigating the murder attend a Hollywood party where a group of directors are engaged in pretentious babble about whether the essence of the city can be found in its space, its absence of space, its shape, the illusion of shape, the smells "of the lost lonely children on the vast, lonely, heartbreaking streets of Beverly Hills," or the light that is "fuchsia and filtered through the pastel gauze of anonymity" (234).

For an author like Carl Hiaasen, satire is no sideshow, it's the main attraction of his books. He writes hilarious crime novels set in South Florida whose aim is to skewer the greedy bankers, rapacious land developers, and corrupt politicians who have transformed a natural paradise into an eyesore, all in the name of progress (and in pursuit of the Almighty Dollar). His works are perfect illustrations of novelist Philip Roth's definition of satire as "moral rage transformed into comic art" (59).

One other type of humor must be mentioned: unintentional humor.

Just as there are characters whose behavior, attitudes, and/or words are funny without them being aware of it, there are writers who, because of haste, incompetence, or simply trying too hard to be clever, just don't realize how funny they sometimes are. Crime novelist Bill Pronzini has done mystery fans a genuine service by publishing two collections—*Gun in Cheek* (1982) and *Son of Gun in Cheek* (1987)—of the best of the worst writing in crime fiction.

Whether it's their use of description, dialogue, or first-person narration, the authors whose howlers Pronzini assembles are such ham-fisted wordsmiths that the results are hilarious. Here is a small sampling from some of the authors he includes in *Gun in Cheek:* Brett Halliday: "He poured himself a drink and counted the money. It came to ten thousand even, mostly in fifties and twenty-fives" (41); Stephen Marlowe: "She was as lovely as a girl could be without bludgeoning your endocrines"(41); Michael Avallone: "She ... unearthed one of her fantastic breasts from the folds of her sheath skirt" (63): R. A. J. Walling: "In plain English, Patterson," said Pye, "nix on the gats" (111).

Finally, there is this over-the-top passage from pulp writer Carl G. Hodges, which should serve as a reminder that a blue pencil or a delete button is often a writer's best friend:

> Then I felt damp fresh air hit the back of my neck and I knew somebody had opened the door. Before I could see who it was, somebody stuck a red-hot poker in my ear and all my brains ran out of the hole. My bones turned to macaroni and I sank down into a gooey mass of tomato sauce that looked like blood. Then somebody began rubbing the end of my nose with sandpaper and there was a big balloon of pain tied to my ear [215].

Part I: Crime Fiction

Rex Stout (1886–1975)

Rex Stout's Nero Wolfe novels are a good place to begin a study of humor in crime fiction because they draw upon the two main streams of writing in the genre. Nero Wolfe was one of the most popular of all the many imitators spawned by Sherlock Holmes. A crime-solving genius who was even more eccentric than Holmes, he appeared in a long-running series that began with the publication of *Fer-de-Lance* in 1934 and continued until Stout's death in 1975 at the age of eighty-nine. (The series eventually totaled thirty-three novels and dozens of short stories and novellas.) Stout's innovation was partnering the cerebral Wolfe with a sidekick and chronicler of his cases named Archie Goodwin who was modeled on the American wisecracking private eye that was just becoming popular at the time. Wolfe's eccentricities, Archie's irreverent wit, and the pairing of two such opposites was a formula that resulted in plenty of humor.

Wolfe lives in a four-story brownstone on West 35th Street in Manhattan, where he has carefully arranged every detail of his life to suit his whims. He employs a household staff of four that in addition to Archie includes a full-time chef and a gardener to help him cultivate his 10,000 orchids, which he tends religiously twice a day between ten and twelve and four and six. He is so large, weighing somewhere in the neighborhood of three hundred pounds, that he has to sit in an oversized made-to-order chair. He has expensive tastes and personal extravagances (he owns an eighteen-carat-gold bottle opener and uses a thin strip of gold as a bookmark): his only bow to plebeian tastes is a fondness for beer.

Though he may be a genius, Wolfe is also self-absorbed, rude, lazy, arrogant, impatient, and set in his ways. As imperious as the Roman emperor whose name he bears, he bellows, grunts, growls, groans, snarls, and scowls at whatever displeases him. His favorite expressions are "Nuts!," "Bah!," and "Pfui!" Among his many dislikes are leaving his house, the outdoors, interruptions during meals, bawling women, gin drinkers, shaking hands, etc. His stubbornness and extreme rigidity provide a rich source of humor in the books, especially when he faces threats to his routine.

Above all, he has a strong sense of his own self-worth: "It is true that I hire out my abilities for money," he informs one client, "but I assure you that I am not to be regarded as a mere peddler of gewgaws or tricks. I am an artist or nothing" (*Red* 30). And unlike those poor gumshoes who at the time were lucky to get twenty-five dollars a day, plus expenses, he demands high prices for his services: he charges one man a thousand dollars just for his opinion about how his son died; he charges another client ten thousand dollars to take her case. Someone has to pay for all those household extravagances.

Wolfe may be an intellectual genius, but he would be nothing without Archie Goodwin, who considers himself "the heart, liver, lungs, and gizzard of the private detective business of Nero Wolfe, Wolfe being merely the brains" (*All* 155). He dashes around town interrogating suspects and searching for clues and evidence. Meanwhile, Wolfe tends to his orchids and mulls over the case while sitting for long periods in his oversized chair, his eyes closed, pushing his lips out and pulling them back in. When the time is ripe, he summons all the suspects to his office and, like the Great Detective (and showman) he is, identifies the guilty person.

As Wolfe's "assistant detective and man Friday, Saturday, Sunday, Monday, Tuesday, Wednesday, and Thursday" (*Three* 4), Archie also pays the bills, answers the mail, records the conversations with prospective clients, dusts, sharpens the pencils, and keeps fresh water in the vase on Wolfe's desk. His main responsibility, however, is prodding his lazy boss to accept a job whenever his finances begin to run low. It takes a small fortune to keep the household going, so Wolfe has to work whether he likes it or not, though his first response is almost always to refuse the job. Watching Archie badger his stubborn boss into taking a case is one of the delights of the series.

But Archie's most important contribution to the series is his role as narrator, where he can make Wolfe palatable to the reader. Without him, the books would collapse under the weight of Wolfe's arrogance, snobbishness, and gargantuan ego. "If Wolfe is the pill," said Donald E. Westlake,

"Archie is the sugar coating" (*Getaway* 135). The sidekick's traditional role has been to shine a loving light on his superior and express his admiration for him. Archie rightfully admires Wolfe's genius, but he's no fawning acolyte and often becomes exasperated by his boss's fussiness, stubbornness, and rigidity. Instead of blindly singing Wolfe's praises, Archie jokes about his quirks, foibles, even his appearance. He pokes fun at his indolence: "He was too damned lazy to live" (*Homicide* 176); the careful way he maneuvers his bulk into his ready-made chair: "His fundament lapped over at both sides" (*Homicide* 8) and then he sucks in whole "bushels" of air; even his sense of humor: "Of all Wolfe's thousand techniques for making himself obnoxious the worst was when he thought he was being funny" (*Golden* 9). "If you think a problem child is tough," Archie complains to the reader, "try handling a problem elephant" (*Homicide* 23).

Archie gets his revenge against Wolfe for his irritating habits in both subtle and not-so-subtle ways. Since he controls the narrative, he can choose to portray Wolfe's appearance in less than flattering ways. For example, he enjoys describing the way a disheveled Wolfe looks first thing in the morning, "barefooted, his hair tousled, with his couple of acres of yellow pajamas dazzling in the sun" (*Three* 8). And instead of simply mentioning that his boss is overweight, he finds a way of emphasizing it—e.g., by saying he weighs a seventh of a ton or 4000 ounces—that makes him appear even heavier than he is. This is certainly not how the fastidious Wolfe would choose to present himself.

He also finds overt ways of annoying his boss. He sharpens pencils that don't need it knowing how much the noise irritates Wolfe. While chauffeuring him around town, he deliberately drives over holes in the pavement just to rattle him. He also takes special delight whenever someone else can irritate his boss. When a woman complains to Wolfe that he's simply asking her questions the police have already asked, Archie is delighted: "I could have given her a hug and a kiss, too.... Anyone who takes Wolfe down a peg renders a service to the balance of nature, and to tell him to his face that he was merely a carbon copy of the cops was enough to spoil his appetite for dinner" (*Champagne* 113).

Sometimes, however, Archie's pranks backfire. After Wolfe childishly rejects a dish his chef has prepared because he used a different spice than usual without consulting him about it beforehand, Archie gets back at him by inviting a twelve-year-old boy who rings the doorbell into Wolfe's dining room, a serious breach of protocol. Wolfe in turn gets his revenge by insisting that Archie record in his notebook each and every detail of the entire lengthy conversation he has with the boy.

The verbal jousting between this classic odd couple is a comic highlight of the series. When Archie gives a succinct answer to a question his boss asks, Wolfe praises him by saying, "That's why I put up with you; you could have answered with fifty words and you did it with one." To which Archie retorts, "I've often wondered. Now tell me why I put up with you" (*Homicide* 76). When Wolfe can muster only faint praise to Archie for his work—"I must say, Archie, satisfactory"—Archie responds, "Don't strain yourself" (*Second* 184). Sometimes the verbal jabs are limited to a basic few words: "I wheeled and glared at him. He glared back. 'Pfui,' he said. 'Nuts,' I said, and turned and went" (*Prisoner's* 2).

Archie's wisecracking style contrasts nicely with Wolfe's more formal diction—e.g., "My distrust and hatred of vehicles in motion is partly based on my plerophory that their apparent submission to control is illusory and that they may at their pleasure, and sooner or later will, act on whim" (*Some* 1)—and pompous demeanor. Archie's pithy descriptions are especially entertaining: "That one ... was a neat little squirt, with a suspicious twist to his lips, who had been fifty years all his life and would be for the rest of it" (*Prisoner's* 53); he describes another man as speaking "in the sort of greasy voice that makes me want to take up strangling" (*Three Doors* 54). Like many of his private-eye brethren he can also come up with a humorous simile from time to time: "She looked like an antelope in a herd of Guernseys" (*Some* 78).

Some of the fun in a long-running series that ordinarily follows a predictable formula comes from those entries that upend it. Wolfe likes being the boss, but when a female client decides to hire Archie instead of him, he finds himself in the unexpected role of Archie's assistant. Wolfe also hates to leave his home; for one thing, there is always the problem of finding a chair large enough to accommodate his large backside. So when he does leave, unexpected things happen with comic results, as in *Some Buried Caesar* (1939) where he finds himself stranded on a boulder in a pasture where a menacing bull lurks after a flat tire causes his car to crash.

Despite their contrasting personalities and sometimes testy relationship, Wolfe and Archie respect (and need) one another; together they form the greatest (and one of the most entertaining) crime-solving partnerships in crime and mystery fiction. Their ongoing popularity is evidenced by the fact that new adventures of the duo (under the authorship of Robert Goldsborough) continue to appear forty years after their creator's death.

Jonathan Latimer (1906–1983)

The 1930s witnessed several major innovations in American crime fiction. In 1933, Raymond Chandler published the first of his private-eye stories that would soon take the fledgling genre in a new direction. One year later, Rex Stout published his first Nero Wolfe novel, showing how the private-eye story could be combined with the classical mystery form with great success. The following year a lesser-known but no less original writer named Jonathan Latimer published the first of five novels featuring a private eye named William Crane that, like the Nero Wolfe novels, found a new way of mixing elements of the traditional classical mystery with those of the emerging private-eye tale. He also added an element he found lacking in many of his hard-boiled predecessors; he felt that Sam Spade was too serious and never had much fun, so he decided to inject plenty of it into his mysteries. (They are closer in spirit to another Hammett novel, *The Thin Man* (1934), as well as to the William Powell-Myrna Loy film versions that began appearing that same year.)

Unlike most other private-eye writers of the time, Latimer did not start out as a pulp writer. A Phi Beta Kappa graduate of Knox College in Illinois, he began working as a reporter, first for the Chicago *Herald-Examiner* and later for the *Chicago Tribune*. In 1935 he briefly served as an editor in the publicity department at the U.S. Department of the Interior before launching a career as a crime novelist with the publication of *Murder in the Madhouse*, his first William Crane novel, in 1935.

Like Hammett's Continental Op, Bill Crane is an operative for a New York detective agency. He claims to belong to "the pleasure school of crime detection" (*Dead* 30) and prefers to do his work in "luxurious surroundings among rich, congenial people. One of the troubles with crime was its prevalence among criminals" (*Dead* 4). But like Sam Spade, who fooled people into thinking he was more crooked than he really was, Crane knows it's good for business if people underestimate him. His detective methods include both looking for clues with a magnifying glass like Sherlock Holmes and the tough-guy approach of the hard-boiled detective. He can pretend to be the great detective C. Auguste Dupin, as he does when he goes undercover posing as a patient in mental institution, but he can also dish out violence like a street thug: e.g., he punches one man in the face, jams his heel on the man's nose and cracks it, then calmly steps away and wipes his shoe on the grass.

Max Allan Collins, who rates Latimer just behind Hammett and

Chandler as pioneers in the field, describes his books as "the most successful melding of the hardboiled novel and the classic drawing-room mystery" ("Screwball"). *Headed for a Hearse* (1935) is a good example. Crane has to solve the mystery of the murder of a woman whose body was found in a locked room, though the gun that killed her was missing from the room. The only other person with a key to the room is her husband, who is convicted of her murder. The realistic tone of the novel is established in the opening scene set on death row where the husband is nervously awaiting his execution scheduled only days later. This introduces a powerful note of urgency to Crane's efforts to find the real murderer in time to save the husband's life.

The humor comes from a different direction. One convention of the private-eye genre that Latimer exploits for comic purposes is the detective's fondness for alcohol. Crane enjoys a drink, but unlike most of his detective brethren at the time, he often becomes drunk and stumbles around. Drunks, however, are not as charming today as they once might have been thought to be. Drinking to excess is no laughing matter and contemporary crime writers like Lawrence Block and Ken Bruen have explored in dramatic fashion the effects of alcoholism on their detective heroes. One reason Latimer may have seized on this feature is that America's experiment in Prohibition had just ended and some, like Crane, may have been making up for lost time. The novels read like product placement ads for alcohol producers, as Latimer always identifies the brand Crane drinks: Seagram's V. O. Rye, Bass Ale, Dewer's White Label Scotch (Crane's favorite), Bushmills' Irish Whiskey, Mumm's Cordon Rouge champagne, Gilbey's Gin. (One other element that is also reflective of the time is Latimer's unfortunate use of derogatory racist and ethnic epithets which are jarring and offensive to today's readers.)

Crane's drinking habits make him the butt of the joke, as in this instance when he begins comically slurring his words: "If he wanted the body watched all he had to do was to say see, so—I mean so, see?" and "Why, I stuck round there at great person'l sacri ... sacro ... risk" (*Lady* 47). Though he thinks it's helpful to pretend to be drunk, that ruse can get out of hand pretty quickly: "He felt very pleased he had fooled them into thinking he was drunk. He giggled a little at the thought of his cleverness, bumped into a man, said, 'Excuse me many times.' He carried out his role so thoroughly he had to be helped into the phone booth" (*Red* 55).

He also suffers painful hangovers after bouts of excessive imbibing. After he wakes up with one particularly severe hangover, a friend asks if he's sure he's still alive. "You can tell I'm not a corpse," he assures him, "a corpse is livelier" (*Red* 140). When he declines a drink, explaining to the woman he's with that he's on the wagon "for at least an hour," she replies, "You look as though you'd been run over by the wagon" (*Red* 152). His taste for alcohol also leads to a comically embarrassing episode in which he finds a bottle of his favorite Scotch in a desk drawer in a mortuary; he takes a healthy swig, only to discover too late that the bottle is filled with embalming fluid.

Much of the comedy is situational. For example, the setting of *Murder in the Madhouse* allows Latimer to introduce a number of patients who provide comic relief. One thinks he's Abraham Lincoln, which leads to some funny situations. In the case of another patient with a Biblical bent, Crane has to pretend to be the Angel Gabriel when questioning him about what he might know about the case. A naked female patient has to be coaxed out of jumping from her window. Later, she shows up, again naked, in Crane's bed and kisses him, thinking he's her dead husband, which causes him to jump from the bed and leap from his bedroom window to the bushes below.

In *The Lady in the Morgue* (1936), Crane slips out of the window of a hotel room where he has been searching for clues when he hears the cops at the door; he scrambles along a narrow ledge to the window of the room next door and enters, surprising a naked woman in bed with a drunken man. He drags the sleeping man into the shower, ties the woman up and gags her, then takes his shirt off and climbs into bed beside her. When the cops knock on the door, he invites them in and convinces them he's been in bed the whole evening. After the police exit, he bows gallantly to the woman and says as he leaves, "I hope I'll see less of you sometime, madam" (*Lady* 36). Later in the same novel, he is riding in a car with the body of a woman he and his partners have stolen from a cemetery. Along the way he engages in conversation with the woman, moving her head up and down in response to his comments about the weather, which prompts another passenger to joke, "I like a babe that can hold up her end of the conversation" (*Lady* 163).

Like Marlowe, Crane is quick with a quip. After a traffic cop stops his car and asks him if the dead woman sitting next to him is drunk, he explains, "She's stiff practically all the time" (*Lady* 164). To a man who tells him he doesn't like him, he replies, "Kraft-Ebbing will never have to write a case history of my passion for you, either" (*Headed* 157). When a patient in a mental institution who suffers from the delusion that he's Abraham Lincoln is murdered, Crane promptly announces he knows the identity of the killer: John Wilkes Booth.

The Crane novels reveal the strong influence of the *Thin Man* films that began appearing shortly before Latimer's series, especially in the casual non-stop drinking that saturates the novels. *Red Gardenias* (1938) introduces an additional parallel when Crane is paired with Ann Fortune, his boss's niece. (Latimer doesn't hide the influence: at one point Ann herself refers to the William Powell-Myrna Loy film pairing.) The two of them go undercover posing as a married couple, and end up tossing wisecracks back and forth like Nick and Nora Charles in the movies. When she orders him to investigate what sounds like the noise of a burglar in the house they are staying in, he complains, "If I'm killed you'll have me on your conscience." "It won't be much of a load," she fires back (*Red* 3). When he later goes off duck hunting with a friend, leaving Ann home to sew, she retorts, "I'll sew nothing ... unless it's wild oats" (*Red* 10).

Chandler had Philip Marlowe utter all those colorful similes he's known for as a way of revealing his personality to the reader. Latimer is almost as clever as Chandler in the simile department, but because he employs third-person narration they are spoken by the narrator, though they are consistent with Crane's offbeat sense of humor, as these examples illustrate: a cup of coffee is "as black as tar, as pungent as garlic, as clear as dry sherry, as hot as Bisbee, Arizona" (*Headed* 233); the snow falls "as though someone was cutting up an ostrich boa with a pair of nail scissors" (*Headed* 119); an expensive Bugatti looks "like a beetle on a gauze bandage" (*Dead* 204); a woman's eyes "were like two frightened prisoners staring out the peepholes of a white adobe jail; waiting for daybreak and a Mexican firing squad" (*Murder* 202); the mouth of another "looked as though it had been lipsticked with a vermilion squirt gun" (*Red* 69).

Latimer ended the Crane series after *Red Gardenias*, possibly because he was lured to Hollywood, where he wrote several screenplays, including those for such noted crime films as *The Glass Key* (1942), *The Big Clock* (1948), and *The Night Has a Thousand Eyes* (1948). He later turned to television work, turning out some ninety-five scripts for the popular Perry Mason series, both original stories and adaptations of the Erle Stanley Gardner novels. Though the Bill Crane novels aren't widely known today, they remain among the funniest screwball mysteries ever written.

Raymond Chandler (1888–1959)

Along with Dashiell Hammett, Raymond Chandler is credited with creating the hard-boiled private eye genre. Although it was Carroll John

Daly who actually introduced the first private eye, Race Williams, in the pages of *Black Mask* magazine in the 1920s, he was soon eclipsed by Hammett, whose stories and novels about the Continental Op and Sam Spade laid the foundation for a new kind of detective hero. At around the same time, Raymond Chandler was an oil-company executive in Los Angeles. But after losing his job at age forty-five, he decided to try his hand at writing. He began studying the detective stories in *Black Mask* and started experimenting with the form. It took him five months to write his first story, "Blackmailers Don't Shoot," which was published in *Black Mask* in 1933. His first Philip Marlowe novel, *The Big Sleep*, came out in 1939.

While the pulp detective stories inspired his own writing, Chandler wasn't necessarily interested in the genre itself. "All I wanted when I began," he confessed, "was to play with a fascinating new language … to see what it would do as a means of expression which might remain on the level of unintellectual thinking and yet acquire the power to say things which are usually only said with a literary air" (*Letters* 43). In the long run, he argued, style was "the most durable thing in writing" and "the most valuable investment a writer can make with his time" (*Letters* 88). "It doesn't matter a damn what a novel is about," he declared. "The only fiction of any moment in any age is that which does magic with words" (*Letters* 59). His aim was to make his words "get up and walk" (*Letters* 174), which they did in memorable fashion.

Though born in Chicago, Chandler moved to London at age seven and lived there until he returned to the U.S. sixteen years later. As a student of the classics who grew up on Latin and Greek, the American language seemed to him like a foreign one which he had to study and analyze: "As a result," he wrote, "when I use slang, solecisms, colloquialisms, snide talk or any kind of off beat language, I do it deliberately" (*Letters* 155). Not only did he master this new colloquial language, he used it to create one of the most original and evocative styles in all of crime fiction, one noted above all for its wit and humor.

A primary reason for this success was his decision to use Philip Marlowe as narrator. Hammett chose third-person narration for *The Maltese Falcon*, which allowed him to keep Sam Spade something of a mystery to the reader. For example, when Spade gets a late-night phone call informing him that his partner Miles Archer has just been murdered, he takes out a packet of brown papers and a pouch of tobacco. He then slowly and methodically rolls a cigarette and lights it. We are never told how he feels about his partner's murder; the narrator leaves it to the reader to infer what he's thinking. Marlowe, by contrast, is an open book, as his first-person narration invites the reader to see the world though his eyes and through his words.

There are, in fact, two Philip Marlowes in Chandler's novels, a private and a public one. Marlowe's spoken words—his tough talk, wisecracks, and witty rejoinders—are meant to be heard by the person at whom they are directed as well as by the reader. They reveal a man with a quick wit who uses language sometimes to be funny, other times to deflect a verbal assault. To a prospective client who complains, "I don't think I'd care to employ a detective that uses liquor in any form. I don't even approve of tobacco," he replies, "Would it be all right if I peeled an orange?" (*Little* 3). "Tall, aren't you?," a woman remarks. "I didn't mean to be," is his quick reply (*Big* 3). When a beautiful woman threatens him with a gun and warns, "Don't ever think I'm fooling,... I'll give you exactly three seconds to do what I say," he replies, "Couldn't you make it a minute? I like looking at you" (*Little* 53).

But it is in the privacy of his thoughts, which only the reader hears, that Marlowe's wit and humor get full play. One major source is Marlowe's witty descriptions of some of the people he meets: "She had a lot of face and chin. She had pewter-colored hair set in a ruthless permanent, a hard beak and large moist eyes with the sympathetic expression of wet stones. There was lace at her throat, but it was the kind of throat that would have looked better in a football sweater" (*High* 6); "To say she had a face that would have stopped a clock would have been to insult her. It would have stopped a runaway horse" (*Little* 186); "A few locks of dry white hair clung to his scalp, like wild flowers fighting for life on a bare rock" (*Big* 6); "It was a blonde. A blonde to make a bishop kick a hole in a stained glass window" (*Farewell* 93).

Chandler's most famous contribution to style was his strikingly original similes. A lazy writer falls back on clichés: e. g., "Smart as a whip" or "drunk as a skunk." Chandler recognized the importance of avoiding clichés like the plague (to use yet another overworked simile): "If you use similes," he once advised, "try and make them both extravagant and orig-/inal" (*Letters* 132). He did both, fashioning fresh similes that painted a vivid image while making the reader smile. Here's a sampling of some of the best, beginning with perhaps his best-known one: "He looked about as inconspicuous as a tarantula on a slice of angel food" (*Farewell* 4); a client pushes a few dollars across his desk "as if she was drowning a favorite kitten" (*Little* 14); "She looked almost as hard to get as a haircut" (*Little* 77); "The smell of old dust hung in the air as flat and stale as a football interview" (*Little* 148); "Her face fell apart like a bride's pie crust" (*Big* 47);

"This car sticks out like spats at an Iowa picnic" (*Farewell* 60); "I belonged in Idle Valley like a pearl onion on a banana split" (*Long* 80). Marlowe's witty wisecracks and colorful similes do more than simply entertain; as Stephen L. Tanner notes, they also give Chandler "a way of ordering and controlling a disjointed, corrupt, and bewildering world. The world of southern California with its sordidness, vulgarity, violence, fraud, and cruelty is turned, when it enters the language of the novel, into a series of triumphant comic simplicities" (173). A good example of a wisecrack that also punctures pretense can be found in *Farewell, My Lovely* where Marlowe is staring at an abstract metal sculpture. When the owner of the work proudly informs him it's Asta Dial's *Spirit of Dawn*, Marlowe zings him with his reply: "I thought it was Klopstein's *Two Warts on a Fanny*" (*Farewell* 50). Chandler said he admired Humphrey Bogart, who portrayed Marlowe in *The Big Sleep*, because like Marlowe he too possessed "a sense of humor that contains that grating undertone of contempt" (*Letters* 75).

Marlowe is a tough guy like Sam Spade and The Continental Op, but he's more vulnerable than either of them. This is shown in his use of self-deprecating humor. For example, as he examines a marijuana cigarette he says, "I slit one down the middle. The mouthpiece part was pretty tough to slit. Okey, I was a tough guy, I slit it anyway. See if you can stop me" (*Farewell* 100). How can you not like someone who can describe himself as "the big boob that goes around asking all the wrong questions" (*High* 157) or who muses, "My face was stiff with thought, or with something that made my face stiff" (*High* 26). Stephen L. Tanner calls this a "cushioning humor" that consists of "a self-deflating wit that disguises the sentimental note in Marlowe and his knight-errantry" (173).

The humor in Marlowe's similes is mainly based on the incongruity of the two items he's comparing. It is also a product of both exaggeration—"Spink laid his cigar aside in an ash tray the size of a bird bath" (*Little* 121); "On the chair beside her there was a white straw garden hat with a brim the size of a spare tire" (*High* 34); "She wore a hat with a crown the size of a whiskey glass and a brim you could have wrapped the week's laundry in" (*Farewell* 87)—and ironic understatement—"The house itself was not so much. It was smaller than Buckingham Palace, rather gray for California, and probably had fewer windows than the Chrysler Building" (*Farewell* 122); "The green stone in his stickpin was not quite as large as an apple" (*Farewell* 21); "He was a big man but not more than six feet five inches tall and not wider than a beer truck" (*Farewell* 3).

Though not a jokester in the traditional sense, Marlowe has what Dennis Porter calls "the stylist's impulse to shape everything he writes in preparation for the delivery of a punch line" (143). After spotting a car parked outside his apartment that he had noticed the previous day trailing him around, he says, "There might be a cop in it, if a cop had that much time on his hands and wanted to waste it following me around. Or it might be a smoothie in the detective business trying to get a noseful of somebody else's case in order to chisel a way into it. Or it might be the Bishop of Bermuda disapproving of my night life" (*Big* 149). When he hears shots fired inside a house, he smashes a window to gain entry and in typical deadpan fashion describes what he sees: "Neither of the two people in the room paid any attention to the way I came in, although only one of them was dead" (*Big* 30).

Marlowe is fully aware of his own comic bent. When Anne Riordan in *Farewell, My Lovely* doesn't buy his explanation for events, telling him it "stands out so far you could break off a yard of it and still have enough left for a baseball bat," he replies, "I ought to have said that one.... Just my style" (186). He even self-consciously winks at his own proclivity for similes by piling one on top of another trying to describe his difficulty in standing up after being drugged: "I was as dizzy as a dervish, as weak as a worn-out washer, as low as a badger's belly, as timid as a titmouse, and as unlikely to succeed as a ballet dancer with a wooden leg" (*Little* 168).

Chandler's generous use of wisecracks, witty repartee, and colorful similes quickly transformed the tough-guy language of the new private-eye genre and introduced the one element heretofore lacking: humor. Marlowe's comic voice has become one of the most memorable and imitated in crime fiction. British writer Simon Brett, one of the many whose fiction was inspired by Chandler, had this to say:

> For me the great achievement of Raymond Chandler is his humor. His books prove that it is possible to put jokes into crime fiction without sacrificing tension, and indeed he frequently manages to use jokes to heighten tension. Nor does he allow humor to detract from character; again it has the effect of reinforcing character. And his jokes are always exemplary lessons in economy of phrasing [Preiss, 205].

Craig Rice (1908–1957)

Though she is little known today and her books are largely out of print and difficult to find, Craig Rice (pseudonym of Georgiana Ann Randolph Craig) was one of the most popular crime writers in America in the

1940s. She was the first mystery writer to be featured on the cover of *Time* magazine in 1946. Noted poet and mystery buff Louis Untermeyer praised her work as "a composite of Agatha Christie's ingenuity, Dashiell Hammett's speed, and Dorothy Sayers's wit" (Breen). She even famously received a fan letter from President Franklin D. Roosevelt thanking her for helping take his mind off his troubles for an evening.

Few today, however, would go so far as Steven Marks, author of a 2010 biography of Rice entitled *Who Was That Lady? Craig Rice: The Queen of Screwball Mystery*, who in the introduction to that book over-enthusiastically proclaimed, "She still stands alone at the top of the humorous mystery heap as the model of how funny murder can be." She doesn't. Yet her novels and short stories about hard-drinking Chicago lawyer John J. Malone and his married friends, Jake Justus and Helene Brand, are worthy of note as being among the earliest examples of the successful mixing of mirth and murder.

In an essay entitled "Murder Makes Merry," Rice observed that, "Murder is not mirthful, and there is nothing comic about a corpse" (239). But then she recounts a murder trial she covered while working as a reporter. The killer, a small drifter who was beginning a life sentence for the crime, was asked what he had done. "I aimed the gun and shot him dead," he replied calmly as the spectators listened in rapt silence. What happened next, he was asked. "He fell down," the man said, and the room erupted into laughter for the next fifteen minutes. Maybe, Rice concluded, humor and homicide do go hand in hand, and she wrote a very funny series of crime novels that proved her point.

Rice introduced her trio of amateur detectives in *Eight Faces at Three* in 1939: Jake Justus, an ex-reporter and ex–press agent who now owns a Chicago nightclub; beautiful blonde Helene Brand, a wealthy heiress who later becomes his wife; and John J. Malone, a Chicago lawyer who eventually becomes the leading character in the series, starring in eleven novels and two dozen short stories. Normally described as "the little lawyer," Malone usually wears a rumpled suit covered in cigar ash and is perennially short of cash, reduced to borrowing a few bucks from his secretary Maggie or from his friend Joe, owner of Joe the Angel's City Hall bar.

Malone shares one trait in common with Jonathan Latimer's Bill Crane: both are seldom without a drink in their hand. Though Malone hides liquor in several drawers of his file cabinet labeled "Confidential," "Unanswered Correspondence," and "Emergency," and replies to a waiter's question about whether he prefers gin, beer, or whiskey with "all three … and make it fast," Rice doesn't go quite as far as Latimer in portraying the disastrously comic effects of alcohol on her main character. Malone's friends Jake and Helene are equally fond of drinking, which in their case often leads to humorous banter reminiscent of that between Hammett's Nick and Nora Charles, especially as portrayed by William Powell and Myrna Loy in the *Thin Man* films that were popular at the time.

The Big Midget Murders (1942) is a typical example of Rice's screwball approach. Following the final evening performance of midget entertainer Jay Otto, known as the Big Midget, at the nightclub Jake Justus owns, Justus accompanied by his wife Helene and Malone enter Otto's dressing room and discover his body hanging from a rope made of eleven stockings, each one a different size. In order to avoid bad publicity, the trio decides not to call the police, but to solve the crime themselves. They hide the body in a large bass fiddle case. Things then get very strange. Before they can remove the body from the dressing room, someone beats them to it. Then the fiddle case is returned but without the body. Later, Otto's body, now dressed in gaudy silk pajamas, is found lying in his hotel room bed. To make matters even more bizarre, all the suspects in his murder have names that begin with the letter "A."

My Kingdom for a Hearse (1956) at first seems to be about a sadistic killer who sends nicely wrapped packages, one containing severed hands, the other severed feet to the office of Delora Deanne, famous as the model of American beauty and idol of American manhood. The situation, however, turns out to be far more complicated than it at first appeared to be. For one thing, there is no Delora Deanne: she is actually a composite of five women who secretly portrayed different parts of her body. Malone assumes the body parts belong to some of those women, but then the five women are all found to be still alive, though the body of another woman related to the case, who died of natural causes, is mysteriously stolen from a hearse. In typical Rice fashion, the details—ranging from the possibility that a voice heard on a phone call may actually be that of one woman imitating another woman who is trying to imitate the first woman's voice to goofy character names like Cuddles Swackhammer, Dennis Dennis, Weasel Firman, and Alonzo Stonecypher—become increasingly comically absurd.

Unlike many of his fictional counterparts, Malone doesn't rattle off a steady stream of wisecracks. His trademark is the malapropism where he comically confuses not just a single word but entire sayings: "Never cross your bridges until the horse is stolen" (*Big* ch. 3); "put the cart before the stable door.... I mean lock the cart after the stable door is stolen" (*Big* ch. 22); "I cross my word. I mean I give my heart" (*Lucky* ch. 8); "Pride goeth before the spring. I mean pride springeth into fall" (*Fourth* 237). The habit is apparently contagious as Jake once remarks that if he has one more thing to worry about, it "will be the camel that tries to grasp at a straw," then smiles and adds, "Malone should have said that" (*Big* ch. 20).

Jake and Helene mainly contribute humor through their good-natured comic banter:

> "Jake," she said thoughtfully, "do you believe in hunches?"
> "Sure," he said. "I used to keep rabbits in them when I was a boy back in Iowa. Rabbit hunches."
> "Damn you," Helene said. "I'm serious."
> "Or, do you mean like the prophet who sat on his hunches and—"
> "Jake, please" [*Lucky* 19].

Another series regular, homicide detective Daniel von Flanagan, also serves a comic purpose. He's a reluctant cop. "It ain't my fault I turned out to be a cop," he moans (*Big* ch.18); the only reason he became one is that a politician owed his father a favor and got him appointed to the police force, and he's been miserable ever since. "Everybody tries to make things hard for you," he complains. "Mix things up and complicate everything" (*My* 126). He even went to court to have the von added to his name because Dan Flanagan sounded too much like a cop's name. He dreams of quitting and starting a mink farm or buying a pecan grove or running a weekly newspaper. In *The Big Midget Murders*, he decides to become a magician, and begins practicing in his office, which leads to one of Rice's characteristically screwball scenes: after attempting to perform a trick involving an uncooperative hen, his office is soon in shambles, chicken feathers scattered all over everything.

In another comic scene, Malone and his undertaker friend toss a pair of thugs who have information Malone wants into the back seat of a hearse and speed off, running through red lights, scattering cars and pedestrians as they careen wildly through the streets of Chicago. When they reach their destination—a funeral home—Malone's friend threatens to embalm the two thugs while they are still alive if they don't cough up the information Malone wants.

Rice also sought to create situations where Malone would encounter oddball characters. For example, in a short story entitled "Don't Go Near," Malone is hired by the owner of a small traveling circus to protect the life of Leopold, his star 550-pound lion after two of his other lions have been killed. The assignment puts Malone in the company of a variety of colorful circus folk with names like Itsy Bitsy, the Wildman, the Weatherman, and the Death-Defying Amazon.

Sadly, Rice's final years were unhappy ones both personally and professionally, and she died in 1957 at the age of forty-nine, her death a result of longtime drug and alcohol abuse.

Norbert Davis (1909–1949)

Norbert Davis, one of Chandler's *Black Mask* contemporaries, could write as tough as any other hard-boiled writer, but in a pair of stories and a trio of novels written in the 1940s, he created one of the funniest private-eye series of all by pairing his detective with a most unusual partner, a fawn-colored Great Dane, large as a yearling calf.

Doan (no first name is ever given) is an employee of the Severn Detective Agency whose boss considers him the best private detective west of the Mississippi. His mild appearance, however, belies his expertise: "He was short and a little on the plump side, and he had a chubby, pink face and a smile as innocent and appealing as a baby's. He looked like a very nice, pleasant sort of person, and on rare occasions he was" (*Mouse* 3). But he is innocent and nice "only when it paid him, and he was as harmless as a rattlesnake" ("Cry" 9).

Sidekicks are not uncommon in crime fiction, but Doan's partner is a special case. Carstairs is a champion dog with an impressive pedigree (with four hundred and eighty-nine blue ribbons to prove it), who has trouble reconciling himself to having for his master such an inferior person who won him in a crap game. When they are out walking, Carstairs always haughtily distances himself either far ahead or far behind Doan so no one would suspect his relationship with him. Carstairs is too snooty to bury his bones in the ground (he keeps them in a safe deposit box) and refuses to eat off the floor because it makes him look like a giraffe taking a drink of water.

Comic banter between the hero and his sidekick is common, but that between Doan and Carstairs is unique, given that one of them can't talk. That, however, doesn't handicap Carstairs too much: he can mumble malignantly under his breath and express his contempt in other ways. For example, he disapproves of Doan's drinking, allowing him only one drink before dinner. When Doan pours a second drink, Carstairs growls at him.

"As for you" said Doan. "You can go straight to hell."
Carstairs growled at him again.

"I'll get drunk if I feel like it," Doan told him. "It's my stomach. Lie down before somebody bops you with a bottle."

Carstairs lowered himself to the floor with a series of loose, bony thuds. He snorted once and then closed his eyes in a resigned way [*Mouse* 147].

Doan describes their relationship this way: "I detest him, and he despises me" (*Sally's* 44). Though Doan routinely calls his canine companion "stupid" and "lame-brain," Carstairs proves to be a valuable partner. He helps support Doan financially thanks to all the female Great Danes whose owners are willing to pay for his services. He's also a valuable assistant on the job, leading Doan safely through a darkened room like a seeing-eye dog or jumping up on a gunman firing at them, distracting him long enough so Doan can shoot him. When Doan wishes to threaten someone, who better to use than a giant dog with fierce fangs and a bone-chilling growl? And when a landlord refuses to rent Doan an apartment, Carstairs lets out an ear-splitting braying sound that Doan promises he'll keep up until the man relents.

The Mouse in the Mountain (1943), also published as *Rendezvous with Fear* (1944) and *Dead Little Rich Girl* (1945), starts out like a comedy. Doan and Carstairs board a bus filled with a motley crew of tourists headed to Los Altos, a difficult-to-reach location high in the mountains of Mexico. His fellow travelers include a female teacher at the Wisteria Young Ladies' Seminary School, a family with a bratty kid, a wealthy heiress whose father made his fortune in flypaper, and her maid, all of them under the guidance of a tour leader whose garbled English is played up for pure humor. "I am Bartolome ... chauffeur licensed and guide most qualified, with English guaranteed by the advanced correspondence school, conversational and classic" (6). But once the bus reaches its destination, the mood abruptly darkens when a gunman begins shooting at Doan, who returns the fire and kills him. When the heiress and her maid are later both murdered, Doan has to find a killer in their midst, which he does with his usual skill.

The plot of *Sally's in the Alley* (1943) is even more preposterous. Doan's agency loans him to the U.S. Government which wants him to travel to the Mohave desert posing as a Japanese spy (he adopts the pseudonym I. Doanwashi) to find the secret location of an ore deposit. This is simply an excuse to allow Davis to introduce characters with colorful names (Parsley Jack, Free-Look Jones, Dust-Mouth Haggerty) and oddball quirks, like the world's politest sheriff—"Excuse me for botherin' you. But I think I'm gonna have to arrest you. Do you mind?"(80)—who belongs to an organization of police officers whose aim is to promote crime among young children. As he explains it, "We got to keep a supply of criminals comin' along all the time so there'll be a big demand for police officers" (86). This being wartime, Doan also tangles with a pair of Nazi spies, one of whom is the Reich's art director and a friend of Hitler from his Munich days.

In *Oh, Murderer Mine* (1946), Doan is hired by a fifty-four-year-old cosmetics tycoon named Heloise of Hollywood to keep an eye on her much younger husband, a man featured in her ads as "Handsome Lover Boy." She wants to keep him out of the clutches of women at the college where he has just been hired to teach. Once again, goofy characters and slapstick scenes—Carstairs runs amok in Heloise's beauty salon when someone tries to tie a pink ribbon on him, scattering an army of screaming naked women in his wake before he ends up slipping and falling into a mud bath, splattering the walls with its contents—share the stage with several violent murders before Doan pieces together the solution to the ridiculous plot.

Two other sources of humor in the books are the flippant voice of the narrator—e.g., "This will probably strike you as highly improbable if you know your Hollywood, but the lobby of the Orna Apartment Hotel, off Rossmore south of Melrose, is done in very nice taste" (*Sally's* 7); "Old Chem was a solid, two-story, grey granite building with an ugly front and a splayed-out rear, and its architect had evidently had the theory that windows were designed to shoot Indians out of and not to facilitate the entrance of fresh air or light" (*Oh* 4)—and Doan's breezy attitude and quick wit—e.g., when questioned about where he studied anatomy, he replies, "Oh, on the street on windy days, and at the beaches and at the burlesque shows" (*Sally's* 137); when asked by a farmer if he ever considered what a pretty sight corn is when it grows in rows," he replies, "I like it better in bottles" (*Sally's* 151).

Joseph T. Shaw, legendary editor of *Black Mask* during its golden years who published five of Davis's stories, admired his ability "in spite of all human trials and tribulations" to look upon life "resignedly and mostly all in fun" and added that, "his sense of humor is prodigious" (Mertz 265). But according to Raymond Chandler, a friend and neighbor, it was likely because Davis "took his murders rather lightly when allowed" (*Letters* 68) that he never became a *Black Mask* regular. Davis's sense of humor can be detected even in his most serious hard-boiled tales, but the Doan and Carstairs books allowed him to give free reign to his comic impulses. These stories are not meant to be taken seriously; readers are simply invited to enjoy reading them as much as Davis obviously enjoyed writing them.

Like his fellow writer of screwball crime fiction Craig Rice, Davis's lively sense of humor couldn't prevent a sad ending. Three years after the publication of the final Doan and Carstairs novel, he took his own life at the age of forty.

Edmund Crispin (1921–1978)

Michael Dirda makes a compelling case for the inclusion of Edmund Crispin in any study of humor in crime fiction: "Compared with the ingenious Agatha Christie or the influential Dashiell Hammett, Edmund Crispin must seem a relatively minor mystery novelist. But are charm and wit to count for nothing? After all, one reads detective stories for many reasons, and there are few writers who can match Crispin's ratio of fun per page" (251).

Edmund Crispin is the pseudonym of Robert Bruce Montgomery, who was born in England in 1921. He attended Oxford University, where he wrote his first Gervase Fen mystery, *The Case of the Gilded Fly* (1944), while still an undergraduate. (The names Gervase and Crispin come from a character named Gervase Crispin in Michael Innis's mystery novel, *Hamlet, Revenge!*) Seven more Fen novels quickly followed over the next eight years. Then after an absence of twenty-seven years, Fen returned for a final appearance in *The Glimpses of the Moon* (1978). Under his real name, Montgomery also had a second career as a composer of music ranging from orchestral and choral pieces to the score for several of the slightly naughty *Carry On* comedy films. For many years he was also a regular mystery reviewer for the Sunday *Times*. He died in 1978.

As a writer of mysteries, Crispin offers little that is new. But the addition of his special brand of humor, which ranges from the sophisticated to the slapstick, makes all the difference. Those of his novels in which humor plays a minor role, like *Swan Song* (1947) and *Frequent Hearses* (1950), are often dragged down by long-winded patches of exposition at the end where the mystery is slowly unraveled. On the other hand, those in which humor is in the forefront have an energy and zest that make for enjoyable reading.

Gervase Fen is an amateur detective. His main job is Professor of English Language and Literature at Oxford University. He doesn't actively seek out cases, but mysteries manage to find him. Some take place in

Oxford, where he lives. Others occur when he's traveling for some reason, e.g., to give a speech at a boys' school or to visit the district he hopes to represent in an upcoming Parliamentary election. In some of his cases, he simply takes a backseat to the police. In solving cases he does admit to a certain amount of luck: "I continue to guess quite nicely, even if I don't actually deduce very much" (*Frequent* 166). His crime-solving skills, however, are not the primary reason to read his books.

Like so much in Crispin's novels, Fen's character is a mixture of the serious and the silly. As befitting a man in his profession, he's fond of literary allusions even when they aren't called for. For example, instead of simply saying, "Wake up," he quotes a line from Thomas Gray: "Awake, Aeolian lyre, awake ... and give to rapture all thy trembling strings" (*Holy* 157). On the other hand, his favorite quote, often repeated—"Oh, my dear paws!... Oh, my fur and whiskers!"—comes from the White Rabbit in *Alice's Adventures in Wonderland* (*Holy* 140).

Crispin may have taken the writing of his mystery novels seriously, but the novels themselves are not intended to be taken that way. As he once declared, "I have no great liking for spy stories, or, come to that, for the more so-called 'realistic' type of crime story. I believe that crime stories in general and detective stories in particular should be essentially imaginative and artificial in order to make their best effect" (Pederson 256). His decision to forgo realism frees him to follow his comic instincts. Like René Magritte's famous painting of a pipe that includes the phrase "Ceci n'est une pipe" ("This is not a pipe"), Crispin's fiction gets plenty of comic mileage out of the frequent reminders to the reader of the made-up nature of what he or she is reading.

Fen regularly jokes about being a character in a Crispin novel. For example, following the narrator's description of him examining his face in a mirror, he wonders whether "he might even live to see the day when novelists described their characters by some other device than that of manoeuvring them into examining themselves in mirrors" (*Glimpses* 48). In *The Moving Toyshop* he amuses himself by "making up titles for Crispin" (79) like *The Return of Fen* and *A Don Dares Death*; when a young woman mentions that she's read about all his cases in the newspapers, he replies, "That's more than Crispin's readers manage to do" (*Love* 179). Asked why he describes a particular rope knot he suspects might have been used to descend into a room from above as the "Hook, Line, and Sinker," he explains, "Because ... the reader has to swallow it" (*Holy* 89). (Crispin isn't amused; in a footnote, he assures the reader that the knot, properly known as the sheet bend, is real and is often used in climbing.)

It isn't just Fen who understands he's only a character in one of Crispin's novels. When Fen and a colleague come to a fork in the road during a car chase, the friend suggests they turn left. "After all," he says, "Gollancz is publishing this book" (*Moving* 85), referring to the left-leaning publishing house that was in fact Crispin's publisher. Another character reminds Fen when he admits he doesn't know the identity of the murderer, "But you must know by now, my dear fellow.... We're practically at the end of the book" (*Glimpses* 207).

Another major source of humor is the third-person narrator who has a flair for the comic mock-epic style in which elevated language or a classical or Biblical allusion is inappropriately applied to something ordinary: schoolgirls frightened by the sudden appearance of their headmistress stood "like those Cornish maids whom the wrath of Jehovah transmogrified in granite for dancing naked on the sabbath day" (*Love* 46); dashing across a busy road, Fen "reached the opposite pavement much as Orestes, hounded by the Furies, must have staggered into Iphigenia's grove in Tauris" (*Moving* 67); walking past a pub because it's too early in the day to begin drinking, Fen gazes back at it "with the lugubrious passion of Orpheus surveying Eurydice at hell-mouth" (*Swan* ch.1).

Not all of the narrator's comic similes are quite so esoteric: "Wolfe thanked him with the civil insincerity of a small boy who has anticipated an aeroplane for Christmas and been given a copy of the Bible" (*Buried* 170); "He looked at Fen as he might have looked at a man who had lit a fire with bank-notes" (*Buried* 38); a buxom village girl is described as having "a frame that was Renoiresque in the outspokenness of its contours" (*Buried* 109).

The narrator's sense of humor is also displayed in descriptions of Fen—"Fen stood with a poker-faced expression which made him look like something loose from a mental home" (*Holy* 203)—and of his beloved red sports car, LILY CHRISTINE III, which is described as being "of exceptional stridency and raffishness" (*Love* 37) and when started "shuddered like a man smitten with the ague" (*Moving* 20). Another comic habit is firing off flippant remarks with a snarky comic edge: "The cathedral clergy are great readers—they have little else to do" (*Holy* 58) and "like most men who have spared themselves the strain of supporting a wife and family, [he] looked younger than his age" (*Glimpses* 39).

But it is Crispin's flair for the farcical that makes several of his novels small comic masterpieces. In *The Moving Toyshop* (1946), for example, poet friend Richard Cadogan decides to pay an impromptu visit to Fen at Oxford. Arriving late one night, he notices a toyshop whose awning had been left down. Entering the unlocked door to investigate, he discovers the body of an elderly woman who has been murdered. Suddenly, he's hit on the head and knocked out. Awakening several hours later, he leaves to report the incident to the police. When they return to the site both the body and the toyshop are gone.

The first clue to the murder appears in the form of a newspaper announcement Fen reads that includes a list of names that he recognizes as coming from some of Edward Lear's nonsense poems, one of which describes a young woman and a dog; as luck (or contrivance) would have it, he spots such a woman walking a dog. He and Cadogan begin following her, leading to the first in a series of madcap chases that are the comic highlights of the novel.

The two of them pursue her into a hall where members of the Handel Society are in the midst of a rehearsal. They squeeze a path through the 300-member choir, knocking over a music stand along the way. Fen even stops to join in the singing, adding an out-of-tune voice to the choir before he's asked to cease. Later, Fen along with a half dozen of his friends, a large contingent of students, and a pair of mysterious men in dark suits whom Fen nicknames Scylla and Charybdis dash off on foot, on bicycles, and in cars in hot pursuit of a fleeing suspect. The chase eventually ends up at a facility for men's nude bathing along the river, where they grab the man before he can escape by boat. The final chase (which inspired the exciting finale of Alfred Hitchcock's 1951 film, *Strangers on a Train*) ends up on a fairgrounds merry-go-round where Fen and Cadogan try to grab the murderer as the carousel keeps spinning round and round.

In *Love Lies Bleeding* (1948), Fen has been invited to the Castreven-ford School to give a talk and hand out awards. Once there, however, he finds himself in the middle of a case involving the disappearance of a sixteen-year-old girl, the murder of two teachers at the school, plus that of a reclusive woman who lived nearby. The novel is filled with oddball characters and comic situations: an escapee from a nearby mental insti-tution who is under the delusion that he is Woodrow Wilson is repeatedly spotted running naked through the area; a voracious pig that eats plenty but won't gain weight is sold, but keeps returning to its unhappy owner; the local rector's house has been inhabited for eighteen years by a polter-geist who keeps throwing household objects at him and his guests.

All these comic elements come together in a farcical climax to the novel when the murderer leads Fen and the police on a wild car chase. The fleeing suspect's car crashes when it swerves to avoid a pig that's blocking the road; the man then flees into the rector's house, rousing the poltergeist to action. He scrambles up onto the roof of the house, where the asylum escapee, who has also taken refuge there, shouts "Boo," causing him to slip and fall off the roof to his death below.

Crispin also employed goofy names (Humbleby, Boysenberry, Elphinstone, Spitshuker, Saversnake, Bartholomew Snerd), clever puns, inside jokes, recurring comic characters, even a variety of cartoon animals (among them a cat named Lavender who distracts a murderer with a gun when he knocks over a vase in his ongoing effort to protect the planet from the threat of Martians that only he can see), all in the service of making his mysteries pure fun to read.

Ed McBain (1926–2005)

Though he wasn't the first to write police procedurals, Ed McBain perfected the formula and influenced virtually every writer in the genre who came after him. (McBain was born Salvatore Lombino in New York City. He legally changed his name to Evan Hunter, under which name he wrote several popular novels (*The Asphalt Jungle*) and screenplays (Alfred Hitchcock's *The Birds*). He used the pseudonym Ed McBain for his police novels and another series about a Florida lawyer named Matthew Hope.) Between *Cop Hater* in 1956 and *Fiddlers* in 2005, the year of his death, McBain published fifty-four novels about a team of police detectives in the 87th Precinct located in the fictional city of Isola, an obvious stand-in for New York City.

While it is certainly true, as George N. Dove observes in his study of the genre, *The Police Procedural*, that "the comic spirit hangs over the saga from start to finish and is never far from the action" (203), McBain is not primarily a comic writer. He described the 87th Precinct series as "a continuing novel about crime and punishment in our times," adding, "What can be more serious than dealing with life and death?" (Carr 15). Police novels like his, he insists, also serve a noble purpose by reconfirming "our faith that a society of laws can work" (Carr 21). None of this, however, requires that he exclude humor from the mix. He employs it effectively, exploring the comic possibilities that later writers in the genre would exploit to an even greater degree.

Each novel in the series includes a note reminding the reader that although the city is imaginary and the characters fictitious, the police routine described in that book is based on established investigatory technique. McBain aims to depict the 87th Precinct detectives as dedicated professionals who do the difficult work of trying to solve every crime committed on their watch. Consequently, he rarely makes fun of them, choosing secondary cop characters to carry the comic weight.

Although Detective Steve Carella is the most prominent character in the series, McBain insists that the entire squad comprises what he calls a "conglomerate protagonist" ("The 87th" 91). The other key members— Meyer Meyer, Bert Kling, Cotton Hawes, Arthur Brown, and Hall Wallis—all have distinctive personalities, but professionally mesh into a solid team, each one contributing to the success of the investigation. There is no star on this team.

Early on McBain realized that humor could be found in the everyday activities of the police. For example, one routine activity in the squad room with comic possibilities is the simple telephone conversation. One of the funniest of these occurs in *Heat* (1981) when Carella calls the telephone company to request a list of calls made from a murder victim's phone. Reminiscent of the classic Mike Nichols-Elaine May comedy routine, the scene exploits the humor that arises out of the increasing frustration of a person desperately trying to find anyone on the other end of the line who can help him.

Another routine activity is the interview, which can ordinarily be a pretty dull exercise. In *Killer's Payoff* (1958), McBain jazzes up such a scene with humor. Detective Cotton Hawes pays a visit to the editor of a men's magazine to question him about a model who had recently been there. Instead of hearing spicy stories about models from a man who boasts, "I veritably cut my way through a cheesecake jungle every day" (58), Hawes has to sit there patiently while the editor peppers him with quotes he has memorized of the opening lines of novels ranging from *Gone with the Wind* to *Ulysses*.

Reading Miranda rights to a suspect is another routine practice that is capable of taking a comic turn. Bert Kling takes time to carefully explain to an eighteen-year-old boy he wants to question exactly what his Miranda rights are. After the boy acknowledges that he understands, Kling says, "You've signified that you understand all the warnings ... and now I ask you whether you are willing to answer my questions without an attorney here to counsel you." "Go shit in your hat," the boy says, "I don't want to answer nothing" (*Hail* 16).

And then there are the harmless but deluded kooks who regularly come to the police for help with their problems, real to them but humorous to others. Sadie the Nut is a good example. For four years, the seventy-eight-year-old toothless woman has been showing up every Wednesday morning to report that yet another potential rapist, all of whom resemble Rudolph Valentino, has attempted to steal her virginity.

McBain's cops take their work very seriously, but not every cop is to be taken that way. For example, a pair of Homicide detectives is required to be present at the scene of every murder, but their role is largely confined to that of sideline observer once someone from the 87th Precinct arrives to take over. The role is ordinarily played by a pair of Tweedledum and Tweedledee dimwits named Monoghan and Monroe who dress alike in black overcoats, black mufflers, and black fedoras and whose conversations are comically pointless and often antiphonal in nature, as in this example:

> Monoghan asked, "You know what you find in a joint like this?"
> "What," Brown asked.
> "Cockroaches," Monoghan said.
> "Bedbugs," Monroe added.
> "Cockroaches and bedbugs," Monoghan summarized [*Jigsaw* 10].

When Monaghan and Monroe are on vacation, they are replaced by Phelps and Forbes, whose conversation sounds exactly like their predecessors:

> "Where's Monoghan and Monroe?" Carella said.
> "Vacation," Phelps said.
> "In January?"
> "Why not?" Forbes said.
> "They both got nice places down in Miami," Phelps said.
> "No reason they shouldn't go there in January," Forbes said.
> "Best time of the year for Florida," Phelps said.
> "Certainly," Forbes said [*Ax* 5].

To underscore their interchangeability, McBain introduces several other pairs of Homicide cops, all with the same kind of alliterative names as Monoghan and Monroe: Carpenter and Calhoun, Mulready and Muldoon, Mastriano and Manzini, Flaherty and Flanagan, Matson and Manson.

Midway through the series, McBain introduced a new continuing character named Fat Ollie Weeks, a detective assigned to the neighboring 88th Precinct. Fat Ollie is crude, overweight, and a consummate bigot, though he doesn't consider himself prejudiced, just discerning. When Carella admonishes him for using a racial epithet and reminds him that the squad room has a diverse mix of people, Ollie replies, "Oh sure, it takes all kinds.... Kikes, spics, niggers ... listen, don't you think I know" (*So Long* 55). He loves to tell ethnic jokes, which he believes are funny rather than offensive, and enjoys showing off his W. C. Fields impression replete with famous Fields quotes like "Ah yes, m'dear" and "m'little chickadee." Unfortunately, most people don't know who W.C. Fields was and think he's doing Al Pacino.

His saving grace is that he happens to be a very good cop who also saves Carella's life on two occasions. He's also a rich source of humor, much of which comes from the way McBain gets inside his head to reveal how he thinks:

> Ollie liked dead people much better than he did most living ones. Dead people didn't give you any trouble. You went into a dead person's apartment, you didn't have to worry about farting or belching. Also, if the vic was a girl, you could handle her panties or pantyhose—like he was doing now—without anybody thinking you were some kind of pervert. Ollie sniffed the crotch of a pair of red panties, which was actually good police work because it would tell him was the girl a clean person or somebody who just dropped panties she had worn right back in the drawer without rinsing them out [*Last 100*].

In *Fat Ollie's Book* (2002), McBain comes up with the brilliant idea of making Ollie, a man who previously thought amazon.com was "a very large broad named Dorothy Kahm" (58), an author. Ollie has written a thirty-six-page "novel" entitled "Report to the Commissioner" which someone steals from the back seat of his car and mistakenly thinks is a blueprint to a diamond heist. McBain entertains the reader throughout the novel by regularly quoting generous portions of hilariously clunky prose that is as unpolished and bloated as Ollie himself.

One of McBain's funniest novels is also one of his best. *Fuzz* (1968) features an arch villain known only as the Deaf Man, who becomes the squad's nemesis in six books. This time he has devised a diabolical scheme in which he sends letters to the 87th Precinct threatening to kill a particular city official if a ransom isn't paid. When the money isn't paid, he goes through with his deadly threat. The various members of the squad desperately want to catch him because in his previous appearance he made every one of them appear "dim-witted and bumbling and inefficient" (*Fuzz* 73).

Before long, he has them once again behaving like inept Keystone Kops. Carella poses as a drunken bum in an effort to apprehend a pair of thugs who have previously set two vagrants on fire. When the assailants approach him, his gun snags in his sweater when he tries to pull it out and he is beaten and burned with flaming gasoline. Another cop misses a suspect's meeting because of a flat tire. Two of the most experienced detectives both lose track of an individual they are tailing. A fellow cop on a stakeout slips on the ice and nearly breaks his leg. Genero, a lousy cop to begin with, shoots himself in the leg when he pulls his gun to apprehend a fleeing suspect. Later, he chases after the pair of thugs who had earlier attacked Carella, unaware that their intended victim this time was the Deaf Man, who thanks to Genero is able to escape and begin planning another assault on the precinct.

McBain perfected a formula that made him the most successful and influential writer of police procedurals ever, leading John C. Carr to proclaim that, "To say that Ed McBain is a giant among popular writers is like saying the Colossus of Rhodes was a pretty fair piece of municipal sculpture" (1).

Donald E. Westlake (1933–2008)

Many crime writers have a healthy sense of humor and are able to create comic dialogue, witty similes, and slapstick situations. Few, however, have the kind of fertile comic imagination that Donald E. Westlake had. Otto Penzler, a longtime friend and editor, proclaimed him "the most consistently humorous writer of mystery and crime the world has ever seen" (Cannon). Humor can be found in many of Westlake's novels, but his most sustained effort is the fourteen-novel series he wrote between 1970 and his death in 2008 about bad-luck burglar John Dortmunder.

For several years, Richard Stark, author of a series of serious crime novels about a cold-blooded professional thief named Parker, sold far more books than Westlake. It irritated Westlake because he was also Richard Stark, the pseudonym he used only for that series. (He also wrote another series about ex-cop-turned-private-eye Mitch Tobin under the name Tucker Coe.) But thanks to Dortmunder it wasn't long before Westlake's sales caught up with Stark's.

The Dortmunder novels were not Westlake's first foray into comic crime fiction. He had already published several stand-alone novels that showcased his comic gifts. *Who Stole Sassi Manoon?* (1969), for example, is about a computer-generated plan for kidnapping a famous actress that is thwarted when a second gang, an elderly couple planning to use the ransom money to finance their retirement, beats the first gang to the punch. Other later examples include *Help, I Am Being Held Prisoner* (1974), about a gang that plans a bank robbery while they have the perfect alibi—they are already serving time in prison but a secret tunnel allows them to come and go as they wish; and *Dancing Aztecs* (1976), his comic masterpiece, which details the efforts of three competing groups to get their hands on a solid gold statue of a dancing Aztec priest. Unfortunately for them, it has been mixed in with a box full of worthless copies, which end up in the possession of sixteen unsuspecting people. The search for the genuine item leads to plot complications that multiply hilariously.

The Hot Rock (1970), the first Dortmunder novel, started out as a Parker book. After writing ten or eleven of the Parker novels, Westlake was looking for a new angle. Since Parker didn't handle frustration well, Westlake thought it might be interesting to see what would happen if he had to steal the same object several times. But he soon came to realize that, "the worst thing you can do with a tough guy is make him funny inadvertently, because then he isn't a tough guy anymore, he's just a jerk" (Silet 262). So he came up with another character who was more long suffering, and gave his dogged but doomed new hero the name Dortmunder (after seeing a German beer with that name) because he felt it "just has a nice gloomy sound to it" (Silet 262).

Born in Dead Indian, Illinois, and raised by nuns in the Bleeding Heart Sisters of Eternal Misery orphanage, Dortmunder now lives in a tiny Manhattan apartment with his longtime companion May, who works as a cashier at the local supermarket. He's a small-time con man and burglar who occasionally picks up a few bucks here and there by posing as a door-to-door encyclopedia salesman and then stealing the customer's down payment or as a repairmen who takes expensive typewriters away with him to be fixed and then pawns them. He's a two-time loser who faces a lifetime sentence if he's ever convicted of another crime.

Dortmunder does possess one special talent: he's a wizard at planning clever ways of pulling off the most complicated heist. He's no inept bungler, just one of the world's unluckiest criminals; something almost always torpedoes his plans. He's the kind of star-crossed guy "on whom the sun shone only when he needed darkness" (*Bad* 1), one whose bad luck "clouded his days and chilled his nights" (*Why* 91). A list of some of the titles in the series provides a pretty good idea about his unhappy plight: *Nobody's Perfect, Why Me?, Drowned Hopes, Don't Ask, Bad News, What's So Funny?*

Failure can be either tragic or comic. The unrealized dreams of a man like Willy Loman in Arthur Miller's *Death of a Salesman* can brings tears to the eyes of the audience. But in the case of a loser like John Dortmunder, only laughter ensues. The fun (for the reader, certainly not for Dortmunder) comes from the inventive ways Westlake repeatedly frustrates Dortmunder. He's like a comic Sisyphus, the ancient Greek king who was condemned for eternity to roll a massive boulder up a hill only to watch it fall back down and have to start all over again.

Dortmunder's plans require the help of a regular gang: Andy Kelp, who steals only doctors' cars because he knows they usually buy luxurious ones, and whom Dortmunder fears may be the jinx that keeps foiling his plans; Stan Murch, the getaway driver whose sole subject of conversation is the quickest route from one place to another; and Tiny Bulcher, a giant of a man whose skill is a simple one: "I pick up heavy things, I move them, I put them down, that's what *I* do. Sometimes I persuade people to change their minds about certain things" (*Drowned* 237). From time to time the gang is expanded to include Dortmunder's chain-smoking girlfriend May and Murch's Mom, who works (naturally) as a New York City cab driver.

In true *Groundhog Day* fashion, each novel in the series features one scene that recurs with only minor variations, underscoring the Sisyphus-like repetitivesness of Dortmunder's existence. The setting is the O. J. Bar & Grill on Amsterdam Avenue where Dortmunder is first greeted by Rollo the bartender. He makes his way past the regular customers at the bar, who are always arguing about burning issues like the etymology of the word "spic" or why the Indy 500 is called the Indy 500, and then strolls by the bathrooms labeled "Pointers" and "Setters." He finally enters the storage room at the back lined with beer and liquor cases where he joins his gang around a table with a green felt top where a new plan (with the same old result) is hatched.

The Hot Rock (1970) is structured like a house of cards that keeps collapsing each time a new one is added to the pile. Dortmunder is hired by an African ambassador to steal a precious emerald that he claims rightfully belongs to his country. Dortmunder and his crew successfully pull off the theft from a museum where the jewel is being displayed. Then things take a bad turn. Just as he's about to be grabbed by the police, Greenwood, the gang member who has the gem, swallows it. Dortmunder now has to figure out a way to break him out of jail. That plan succeeds, but Greenwood then confesses that he doesn't have it—he actually hid it in the police station after his arrest. Now Dortmunder has to break into a police station in the middle of Manhattan, which requires him to find a helicopter. Naturally, the emerald isn't there; it turns out that Greenwood's lawyer grabbed it and he's now hiding out in an insane asylum. This time, with the aid of a miniature train, the gang kidnaps the lawyer, but he no longer has it: it's locked in a safe-deposit box in a bank. And so it goes, one frustration after another.

In *Bank Shot* (1972) Dortmunder and his associates plan to rob a bank that is temporarily being housed in a trailer. They decide to steal the trailer, drive it away, paint it, put up curtains, and then hide it in plain sight in a trailer park. The plan succeeds, but then it begins raining, which washes off the trailer's paint, so they have to hide it elsewhere. Then when they blow open the safe, the explosion sets the money on fire. The gang puts it out, salvaging some of the damp charred bills. Then the trailer begins slipping down the hill and into the ocean, where it is carried out to sea. For all of their hard work, each of them ends up with only $200.

Jimmy the Kid (1974) is one of Westlake's most playfully inventive entries. Andy Kelp stumbles upon a novel by Richard Stark entitled *Child Heist* about a criminal named Parker who successfully pulls off the kidnapping of a twelve-year-old boy. The joke, of course, is that Richard Stark is the pseudonym Westlake used for his Parker books. *Child Heist* is a fictitious Parker novel, but Westlake includes several chapters written in the Stark style to lay out the groundwork for Dortmunder's latest disappointment.

At first, Dortmunder refuses to read the book, insisting that he, not some fiction writer, is the planner of the group's activity (another sly joke by Westlake). But he eventually agrees that the scheme laid out in the Stark book seems foolproof. He studies the details and then selects his own twelve-year-old victim. But as usual in Dortmunder's world, nothing goes as expected.

The first thing that goes wrong is that the Cadillac young Jimmy Harrington is riding in is too wide to fit into the truck that is supposed to take it to the gang's hideout, as the Stark novel depicts. Even though Dortmunder and his buddies took the trouble to actually memorize the dialogue that worked so well in the Stark novel, the rubber Mickey Mouse masks they all wear make whatever they say completely unintelligible. More mishaps follow: the phone call to the car carrying Jimmy's father to tell him where to drop the ransom money off can't get through because the father is talking on the phone to his secretary. When his car drives past the designated location for the money drop, it has to turn around, but is then stopped by a traffic cop for speeding. Eventually, things get back on track, but when the suitcase carrying the ransom is tossed from the car at the designated spot, it hits Dortmunder in the head, knocking him out. But the biggest difference between the Stark novel's plan and Dortmunder's is that young Jimmy is a genius who reads the *New Yorker* and *Scientific American* in his spare time. The Dortmunder gang is no match for this smart kid, who turns his kidnap experience into a Hollywood film.

In *Drowned Hopes* (1990), Dortmunder's 70-year-old former cellmate Tom Jimson who has just been released from prison comes to him with a deal. (The name Tom Jimson is a nod to Jim Thompson, whose novel *The Grifters* Westlake was at the time adapting for the screen; he later earned an Academy Award nomination for his screenplay.) Before going to prison, Jimson buried $700,000 and wants Dortmunder's help in digging it up. The problem is the town where it was buried now lies fifty feet under water after a nearby river was damned to create a reservoir. The comic complications intensify with each effort to get cash to fund the enterprise from the various hiding places where Tom stashed it: at one point Dortmunder has to retrieve the cash from inside the left nostril of Lincoln's face on Mount Rushmore.

Westlake is more than a simple jokester. Though his special talent is devising elaborate plots that find the humor in the interaction between character and situation, his sense of humor is notable for its wide range. "His taste in humor is catholic," his wife Abby Adams once wrote, "embracing brows low, middle and high, from *Volpone* to Laurel and Hardy" (76). Lew Stahl, editor of a posthumous collection of Westlake's non-fiction, added this observation:

> Westlake hardly ever wrote a full page of anything—be it fiction or a business letter—without finding a way to get some humor into it. He just seems to have seen the world that way: everything is a tiny bit ridiculous, because, well, look at us? We're not really very good at this living stuff, are we? Yet we have the audacity to make plans and think we're in control. That illusion is the source of so much of Westlake's humor. Everything is always going wrong, and that in and of itself is funny, if you look at it the right way. As he put it in his piece on Stephen Frears, "If we aren't going to enjoy ourselves, why do it?" He really seems to have written, and lived, with that motto in mind [Belth].

Westlake has a childlike attraction to silly things like funny names: J. Radcliffe Stonewiler (an attorney), Lance Sheath (a film star), Panchard L. Whiskum, Griswold Porculey, Sheikh Rama el-Rama el-Rama El, Lotte de Charraiveuneuirauville. He also exploits the comic absurdity of simple names. For example, he gives one character the name Francis Xavier Mologna (pronounced Maloney), which requires him to correct everyone he meets who invariably fail to pronounce it correctly. And who else but Westlake would name a character Irene only so that the cop questioning her can bid her farewell with the words, "Good night, Irene," or give a character the name Myrtle Street and then have her reside on Myrtle Street?

He also loves funny sounds, and finds humorous ways of describing them: e.g., the sound a wrench makes trying to loosen a bolt: "WANG! WANG!WANG! SKRAWK-SKRAWK" (*Drowned* 193); a congregation standing and then sitting back down in church: "Shckr—shckr—shckr*oop*" and "Schlff—schlff—*fflrp*" (*Drowned* 108); or the racket at a construction site: "a backhoe kept lumbering around in the way of the traffic flow, backing up (beep beep beep beep) and going forward (   ) and backing up (beep beep beep beep) and going forward (   )" (*Don't* 70).

Westlake's comic sense of absurdity is also displayed in such simple things as this brief exchange between Dortmunder and Andy Kelp:

"What's the guy's name?"
"Guy."
"Yeah, What's his name?"
"Guy Claverack" [*Don't* 198].

And in this more extensive description of a beautiful day which builds up to an ironic punch line:

Two solid weeks of beautiful weather. Clear sunny days, low humidity, temperature in the seventies, air so brisk and clean you could read E PLURIBUS UNUM on a dime across the street. Clear cloudless nights, temperature in the fifties, the sky a great soft raven's breast, an immense bowl of octopus ink salted with a million hard white crystalline stars and garnished with a huge moon *pulsing* with white light. It was disgusting [*Drowned* 299].

He also writes some of the funniest similes around: "the chateau was as ready as a fifteen-year-old boy after two hours of foreplay" (*Don't* 247); a plane takes off, "galumphing away like Sidney Greenstreet playing basketball" (*Hot* 276); a person glowers "like a man falsely accused of being the one who farted" (*Why* ch. 23); a foreign language sounds "like crickets in armor jousting" (*Don't* 95); an elderly woman is "as mad as an African general and as incontinent as Atlantis" (*Nobody* 173).

Even his failed similes are funny, as in this example where the narrator attempts to compare a seventy-six story Manhattan skyscraper to an ocean liner:

The bottom two floors were all machinery and metal ladders, like the bowels of a great ocean-going passenger liner—which in many ways is what a skyscraper is, massive and self-contained and compartmented, except that the skyscraper is always moored in the same place, and of course it's standing on end, and come to think of it skyscrapers don't float, and maybe they aren't anything like each other at all. Forget the whole thing [*Good* 158].

In the end, Westlake's all-too-human criminals provide what Michael Dunne calls the "smiling comedy of recognition" (175) which reminds his readers of their own limitations and failures, yet allows them "to laugh rather than to cry at perhaps the most depressing truth of the human condition, the fact that Nobody's Perfect" (180).

Joseph Wambaugh (1937–)

Professions often have their own distinctive brand of humor, but none is more colorful than cop humor. No one has captured that style of dark, raunchy humor better than Joseph Wambaugh, a fourteen-year veteran of the Los Angeles police department, who became a best-selling novelist while still working as a cop.

There are many writers of police procedurals, the most famous of whom is Ed McBain, author of the groundbreaking 87th Precinct series that began in 1956. As we have seen, there is plenty of humor in those novels, as there is in other police procedurals like Chester Himes's Grave Digger Jones and Coffin Ed Johnson series set in Harlem and the Martin Beck series by the Swedish writers Maj Sjöwall and Per Wahlöö, whose klutzy patrolmen Karl Kristiansson and Kurt Kvant offer some Keystone Kop style humor.

Wambaugh, however, doesn't write police procedurals. For one thing, he doesn't limit himself to a single police squad as most writers of procedurals do. His cops are mainly uniformed patrolmen (and sometimes patrolwomen) who are not directly involved in criminal investigation, so the process the police use to solve a crime doesn't play a major role. Instead, Wambaugh prefers to call what he writes, "the modern police novel." As he explains it:

> Before I started writing about the police there were police procedurals. Those stories told how the cop acts on the job. I was the first one to flip it. I decided what was more interesting was to tell how the job acts on the cop. So we spent a lot of time in characters and people's heads rather than worrying about plot. My position is that if you get the character right, he will lead you into plot. That became a different kind of police novel. You are with them on the job, off the job, in intimate moments [Trachtenberg].

The portrait he paints of cops on the job focuses primarily on their personalities, and one of the most distinctive features his beat cops share is a dark sense of humor. Wambaugh describes it this way: "It's gallows humor, it's defensive humor. You find it in morgues, emergency rooms, and in the Marine Corps, where I served. You find it wherever people need humor to ward off fear or despair" (Trachtenberg).

His cop humor may remind readers of *M*A*S*H*, both the 1970 film directed by Robert Altman and the classic television series that ran from 1972 to 1983. The characters in *M*A*S*H* are members of a surgical team laboring during the Korean War who develop a mordant sense of humor as a way of fortifying themselves so they can continue their sometimes gruesome work. The difference in the case of Wambaugh's cops is that he has greater freedom than the television writers to emphasize the raunchy, obscene, racist nature of their humor. For them, political correctness be damned!

The language Wambaugh's cops speak is obscene, their behavior boorish, their attitudes sexist, racist, and homophobic. All of this, however, is also very funny. The humor begins with the colorful Dickensian names they hang on one another: Roscoe Rules, Whaddayamean Dean, Spermwhale Whalen, Whipdick Woofer, the Gook and the Spook (a team of a Japanese and a black cop), the Weasel and the Ferret, and Balls Hadley and No-Balls Hadley, their way of distinguishing between a male and a female cop with the same last name. Their slang is equally distinctive— "scrotes" (short for "scrotum," the term they use to describe the unsavory types they have to deal with), "badge bunnies," "saline Suzies," and "yuckbabes." They also create their own names for Hollywood ("Babelwood" and "Hollyweird"), Santa Monica Blvd. ("Sodom-Monica"), and a favorite cop bar ("The House of Misery").

But it is their distinctive style of mordant humor that stands out. Here's a small sampling: after discovering the body of a man who had committed suicide by hanging himself, a cop says, "He probably reached the end of his rope" (*Choirboys* 66); a cop holds up a mayonnaise jar that contains part of a woman's lip bitten off during a fight with another woman and asks his partner, "Ever hear of somebody lipping off to you?" (*Choirboys* 165); another cop knocks on a woman's door to inform her that her husband has just been killed in a knife fight: "You the widow Brown?" he asks. "No, I ain't a widow," she says. "The hell you ain't," he replies (*Choirboys* 279); on the eighteenth birthday of some young gang members he knows, the same cop would send a Xerox of the page of the LAPD manual which talks about shooting at adults only, along with a bullet and a greeting card on which he'd write, "You are now, by law, an adult. Have a nice eighteenth birthday, asshole" (*Choirboys* 288).

Cop humor isn't always so dark. It can also be playful. For example, some of Wambaugh's cops like to entertain themselves by approaching a drug house, shouting "Police," then listening to the toilets flushing up and down the street. Or by displaying a sign in the window of their cruiser that reads, "Driver carries no cash," when traveling through certain rough neighborhoods. Sometimes it is both dark *and* playful. In *The Black Marble* (1978), one cop with a macabre sense of humor hides the severed head of a murder victim in a bag of tortillas belonging to a female clerk in the department. Then he waits to enjoy the unsuspecting woman's reaction when she digs into the bag for a snack. She transfers to another department once she learns the cop has come into possession of a severed penis. In *The Glitter Dome* (1981), a cop pulls the torso of a murdered woman out of a trash bin and begins spinning her around while singing "Shall We Dance?" from *The King and I*.

Wambaugh's first two novels, *The New Centurions* (1971) and *The Blue Knight* (1972), were largely realistic depictions of actual police work. *The Choirboys* (1975), his first novel written after his retirement, is also the first to fully display his skill at combining dark humor and human tragedy. The novel follows the actions, both on and off the job, of ten L. A. patrol officers. Their primary extracurricular activity is what they call "choir practice," a gathering in MacArthur Park following their shift where they can blow off steam, mainly by griping, getting drunk, and cavorting with a pair of plump cocktail waitresses named Ora Lee Tingle and Carolina Moon. These drunken celebrations are often hilarious, but what gives the novel its powerful impact are the emotionally painful things they encounter on the job (like discovering the bodies of a mother and her three young children who have been brutally murdered in their home), which helps us understand their need for such escapes as "choir practice."

The book is filled with extended comic episodes. One incident involves a pair of choirboys who are injured while attempting to corral the notorious Filthy Herman, a three-foot-tall amputee who is well-known to the cops as "a legless wienie wagger" who periodically gets drunk and exposes himself in colorful ways. This time, naked except for a Dodger baseball cap, he's found proudly screaming, "My cock's dragging the ground, how about yours?" (*Choirboys* 127). In another episode, one of the choirboys on loan to the vice squad attempts to arrest two prostitutes, one of them eight-months pregnant. One yells "rape," and the two of them take off running, leading to a Keystone Kops–like chase through the streets of L. A. that eventually draws twenty-one police cars to the scene.

Despite the novel's heavy dose of humor, Wambaugh makes it clear that there is nothing funny about the emotional demands of the cops' demanding job, stress that is caused not only by dangers on the streets but also by their short-sighted and small-minded superiors. The comedy eventually gives way to tragedy when one of the choirboys takes his own life, which prompts a final choir practice during which a drunken cop accidentally kills an innocent man, resulting in dire consequences for many of the participants.

Wambaugh has said that *The Choirboys* was heavily influenced by Joseph Heller's *Catch-22*. Like Heller's comic masterpiece about the absurdity that often accompanies warfare, *The Choirboys* features numerous examples of absurd behavior, as well as plenty of higher-ups (with appropriate names like Lieutenant Finque and Suckass Sneed) who represent ridiculous authority figures hopelessly out of touch with the reality of what their underlings are facing. The novel also includes lines of twisted logic like these—"The regulations were perfect. No one could understand them" (7) and "Sam Niles was starting to like his friend Baxter Slate so much he never wanted to see him again" (250)—which read like they might have actually come from the pages of *Catch-22*.

Wambaugh's cops often become embroiled in dangerous situations that unexpectedly turn comic. A memorable example can be found in *The Delta Star* (1983), where a pair of cops (one black, one Asian) attempt to arrest a giant of a man who operated as a hit man for the Aryan Brotherhood when he was in prison. The arresting officers are soon joined by reinforcements and the resulting struggle turns violent. But with the Asian cop ineffectually trying to stop the giant with Bruce Lee–like martial-art maneuvers that work only in the movies, another cop inadvertently spraying a blast of mace into his own armpit, and a female cop riding on the giant's back like a jockey on an elephant, the scene quickly degenerates into slapstick farce. The comic capstone comes when the giant's wheelchair-bound mother enters the fray, cheering on the cops with shouts of "KICK HIM!... USE YOUR FEET! PUNCH HIS EYES OUT!" and "WELL, YA AIN'T GONNA STOP NOW, ARE YA, YA CHICKENSHITS?" (*Delta* 148).

Ten years after publishing what he thought was his final novel, Wambaugh wrote *Hollywood Station* (2006), the first of five novels that appeared in quick succession about a group of cops in the Hollywood Division. Unlike his early novels where he drew upon his own experiences, this time he relied upon the stories of other cops. For each of these novels, he would gather upwards of fifty cops in groups of three and four and over dinner and drinks would listen to their tales of life on the job. He would then fashion a plot that would largely serve as a simple framework for a succession of some of the funniest stories of modern cops on the job. Their turf being Hollywood, which they call Hollyweird, these cops encounter more than their fair share of oddball characters, including an army of street performers on Hollywood Boulevard dressed like movie stars, cartoon characters, and superheroes. The cops find themselves having to deal with complaints that Darth Vader is exposing himself, Batman is assaulting Spiderman, and Bugs Bunny is selling drugs to Pluto.

For all their outrageous humor, Wambaugh's novels aren't simple comedies; they are warts-and-all portraits of cops at work and play whose humor helps them maintain their sanity in a world that can quickly rob them of their innocence. Many of them adopt a cynical attitude; some of them develop hardened souls. But they never lose their sense of humor. They also serve to illustrate what Wambaugh said he learned from his own experience as a cop: "no matter how distressing the job can become, and how emotionally dangerous, doing good police work is still the most fun a person will ever have in a lifetime" (High).

Robert B. Parker (1932–2010)

Robert B. Parker is widely considered to be the fourth member (along with Dashiell Hammett, Raymond Chandler, and Ross Macdonald) of the Mount Rushmore quartet of Great Writers of American private-eye fiction. His version of the hard-boiled hero is a tough and dedicated Boston-based private detective named Spenser ("with an S like the English poet") who fits firmly into the knightly tradition first established by Chandler's Philip Marlowe. Parker's connection to Chandler is strong: he wrote his Ph.D. dissertation on Chandler, Hammett, and Macdonald and was commissioned by the Chandler estate to complete *Poodle Springs* (1989), Chandler's unfinished Marlowe novel, and to write a sequel to *The Big Sleep*, entitled *Perchance to Dream* (1991).

Despite adopting many of the same features of style and character associated with Marlowe, Spenser differs from his predecessor in key ways: thanks to a loving relationship with long-time girlfriend Susan Silverman, he's no loner stuck in a monastic lifestyle like Marlowe who in one of his darker moments complained, "Nobody came in, nobody called, nobody cared whether I died or went to El Paso" (*High* 150); thanks to a much sunnier disposition than most early private eyes, he's also an inveterate jokester. Marlowe could crack wise, but much of the humor in his books is specifically aimed at the reader. Spenser by contrast is a public quipster who enjoys an audience so much he's even forced to concede that, "Sometimes I try too hard to be funny" (*Mortal* 17).

As noted previously, first-person narrative is as much about the narrator as the story he tells, for the reader gets to observe a mind at work. Spenser is no "just-the-facts-ma'am" narrator. He seldom passes up an opportunity to make a joke even when he's simply describing the most ordinary of events:

> I had breakfast in a diner, nothing could be finer, took two aspirin and set out after Frank Doerr. A funeral parlor in Charlestown Quirk had said. I brought all my sleuthing wiles to bear on the problem of how to locate it and looked in the yellow pages. Elementary, my dear Holmes. There it was, under Funeral directors; Francis X. Doerr, 228 Main Street, Charlestown. There's no escape Doerr [*Mortal* 110].

Surveillance is never particularly enjoyable, but it is for the reader when a man with a sense of humor like Spenser describes the experience:

> It was hard watching both the door and the corridor traffic. I was getting tired of holding the gun. My hand was stiff, and with the thing cocked I had to hold it carefully. I thought about shifting it to my left hand. I wasn't as good with my left hand, and I might need to be very good all of a sudden. I wouldn't be too good if my gun hand had gone to sleep, however. I shifted the thing to my left hand and exercised my right. The gun felt clumsy in my left. I ought to practice left-handed more. I hadn't anticipated a gun hand going to sleep. *How'd you get shot, Spenser?* Well, it's this way, Saint Pete, I was staked out in a hotel corridor but my hand went to sleep. Then after a while my entire body nodded off. *Did Bogey's hand ever go to sleep, Spenser? Did Kerry Drake's?* No, sir. *I don't think we can admit you here to Private-Eye Heaven, Spenser* [*Judas* 41].

Marlowe ordinarily employed wisecracks to cheer himself up or to deflect a threat. Spenser simply loves to joke around. When told, "You don't have to be a wise guy," he replies, "I know... I do it voluntarily" (*Stardust* 55). When a busty receptionist in a chiffon dress asks him, "May I help you?" he answers, "Yes you may," then quips, "but it would involve wrinkling your dress" (*God* 108). After Rachel Wallace, the feminist author he's been hired to protect, objects to his having punched a man and chastises him by saying, "You were a stupid thug. I will not have you acting on my behalf in a manner I deplore. If you strike another person except to save my life, I will fire you at that moment," he responds, "How about if I stick my tongue out at them and go *bleaaah*" (*Looking* 45).

Like Marlowe, Spenser is also adept at using humor to fend off a threat or deflate the self-important and pretentious. "I'm getting sick of you, Spenser," one man declares, "I'm sick of the way you look, and the way you dress, and the way you get your hair cut and the way you keep shoving your face into my work. I'm sick of you being alive and making wise remarks. You understand what I'm saying to you, turd?" "What's wrong with the way I dress?," Spenser asks (*Mortal* 113). When a CIA agent introduces himself by announcing, "I'm with the three-letter agency," Spenser belittles the man's self-importance by replying, "You with the Tennessee Valley Authority... Well damn, I always wanted to meet someone like you. TVA is my favorite" (*Catskill* 151). When a college president, impressed by Spenser's answer to a question, makes the mistake of telling him, "You speak rather well," he needs only two words—"You too"—to brush off her patronizing attitude (*Small* 37).

Spenser also uses humor in his descriptions, whether in a brief snapshot—"She was wearing something in purple suede that was too short for a skirt and too long for a belt" (*Godwulf* 6)—or in a longer passage that ends with a comic zinger, like this one:

> In the center of the line was a large man with a square jaw and thick brown hair. Looked like he'd been a tight end perhaps, at Harvard. He wore a dark suit and a pale gray silk tie. His cheeks were rosy, and his eye was clear. Probably still active in his alumni association. A splendid figure of a man, the rock upon which the picket line was anchored. Surely a foe of atheism, Communism, and faggotry. Almost certainly a perfect asshole [*Looking* 36].

Spenser tends to be full of himself, so it's a good thing he's willing to turn his mockery back on himself. Complimented for looking like "somebody in a Tarzan movie," he self-deprecatingly replies, "Cheetah" (*Godwulf* 105). He even jokes about his sex appeal: before heading off to a Red Sox game, he checks himself in a mirror: "Adorable," he says, then adds, "Lucky it wasn't ladies' day. I'd get molested at the park" (*Mortal* 8).

He also makes fun of (1) his powers of observation: "Cathy Connelly was apartment 13. I guessed second floor, given the size of the building. I was wrong. It was third floor. Close observation is my business" (*Godwulf* 120); (2) his interviewing prowess: after a sixteen-year-old girl responds to all of his questions with either a shrug of the shoulders or a shake of the head, he says, "When I turn on the charm they melt like butter" (*Promised* 22); (3) his supposed expertise in reading the opposite sex: a request from a woman to put another log on the fire gets him thinking: "It was a way of establishing relationships, I thought, as I got a log from the basket and set it on top of the fire—get me to do her bidding. I'd known other women like that. If they couldn't get you to do them little services they felt insecure. Or, maybe she just wanted another log on the fireplace. Sometimes," he concludes, "I'm deep as hell" (*Godwulf* 43).

He's especially good at poking fun at his own flair for using wisecracks. When informed that star Boston Red Sox pitcher Marty Rabb might have secret gambling connections, all he can think of to say in response is "Rabb." Then he adds, tongue firmly lodged in cheek, "Snappy comebacks are one of my specialties" (*Mortal* 4). He also concedes that not everyone finds what he says to be as humorous as he does: "No one laughed; I was getting used to that" (*Looking* 36). After failing to come up with a witty rejoinder to one remark, he confesses, "I couldn't think of anything to say, so I didn't say anything," then adds, "It was a technique I ought to work on" (*Godwulf* 123).

A certain amount of confidence is good, as for example when Spenser tells a prospective client, "I'm not only the best you can get; I'm the best there is" (*Judas* 6). Sometimes, however, his smug self-satisfaction becomes almost too much. A man who can boast, "If I hadn't been me, I'd have wished I were" (*Playmates* 2) or who can say to Susan Silverman, "It is a lot better to be you and me than to be most people" (*Paper* 180), occasionally needs to be brought back to earth. Archie Goodwin was ready to cut Nero Wolfe down to size whenever his britches got too big. Fortunately, Spenser is able to do it to himself. Otherwise his bravado and braggadocio would make him insufferable. As Parnell Hall has noted. Spenser's jests, "humanize him, mask his heroism, diffuse the macho image that is rightfully his. Without humor, he would appear a self-righteous prig, adhering to a strict moral code. With it, he is a jaunty, cocky son of a bitch, constantly ridiculing himself while he ridicules others" (ch. 4).

Parker gave Spenser a pair of loyal sidekicks who also contribute to the humor in the series. Susan Silverman, his longtime therapist girlfriend, plays a key role as interpreter of Spenser's heroic code and enthusiastic cheerleader of his brave efforts. Her presence also serves to distinguish him from the crowd of lonely private eyes who have nothing but a bottle of whiskey to snuggle up to when they come home. Spenser has Susan, and their playful to-and-fro is a trademark of the series. In this scene, the couple has just enjoyed a bit of spontaneous lovemaking that has ended on the couch. Susan worries about having frolicked in front of their dog Pearl (another series regular):

> "Maybe she showed a little class," I said, "and looked away."
> "I seem to recall her barking at a very critical juncture."
> "For heaven's sake," I said. "I thought that was you."
> Susan giggled into my shoulder where she was resting her head.
> "You yanked me right over the counter," she said.
> "I didn't yank," I said "I swept."
> "And spilled the wine and broke the wine glass."
> "Seemed worth it at the time," I said.
> "Usually I like to undress and hang up my clothes neatly."

"So why didn't you resist?" I said.
"And miss all the fun?" [*Paper* 208].

But it is Spenser's coldly efficient African American sidekick Hawk who provides the most interesting comic possibilities. Hawk highlights Spenser in multiple ways, including establishing the line a man with a moral code like Spenser won't cross. In *Early Autumn,* for example, Hawk orders Spenser to shoot the man he's standing over. "I can't kill a man lying there on the floor," Spenser says. "I can," says Hawk (201). And he does.

Hawk also gives Parker plenty of opportunities to include the kind of good-natured racial banter that is possible only between longtime friends who respect one another. For example, Spenser observes Hawk nattily dressed in a three-piece suit with a lavender tie and a white straw hat tipped forward over his face. "Excuse me, Mr. Fetchit," he says, "I've seen all your movies and was wondering if you'd care to join me for a bite of watermelon." Hawk responds, "Y'all can call me Stepin, bawse" (*Judas* 75). When Spenser tries to advise his friend how to do his job, Hawk retorts, "Yowsah, boss, y'all awful kind to hep ol Hawk lak yew do." "Why don't you can that Aunt Jemima crap," Spenser parries. "You're about as down-home darkie as Truman Capote" (*Judas* 81).

Spenser has proven to be one of the most entertaining and durable of all American private-eye heroes. Beginning with his debut in *The Godwulf Manuscript* in 1973, he would eventually be featured in forty novels before Parker's death in 2010. He also appeared in a popular 1980s TV series, *Spenser: For Hire,* starring Robert Urich, and in four made-for-TV films a decade later with Joe Montegna as Spenser. He even continues to live on in new novels now being written by Ace Atkins.

Elmore Leonard (1925–2013)

At the time of his death at age eighty-seven in 2013, Elmore Leonard was America's most celebrated and influential crime writer. In a career that spanned sixty years, he wrote dozens of novels that changed the style and sound of American crime fiction. A rarity among crime writers in that he never produced a series and seldom used characters in more than one novel, he is celebrated for his rich variety of settings, characters, and crimes. But what his books all share in common is a pervasive sense of deadpan humor.

Because both writers are noted for wisecracks and funny remarks, Leonard is often compared to Raymond Chandler. However, aside from the use of comic language and the influence their fiction has had on writers who came after them, they are quite different. The biggest distinction can be seen in their use of narrative. Chandler's novels are narrated in first-person by Philip Marlowe and are thus limited to his point of view, attitude, and comic sensibility. He is almost exclusively the source of humor, which is characterized in large part by witty wisecracks and clever similes.

Leonard, by contrast, never uses first-person narration, rarely employs similes, and mainly avoids using recurring characters. Instead, he assembles a variety of characters who love to talk, switches back and forth among their various points of view, and never gets in their way. You never hear his voice. The result is a body of comic crime fiction that is unsurpassed in the genre.

Leonard grew up admiring Ernest Hemingway's direct style of writing and would often open one of his novels and read a page or two just to get in the right mood while writing his own books. But he quickly realized there was a key difference between Hemingway and himself: Hemingway had no sense of humor. It was comic writers like Mark Harris, Kurt Vonnegut, Jr., and Richard Bissell (whose *High Water* he named as one of his favorite novels) whose sense of humor aligned with his. Leonard began his career as an author of western novels and short stories, where humor plays little role. But when he turned to writing crime fiction, and especially after reading George V. Higgins's *The Friends of Eddie Coyle* in 1972, he found the perfect vehicle for his distinctive sense of humor.

Leonard has a gifted ear for the sound of real people talking. Instead of plotting his novels in advance, his usual method is to come up with a setting and a situation and then begin looking for characters he might use. In an essay he wrote entitled, "What Elmore Leonard Does," he has his characters explain his method of writing: "He makes us do all the work," they say. "Puts us in scenes and says, 'Go ahead and do something'" (Halpern). He auditions them, listening to the way they talk, looking for those blessed with the gift of gab. "Anyone who can't hold up his or her end of a conversation," Leonard says, "is liable to be shelved, or maybe shot" ("Making" 28). The results are pure comic magic.

He's smart enough to know that while educated characters—lawyers, teachers, doctors—might have intelligent things to say, they wouldn't necessarily say them in colorful ways. He's drawn more to those closer to the streets or on the shady side of the law for inspiration. And then he doesn't *make* them talk, he *lets* them talk in their own distinctive lingo and dialect. Blacks and whites, cops and crooks, sassy women and street hustlers— what a chorus of colorful voices. He also loves characters—drug dealers, music promoters, bail bondsmen, hit men, loan sharks—who speak the language of their profession.

Split Images (1981) offers a good example of how Leonard uses his characters. Walter Kouza, a nineteen-year-veteran of the Detroit Police Force now working in Palm Beach, Florida, is a cranky sourpuss who was originally slated to appear in a single scene. But once he began talking, Leonard realized he had a gold mine of a character who added a comic touch whenever he opened his mouth. He isn't a jokester, but as one character puts it, "Walter doesn't know it, but he's a very entertaining guy" (*Split* 125).

Whether explaining his general attitude towards life—"I haven't been surprised at anything since I found out girls don't have weenies" (27)—or answering a question about his record as a cop—"I shot nine people.... Eight colored guys, one Caucasian. I never shot a woman." Asked how many he killed, he says proudly, "I shot nine, I killed nine" (22)—Walter jazzes up the story. His extended monologues are among the comic highlights of the novel. Here he's providing commentary for a video he secretly shot of a woman standing on her patio for his boss:

> "Hang onto your pecker," Walter said, "the show's just starting.... Takes the top off.... You ever see anything like that in your life? Defy the laws of fucking gravity. Look at that...."
> "No tan lines," Robbie said.
> "You aren't kidding no tan lines," Walter said. "Now, hooks her thumbs in there.... You got any music? We should have some music go with this. Boom. Da-da da-boom. Off comes the little panties. Look at that, the red hair and the black bush. She could have quails in there, hiding" [191].

Leonard is also adept at mixing spoken dialogue with internal commentary. In *Freaky Deaky* (1988), Donnell Lewis is an ex–Black Panther radical from the 1960s who has found salvation, not in Jesus but in Woody Ricks, a multimillionaire whose brain has become so befuddled by alcohol he needs someone like Donnell to watch over him. Donnell serves as Mr. Woody's chauffeur, cook, bill payer, etc., but what he's really doing is trying to worm himself into the rich man's will. The following exchange begins with Mr. Woody announcing he wants to get married to a woman who has accused him of raping her:

> "Before you get married, how 'bout we get this new will done?"
> "I could put her in it."
> "You could. Let's see you have anybody closer to you."

"I can't think of any."

"Go through the alphabet. *A ... B ... C ... D.* Anybody you like start with *D*, Mr. Woody?"

"Did you know I was suppose to wear glasses?"

"We thinking of *D*s, Mr. Woody. Come on, let's think of somebody." Donnell waited. If the man was any dumber you'd have to water him twice a week.

"What do I need glasses for, I can see all right. That's why I'm not gonna take singing lessons."

Man had chicken lo mein for brains [*Freaky* 211].

Rather than relying on the same group of continuing characters as many authors do, Leonard looks for fresh voices and new combinations of characters. Like a master chef, he assembles his ingredients, adds a variety of spices, and serves up a savory new treat. For example, in *Tishomingo Blues* (2002), Dennis Lenahan, a world champion high diver who leaps from an eighty-feet perch into a small pool, brings his one-man show to the Tishomingo Lodge and Casino in Tunica, Mississippi. Here he soon encounters Robert Taylor, a black drug dealer from Detroit who arrives in town driving a black Jaguar and carrying a photograph he claims shows the lynching death of his great grandfather. (He also has a briefcase with a gun inside.) He intends to show the photograph to the owner of a modular-home building business (and local drug kingpin) whose grandfather he claims was behind the lynching.

Add a few more colorful characters like Chickasaw Charlie Hoke, celebrity host at the casino, a gasbag who can't stop talking about his pitching heroics for the Detroit Tigers in the final game of the 1984 World Series, an eccentric bunch of locals with names like Junebug and Newton Hoon, some Dixie Mafia types, their wives and girlfriends, and then top it off with an army of Civil War re-enactors who have come to town to recreate the 1864 Battle of Brice's Cross Roads and you have a recipe for a crime story filled with local color, plenty of down-home dialogue, and a heaping portion of humor.

Here's one example, this from gabby young woman named Traci who is complaining about having to wear a hoopskirt for the reenactment:

You try to get in one of those little shithouses with a hoopskirt on. You have to lift it up in front real high and go in sideways. But then you're in there the skirt takes up all the room. What I did was get up on the seat and squat over it to pee.... I went in that store where they have all the little statues of famous generals and stuff? I have all kinds of ashtrays with Confederate flags on 'em, so I bought a plate I thought might be used as one, had Robert E. Lee, Jefferson Davis and Stonewall Jackson on it, and the flag, of course. I use to have a G-string with a Confederate flag on it guys liked a lot when I was dancing go-go. They'd salute it. I was only fourteen but already had my tits [*Tishomingo* 248].

This chatter does nothing to forward the action, nor does it have anything to do with the main characters, but it certainly raises the humor level of the novel.

Nobody's characters are better at delivering funny lines in a deadpan manner than Leonard's. Asked if she killed the man she shot when he didn't drop the gun he was holding, a female cop replies, "No, he survived. He's doing mandatory life," then adds, "with a limp" (*Split* 150). A husband says to his wife: "Jesus Christ, can't you drink without getting smashed every time?" "What would be the point?" she replies (*Mr.* 92). A disgruntled woman complains to her estranged husband, "You never said a kind word about mama in your life." "I couldn't think of any," he says (*Stick* 181). Chili Palmer, loan-shark-turned-movie-producer in *Get Shorty* (1995), is one of the best at the art of the poker-faced delivery. When a beefy stuntman tries to block his exit on a stairway, he grabs the man's crotch, which is conveniently located right at his eye level, and sends him tumbling all the way down to the bottom. "Not bad for a guy his size," he says. Then he explains to those who were watching what happened: "I guess the guy fell" (*Get* 217).

Some of Leonard's comic characters provide humor simply because of who they are, not what they say. Searcy J. Bragg, Jr., better known as the Mutt, is a hit man in *Pagan Babies* (2000) who's in serious need of vocational counseling. He once tried armed robbery, but gave it up after he showed his gun to the girl behind the counter in a drugstore and she simply looked at it and said, "Yeah?" "Aw, fuck it," he said, and walked away: "That girl was too dumb to rob" (141). He agrees to kill a man for $25,000, but later has to be told he should have demanded half in cash *before* doing the job. He doesn't own a gun, but assumes the man he's hired to kill will have one he can use. He decides to hire a driver because his pickup truck needs to be jump-started every time he gets in it, and with a driver he also won't have to worry about finding a parking place. After spending a short time with him, his frustrated driver concludes, "You had to pay close attention to what the Mutt said and ask the right question. Then it made sense, even if you still couldn't fuckin believe it" (*Pagan* 223).

Leonard ordinarily uses a character's own words as a way of revealing that particular individual. Sometimes, however, he uses those words for a secondary purpose. For example, *Get Shorty* is about the movie business. Having Hollywood characters spout off about movies not only helps to reveal their individual personalities, their words satirize the phoniness of the whole industry. For example, when a pretentious movie star talks about one of his films this way—"Take a look at *The Cyclone* again, the way a visual fabric is maintained even while the metaphor plays on different levels, with the priest, with the mother ... so that you never lose sight of the picture's thematic intent" (182)—Leonard is able to skewer both the individual as well as an industry where authenticity is in short supply. Hollywood's notoriously patronizing attitude toward writers is spoofed in the following passage spoken by the owner of a limo service who decides to write a screenplay:

> You asking me ... do I know how to write down words on a piece of paper? That's what you do, man, you put down one word after the other as it comes in your head. It isn't like having to learn how to play the piano, like you have to learn notes. You already learned in school how to write, didn't you? I *hope* so. You have the idea and you put down what you want to say. Then you get somebody to add in the commas and shit where they belong, if you aren't positive yourself. Maybe fix up the spelling where you have some tricky words. There people do that for you [*Get* 143].

Leonard also has a special talent for cop humor. In 1978, a Detroit newspaper commissioned him to write a piece about the local police. He planned to spend a few days visiting Detroit Police Headquarters; instead he ended up hanging around for two-and-a-half months soaking up the colorful language and distinctive speech rhythms of the cops and criminals who passed through. Though he doesn't routinely feature cops in his novels, when he does he likes to highlight their distinctive brand of humor, a good example of which can be found on a sign taped to a file cabinet at police headquarters in *Mr. Paradise* (a novel dedicated to the Detroit Police Homicide Section): *"Too often we lose sight of life's simple pleasures. Remember, when someone annoys you it takes 42 muscles in your face to frown. But it only takes 4 muscles to extend your arm and bitch-slap the motherfucker upside the head"* (*Mr.* 28).

Leonard's cops are experts at pithy statements: "I learn something today. You can fit a Glock Forty up a guy's nose" (*Mr.* 114); Asked what happened to the man who shot and wounded him, a cop replies, "He died on the way to the hospital.... I think he lost his will to live" (*Glitz* 30); "Somebody was going to do Curtis sooner or later.... What's the difference? Go down the morgue, see all the fucking Curtises they got there" (*Split* 259). Finally, here's some homespun wisdom, cop style: "Wonderful things can happen ... when you plant seeds of distrust in a garden of assholes" (*Glitz* 161).

Leonard's novels have been described as "mini-epics on human folly" (Carr) and as "intricate variations" on the twin notions that in this country "there is hardly anyone who won't sell his soul for a quick buck and that the consequences of such a transaction are invariably comic and disastrous" (McGrath). No matter how they are described, each Leonard crime novel will assuredly contain colorful characters who will give his readers plenty to smile about.

William Marshall (1944–)

There are several good reasons for reading William Marshall's Yellowthread Street mysteries, a series of sixteen police procedurals published between 1975 and 1998: 1) They are set in an exotic location, the British colony of Hong Kong, a thirty-square-mile island in the South China Sea just off the mainland of Communist China. The island was under British administration until 1997, when it was transferred to Chinese control. It has a population of over four million residents, which is swelled by the arrival of millions of tourists each year; 2) The mysteries the police have to solve are bizarre and truly baffling; 3) The novels explore some of the social, political, and cultural tensions that exist between the native Chinese and their British overseers; 4) Above all else, they are arguably the funniest police procedurals ever written.

An Australian by birth, Marshall was born in Sydney in 1944 and later lived for many years in Hong Kong. He has worked at a variety of jobs including journalist, morgue attendant, and teacher at an Irish maximum security prison, where he taught a class once a week. Commenting on that experience, he confesses that he's not sure he ever taught the inmates much of anything, but jokes that, "apparently their confessions were of better quality afterwards than they had been before" (Ross 257). When he began reading mysteries, he says he found a lot of writing in the genre to be "very arid" and also felt that it "takes itself rather too seriously." He decided to apply a decidedly offbeat sense of humor to his own writing, which no one would ever describe as "arid." Marilyn Stasio called him "an inspired poet of the bizarre" and Ed Christian credited him with having "the most fertile imagination in the history of detective fiction" (5).

The Yellowthread Street police station is located on the southern side of the island in a fictional area called Hong Bay, which the tourist brochures warn visitors to avoid after dark. It is here where a police squad under Detective Chief Inspector Harry Feiffer, an Englishman who was born in Hong Kong, tries to maintain order. His chief assistant is Christopher

O'Yee, an Eurasian of Chinese and Irish heritage who was born in San Francisco. Other members of the squad include the bumbling and constantly squabbling pair of Phil Auden and Bill Spencer, who are responsible for most of the slapstick humor in the series.

The following description of Yellowthread Street emphasizes the chaotic background against which the outlandish events that occur in the series play out:

> Below him, in the street, there were people everywhere ... in the clatter and crash and color and life and smell and heat of Yellowthread Street, buyers, sellers, loaders, unloaders, walkers, saunterers, amblers, perambulators, packers, pickers, pedestrians. There were shops, stalls, storehouses, smells—the smells of spices and sweat, smoke. There was movement, sound, a roar of a thousand voices all talking and negotiating and treating and trading at once: in their intercourse and presence there were ten thousand years of history and culture and learning and lore and loudness [*Nightmare* 28].

Highly unusual cases have become common in the recent police procedurals of Fred Vargas and Christopher Fowler, but the origin of the trend can be traced back to Marshall, whose series began with *Yellowthread Street* in 1975. Airplanes filled with dead passengers begin landing in Hong Kong in *Thin Air* (1977). *Skulduggery* (1979) opens with the discovery of a homemade raft that has drifted ashore with a twenty-year-old skeleton on it surrounded by an array of strange objects: ten sweet potatoes, a set of dentures, a dead fish, and what appears to be a vampire's tooth. In *Sci Fi* (1981), set during the All-Asia Science Fiction and Horror Movie Congress taking place in Hong Kong, a man dressed in a silver spacesuit shoots down a plywood flying saucer with a flame thrower, then turns and immolates a street sweeper. Shortly afterwards he kills two film producers the same way and then sets fire to a million dollars in cash on display in a glass case in a hotel lobby.

The Yellowthread novels can be called police procedurals only in a limited sense since the serious criminal investigations are largely carried out by only one cop, Feiffer, who is relentless and determined in his efforts to solve the bewildering crimes committed in Hong Bay. The rest of the squad, especially Auden and Spencer, who become involved in one screwball case after another, are mainly responsible for the humorous action. Like Laurel and Hardy, they have a knack for getting into one fine mess after another, and their utter confusion and frustration in the face of the bizarre situations they encounter is a dependable source of humor throughout the entire series.

In *Skulduggery*, for example, Auden is slowly driven nuts after spending six hours riding up and down in an elevator trying to figure out how a mugger has been able to rob passengers when the door opens on the third floor even though that door is nailed shut and seemingly can't be opened. In *The Far Away Man* (1984), Auden's problems begin when for no good reason he decides to examine forty-seven handguns and assorted automatic weapons that have been seized by the police. He takes them all apart but then, to no one's surprise, can't figure out how to put them back together again. He's punished for his idiocy by being sent out to investigate a bizarre series of events: at a deafeningly noisy fourteen-story apartment complex known as Kamikaze Mansions, there have been multiple reports of suicides involving victims jumping to their deaths. In each case, the screams of the victim and the loud thump of the landing is heard, but no body is ever found. One can only laugh at the bewildered and increasingly frustrated Auden's search for an answer while he hears invisible bodies continuing to fall out of the sky. Things become truly cartoonish in *Nightmare Syndrome* (1997) where Auden spends the entire novel mired in sewage and sludge thanks to a plumbing disaster at police headquarters. Things are made worse when he also uncovers a twelve-foot-long bomb hidden behind the wall which needs to be defused before it explodes.

Christopher O'Yee's family situation also contributes to the humor. His wife frequently complains that he spends too much time at work, ignoring her and their seven children. During a rare breakfast together at home, his kids stare at the stranger at the table. "Mummy, who is this man?" his youngest daughter asks. Her mother in turn questions the man: "You are their father, aren't you? It was you, wasn't it? It's so hard to remember that far back" (*Hatchet* 57). On another occasion, he attempts to placate his angry wife when she calls him at work to complain about his absence by foolishly telling her he has obtained tickets for the entire family to attend a big movie premiere the following night. Unfortunately, he lied and now there are no tickets available anywhere, forcing him to spend much of the rest of the novel frantically calling his underworld contacts with names like Porno Lillie Rodriguez, One Eared Hot Time Alice Ping, and Flick Knife Fong The Fence in a desperate hunt for tickets.

Marshall's capsule descriptions of even minor characters are also often funny: "Alice made a grunting noise and took a cigarette from a pocket in her coat. It looked minute in her mouth, like an elephant using a toothpick, and when she inhaled the smoke did not come out again. It went inside that massive block of lard and was too scared to come back near the teeth in case they snapped at it" (*Yellowthread* 26); "He was a thin man surrounded by fat bags of rice. He had rice in his hair, in the front pocket of his apron, under his fingernails, on his face, and no doubt in his shoes. He looked very ricey" (*Yellowthread* 31).

It is, however, Marshall's highly amped narrative style that establishes the overall comic tone of the series. He writes in very short scenes and nimbly switches back and forth among them to give a manic energy to his novels. Frequent use of italics and bold print like this example also magnify the frenetic pace:

> In the sewer, coming towards Spencer with his hands held up like hammers, Auden said (he thought), "*What do you mean, all of the great secrets of Life can be decoded and deciphered and understood in the one single great act of defusing an undefusable bomb?*" but what he actually said was, "WHADDABOMBMEANINGACTOFSIN-GLEGREATLIFEDECIPHERING DECODING ... FUCKINGKILLYOU!!!..." [*Nightmare* 107].

Whether mimicking the sound of gunfire—"The bullets went chop! chop! chop! choppety-chop! chop! chop! chop!" and the brass cases "went tinkle, tinkle, on to the floor" (*Yellowthread* 101)—or describing slapstick action—as in this scene where Auden is clinging to an unexploded bomb hurtling through the sewage in police headquarters after a plumbing disaster: "the bomb turned a corner in a surf wave of slime and, hitting a solid brick wall, sent up a tsunami of brown, green, black, and all the shades in between of muck, mire, morass, and a millennia-old mountain of malodorous matter" (*Nightmare* 41)—Marshall fashions a prose style that is perfectly suited to the frequently cartoonish action.

The Yellowthread novels aren't designed as spoofs of the police procedural genre, nor do they attempt to capture authentic cop humor the way Joseph Wambaugh's novels do. They are comic novels built around bizarre crimes that at the same time often address serious cultural and political issues. But like the two cultures that inhabit Hong Kong, the comic and the serious exist side by side in Marshall's madcap world.

Simon Brett (1945–)

Simon Brett hit upon a highly successful formula for his long-running series of British mysteries featuring a struggling actor named Charles Paris that began in 1975 with the publication of *Cast, In Order of Disappearance*. A fiftyish actor long separated from his wife, Charles drinks too much and is always on the lookout for what he calls beautiful young "crumpets" whom he hopes to meet on the few acting jobs he manages to get. He's also the kiss of death when it comes to any production he's in, for invariably someone dies in what initially appears to be an accident. The curious Charles takes it upon himself to look into matters; usually determines that the death wasn't accidental, and snoops around until he identifies the killer. What elevates the series above the ordinary and predictable are the glimpses the novels provide into the world of entertainment and the hilarious skewering they contain of many aspects of that world.

Brett acted in several plays while a student at Oxford, but most of his professional work occurred behind the scenes as a radio producer for the BBC. A scribbler since childhood, he also wrote four unpublished novels. In 1974, while working with actors on a radio series based on Dorothy Sayers's Lord Peter Wimsey books, he came up with the idea for a novel about an actor detective. Though he didn't begin with the intention of writing a series of novels about Charles Paris, he found he couldn't abandon the character because, he says, "Nobody else ever gives him any work" ("Origins" 185).

As an amateur detective, Charles is no Sherlock Holmes. He's not driven by a sense of intellectual superiority nor any desire to upstage the police; he's simply curious about things like sudden death, and an actor with his never-give-up attitude can certainly be expected to be a persistent snoop. His method is simple: he works his way through a series of likely suspects, following his suspicions down one blind alley after another until he finally stumbles upon the guilty party: "I think I must have barked up every tree in the park before I found one with anyone in it," he says (*So* 559). But despite downplaying his detective skills—"I'm an actor, not a detective. If I were a detective, I'd have been sacked years ago for incompetence.... I have as much aptitude for detective work as a eunuch has for rape" (*So* 507)—his record of solving murders is impressive.

Charles isn't necessarily a bad actor and he performs each job he manages to get like the professional he is. But a lethal combination of lousy luck, bad breaks, some negative reviews, and a totally incompetent agent have relegated him to bit parts and embarrassing jobs. In *Dead Giveaway* (1985) he's hired not as one of the celebrity guests but as a contestant on a television game show that resembles the classic "What's My Line?" because the program needs an actor whom nobody would recognize. In *Situation Tragedy* (1981), he gets to speak only fourteen lines in each episode of a TV sitcom. In *Corporate Bodies* (1991), he portrays a forklift operator in a company corporate video. In *Murder in the Title* (1983), he plays a corpse.

Each job, however, affords him an ideal perspective from which to observe (and comment on) the challenges, frustrations, insanities (and inanities) of whatever production he's involved in. *Situation Tragedy* offers a behind-the-scenes look at the trials and tribulations of putting on a TV sitcom. In *A Decent Interval* (2013), two winners of TV talent competitions are hired to star in a new production of *Hamlet,* in which Charles has dual roles as the Ghost of Hamlet's father and the First Gravedigger. It's bad enough that the director has a set built like the inside of a skull to reflect his notion that the play takes place in Hamlet's head, the two leads are played by "media mushrooms which had sprung up overnight" (36). The woman playing Ophelia wants to sing songs from her forthcoming CD instead of the mad songs Shakespeare wrote for the character.

Charles himself is the butt of some of the humor in the series. Among the funniest lines at Charles's expense are those from the negative reviews he received for some of his early acting jobs: On his appearance in *Waiting for Godot:* "Never mind Godot, I spent the entire evening waiting for some distinguished acting" (*Situation* 121); "In this Restoration comedy Charles Paris looked in need of restoration" (*Decent* 3); "With Charles Paris as Julius Caesar, I was surprised Brutus and his cronies didn't take action earlier" (*Decent* 54).

Some of the humor in the series arises out of the action. A pair of scenes from a production of *Macbeth* in *What Bloody Man Is That?* (1987) stand out. One of the many small roles Charles plays is that of a head that appears in a cauldron bubbling with dry ice vapor. The apparatus designed to propel him through a trap up into the cauldron moves too quickly, causing him to bang his knuckles on the edge of the trap's opening. When he involuntarily blurts out a loud "Shit!" as he emerges, the audience of schoolchildren in attendance roars in appreciation of the best bit of Shakespeare they've ever seen. In the novel's final scene, a performance before another audience of schoolchildren degenerates into pure farce that is triggered when the actor helping Charles in his role as the Bleeding Sergeant in the opening scene of the play looks at him and then closes his eyes to reveal the words "Fuck" and "Off" neatly written on his eyelids. Additional hijinks, on stage and in the audience, ensue with hilarious results.

In *Dead Room Farce,* (1998), Charles's role in a sex farce titled *Not on Your Wife!* offers plenty of comic craziness. The novel opens with Charles, his trousers down around his ankles, scurrying for cover when the doorbell rings during an assignation with a married woman. Several scenes from the play, filled with lines of unmistakable sexual innuendo, are included in the novel, adding to the humor of the book.

Jokes don't ordinarily play a large role in a crime novel, but they do when that novel features comedians, as *A Comedian Dies* (1979) does. Each chapter begins with a joke. The main character is a comic whose scenes are filled with jokes, good and bad. For example, his zippy banter with a TV host includes such exchanges as this: Question: "Comedians yearn to be taken seriously.... Do you want to play Hamlet?" Answer: "What at" (*Comedian* 58)? We also get a generous sampling of some old comic chestnuts like this: "They crossed a tart with a gorilla. Got one who swings from lamp-posts and does it for peanuts" (*Comedian* 88).

The sardonic narrative voice that conveys Charles's thoughts and opinions is another reliable source of humor. It can be heard, for example, in similes like these: On a woman's low-cut dress: "She was not over-endowed and her bosom was spread thin like a birthday cake run out of icing" (*Comedian* 13); "The police welcomed amateur detectives about as avidly as elephants welcome umbrella-stand manufacturers" (*Comedian* 121); Or the modern style of photographing actors that makes them look "as if they've just come off a building site or are about to start life sentences for rape" (*Star* 336).

This snarky voice also skewers the pompous and the pretentious. Here it is on producers: "Though many television producers can read scripts, it's a very rare one who can manage a whole book" (*Situation* 93). Award shows also come in for a bashing:

> The well-loved television personality would introduce another well-loved television personality who had nothing to do with the awards; this new well-loved television personality would then deliver a couple of scripted jokes and receive an envelope in which there were the names of three nominations for the award; he would then read out the names in reverse order; whereupon a third well-loved television personality, the one who had won the award, would rise from his convenient seat in well-feigned amazement and go forward to receive his chair-spring. If he were a man, he would then make a very boring little speech thanking all of the production team who had made it possible; if she were a woman, she would start to make a boring little speech thanking all of the production team who had made it possible, but after a few words dissolve in tears [*Comedian* 105–06].

Modern theater audiences are also ridiculed, as in this writer's complaint about those who can be expected to flock to his musical based on Oliver Goldsmith's *She Stoops to Conquer* that is being remade to suit a popular TV personality:

> The audience that comes to this show will be so force-fed with television they won't notice what it's about. They'll spend all their time waiting for the commercials. They'd come and see him if he was peeling potatoes onstage. They'd come and see anything that they saw on their screen. A jug of water, *as featured on the Nine O'Clock News*, that's what they'd come to see [*Star* 245].

Sometimes Brett's satiric strategy is simply to allow a blowhard to talk, as in this playwright's description of his play based on the Boston Tea Party: "The central allegorical symbol was the fact that the Boston Tea Party was perpetrated by white men disguised as Indians. White usurping the place of red. Like corpuscles. I used the analogy of leukemia" (*So* 473). Or this from an egocentric director: "My style of direction doesn't need a good play. In fact the play can get in the way. It's only a starting point from which the totality emerges—the iron filing dropped into the acid which produces the perfect crystal" (*So* 445).

The prolific Brett also created three other mystery series: humorous cozies featuring an elderly widow named Mrs. Pargeter; another series set in the seaside village of Feathering where the crimes occur; and a farcical series set just after World War I that features a brother-sister team of amateur sleuths named Blotto and Twink. But it is the Charles Paris novels where he most effectively combines satisfying mysteries with a humorous look at the backstage world of entertainment. Charles's experiences as an actor may have left him bruised and battered, but they have only sharpened his sense of humor, which have made the novels about his adventures as an actor/detective over the past forty years so much fun to read.

Lawrence Block (1938–)

Lawrence Block's writing career parallels that of his longtime friend Donald E. Westlake in several interesting ways. They first met in 1959 in the office of the Scott Meredith Literary Agency where both were employed as manuscript readers. Both published fiction under pseudonyms for the paperback markets at the time, including a handful of sex novels, some of which they even wrote together. They were amazingly prolific writers, each publishing in the neighborhood of 100 novels. Both created several different series of crime novels. And both created a popular series of comic crime novels that featured a criminal protagonist: Westlake gave us a robber named John Dortmunder, Block a burglar named Bernie Rhodenbarr.

There are, however, significant differences in their approach to humor. John Dortmunder is not a funny man, but his frustrating failures and his reactions to them are. Bernie Rhodenbarr, on the other hand, is a very funny man. Unlike Dortmunder, he almost always succeeds in his criminal endeavors, but the unexpected complications that ensue in his case are anything but funny. The laughs come from his first-person narration, which like that of Marlowe, Spenser, Kinsey Millhone, and others, reflects his distinctive sense of humor, which puts a comic spin on serious matters.

Block's best-known character is a New York private detective named Matt Scudder, whom he introduced in 1976. Scudder is an ex-cop who is haunted by guilt after accidentally shooting and killing a seven-year-old girl. He's also an alcoholic, though he quits drinking after the first few books and for the rest of the series regularly attends AA meetings in a continuing struggle to remain sober. There is nothing funny about his life or the cases he becomes involved in. Nor is there much humor in Block's other two series. One features an insomniac globe-trotting secret agent named Evan Tanner whose sleep center was destroyed during the Korean War, the other an introspective hit man named Keller.

When Block sat down to write what became *Burglars Can't Be Choosers* (1977), he had no intention of launching another series, nor did he plan to write a comic novel. All he hoped to do was tell a story about a burglar who broke into an apartment where a body is discovered when the cops walk in, forcing him to bolt and then try to solve the murder to save his own hide. But from the very first moment Bernie Rhodenbarr began to talk, his voice and attitudes were funny, and a new series, much lighter in tone than Block's others, was born. Block once suggested that comedian Jerry Seinfeld would be a perfect choice to play Bernie in a movie version of his books; Hollywood had other ideas, casting instead a black woman (Whoopi Goldberg) to play Bernie in *Burglar* (1987).

"I'm a born burglar, God help me, and I love it," Bernie proudly declares (*Rye* 41). "Some guys can hit a curveball," he explains. "Others can crunch numbers. I can open locks" (*Ted* 47). He freely acknowledges the criminality of his chosen career—"Burglary is morally reprehensible and I'm aware of the fact"—but he adds this defense: "I wasn't stealing the pennies off a dead man's eyes, or the bread from a child's mouth, or objects of deep sentimental value. I'll tell you, I love collectors. I can ransack their holdings with such little guilt" (*Mondrian* 36). Aside from one stint in prison, which taught him that "Don't Get Caught" is a better lesson than "Thou Shalt Not Steal," he has managed to enjoy a very successful career.

Bernie's breezy narrative voice effortlessly mixes humor with more serious matters. In *The Burglar in the Closet* (1978), for example, he is forced to hide in a woman's closet when she unexpectedly returns while he's burglarizing her apartment. He describes his plight with a comic simile: "And there I was, standing snugly in my closet like the world's most cautious homosexual" (26). While trapped inside, he's forced to listen to the woman's lovemaking with the man she has brought home, which leads to this commentary: "They did what they'd come to the bedroom to do, and that's all you're going to hear from me on that subject. It was no fun listening to it and I'm certainly not going to try to re-create the experience for you" (20).

But the jokes abruptly end when he hears a scream, a thudding noise, and then silence. When he exits the closet, he finds the woman dead on the floor, a dentist's scalpel sticking up out of her chest. He leaves before the cops arrive, but an attaché case he had filled with the dead woman's jewelry he was in the process of stealing is missing, presumably taken by the killer. He needs to find the killer before the police do and recover the case, which will likely have his fingerprints on it.

Bernie's playful narrative voice also helps him establish a sympathetic intimacy with the reader. After describing how he takes great care not to leave any evidence of his presence at the scene of a burglary, but then steals some cash, he addresses the reader directly: "Ah, you've spotted an inconsistency, haven't you? All right, I'll tell you why I took the eighty-five bucks. I've never believed in overlooking cash. That's why" (*Choosers* 121); on another occasion, he says this to the reader: "How did four flights of stairs get me from Sixteen to Eleven? No thirteenth floor. But *you* knew that, didn't you? Of course you did" (*Mondrian* 25). He even comments on his own role as narrator:

> I know, I know. You're wondering where the attaché case came from. Didn't Doll and I just spend part of the afternoon searching fruitlessly for it? Well, much as it pains me to admit it, I haven't played entirely fair with you. My day actually got underway a little earlier than you (and Doll Cooper) may have been led to believe. See, I left out a few things in the telling ... [*Ted* 221].

Some first-person narrators try too hard to be funny, busting a gut to come up with clever wisecracks or witty similes. Bernie's humor is less forced as he effortlessly incorporates it into his narrative. He has a gift for comic similes—"He sounded about as enthusiastic as if I'd offered him a lifetime of cauliflower" (*Mondrian* 228)—and quick humorous come-backs—"It's an unusual name, Rhodenbarr. What's the derivation?" "It was my father's" (*Ted* 253). He is often self-deprecating—"I got out of bed and went to the toilet." (I would avoid mentioning this, but it was the first time in a long time that I knew what I was doing) (*Choosers* 58)—and a lover of wordplay—"I managed to turn up half a box of Uncle Ben's Converted Rice (formerly Buddhist and now Presbyterian, I suppose)." When he opens the box, he discovers that "Uncle Ben had been further converted, this time from rice to roach shit" (*Choosers* 52).

His breezy sense of humor also colors his observations of the world around him: he notes that an apartment building is so poorly constructed it has walls "you could detect a fart through, even if you were deaf" (*Prowl* 128). His descriptions of the people he meets are also funny: "We were blessed with a driver who clearly believed that his best hope lay in reincarnation, and the sooner the better" (*Ted* 191); "As usual, he was wearing a dark suit; as usual, it looked to have been custom-tailored for someone else" (*Ted* 295); "He had bigger shoulders than most people, and very widely spaced eyes, as if while in the womb he'd toyed with the idea of becoming Siamese twins and decided against it at the last minute" (*Closet* 70); and then there's this description of a woman dressed entirely in red and black: "Her favorite birds, I felt certain, were the red-winged blackbird and the scarlet tanager. Her favorite author would have to be Stendhal" (*Spinoza* 123).

In *The Burglar Who Liked To Quote Kipling* (1979), the third book in the series, Bernie becomes the proud owner of an antiquarian bookstore in Greenwich Village. He's now a legitimate businessman, but that doesn't interfere with his primary profession, which he pursues in the evenings. (His illegal earnings not only help pay the rent on the store, eventually they allow him to purchase the entire building that houses it.) Bernie's love for books also gives Block an excuse to include some literary humor. For example, *The Burglar Who Traded Ted Williams* (1994) opens with a customer at his store saying to Bernie, "Not a bad-looking *Burglar.…* I don't suppose you'd happen to have a decent *Alibi*" (1)? It takes the shocked Bernie a moment or two to realize the man isn't accusing him of committing a crime, he's simply asking whether he might have those two Sue Grafton mysteries in stock. Later, during a conversation about Grafton's alphabetic mysteries with a friend who can't recall the title of the one that features a proctologist who commits murder, he suggests this possibility: "'H' is for Preparation."

On another occasion, Bernie mentions Nolita, then assures the reader that it's not "as you might suppose, a Nabokovean tale about a prepubescent girl who won't have anything to do with Humbert Humbert" but an area of Manhattan located north of Little Italy (*Prowl* 185). He even works in a reference to Robert Frost: when a neighbor of Bernie's fence, who has just been murdered, tells him that even though he was a criminal he was a good neighbor. Bernie reminds him that, "You know what they say. Good fences make good neighbors" (*Spinoza* 119).

Bernie's also a witty conversationalist, and two of the series regulars offer ample opportunity for humorous banter: Ray Kirschmann, the policeman who discovered the dead body in the apartment Bernie was burglarizing in his first appearance, continues to show up each time Bernie becomes a suspect in another murder; and Bernie's best friend Carolyn Kaiser, a lesbian dog groomer whom he regularly meets for lunch and often for an after-work drink. Because there is no sexual tension between the two of them, there's no romantic banter like that between Spenser and Susan Silverman, instead just plenty of good-natured back and forth. Carolyn also has a flair for comic remarks: When an insurance executive uses the phrase *Qui bono,* she quips, "That was Sonny's first wife, before he was married to Cher. Right?" (*Mondrian* 277).

Bernie Rhodenbarr is no brooding gloomy Gus like John Dortmunder. He's easy-going, comfortable in his own skin, a man who leads such a contented life it's easy to forget that he's a career criminal, though an avowedly non-violent one. But thanks to an engaging sense of humor, he makes everything in his world, including burglary, fun to read about.

Martha Grimes (1931–)

Martha Grimes is an American author who, like fellow countrywoman Elizabeth George, has found success with a series of mystery novels set in England. Though they take place in various quaint British villages, Grimes's novels are far from traditional cozies. They are what Sarah D. Fogle calls a joining of "manners and mean streets" (2), a blending of the English cozy tradition with the more realistic American style that features as primary crime solver a Scotland Yard Inspector named Richard Jury. Her settings may be small remote villages, but the violent murders are more likely to be committed in or around the local pub than in a country house or vicarage. (The title of each of her novels is the colorful name of the pub featured in that novel.) A witty style and a cast of eccentric characters are used to balance the darker crimes she describes.

Grimes's murders are far from polite affairs. In *The Man with a Load of Mischief* (1981), the first novel in the series, one victim is strangled and found with his head shoved into a keg of beer at the Man With a Load of Mischief pub; a second is propped up in place of a mechanical figure above the Jack and Hammer pub just days before Christmas. In *The Dirty Duck* (1984), three female members of an American tour group are viciously killed by an assailant who slits their throats from ear to ear and then opens up their chests.

Grimes's sense of humor begins with the names of characters and places, beginning with the names of the real pubs she employs as titles for her novels: *I Am the Only Running Footman; The Dirty Duck; The Five Bells and Bladebone; The Man with a Load of Mischief; The Old Contemptibles*, etc. She gives a London men's club the name Borings and is especially gifted in coming up with colorful names for characters (e.g., St. John St. Clair, Fiona Clingmore, Bertie Makepeace, Robespierre and Rasputin Cripps) who are, as Ray B. Browne observed, "delineated in Hogarthian outlines, vitalized by Dickensian gusto" (266).

Grimes had originally intended to make Melrose Plant, an aristocrat who gave up his titles (Earl of Caverness; twelfth Viscount Ardry) and is now a professor of French Romantic poetry at the University of London, the central character, an amateur sleuth who would be assisted at times by a Scotland Yard detective. But it soon became apparent to her that the detective, Richard Jury, would make a far better choice as principal investigator.

Plant, who often assists Jury in his various investigations, isn't a comic character, but his annoying Aunt Agatha, with whom he lives on his estate in the village of Long Piddleton, is. An American by birth, she married into Plant's family and is now hell bent on ensuring that she will inherit Plant's estate, even though she is twenty years older than he is. As Mimosa Stephenson points out, her "snobbishness, acquisitiveness, inquisitiveness, and gluttony" entertain the reader while also providing "a comic satire on the worst features of the class system in England" (125). Her antagonistic sparring with her nephew produces frequent laughs in the series. For example, when she walks into a pub just as a woman is explaining to Plant how her mother always flayed a skunk to ward off ghouls, he quips, "Well ... not quite all of them, I see" (*The Man* 191). When she starts jabbering at him alongside a river, he wonders if the river is deep enough to drown in. "But why bother?" he concludes. "In another five minutes he'd be bored to death, anyway" (*Dirty* 9).

Jury's police colleagues provide another source of humor, especially his primary assistant, Detective Sergeant Alfred Wiggins, a man who has managed to "turn hypochondria into an art or even a sport" (*Old* 31). He travels with an array of pills, syrups, herbs, and potions to ward off the effects of ailments, real and imagined. "Some men went for their guns under stress, some for their cigarettes. Wiggins went for his cough drops" (*Dirty* 133). Wiggins is more than a recurring joke, however. He's a soothing presence to witnesses and quickly gets on a first-name basis with crime victims. Not only does he put them at ease, he always has a spare handkerchief at the ready.

Each novel usually features at least one visit to the office of Jury's boss, Chief Superintendent A. E. Racer, a vain, insecure, lazy man whose only talents are delegating tasks to others and keeping his desk spotless. When he orders Jury to leave his office so he can get back to work, the narrator comments wryly, "The pristine condition of his desk did not attest to this" (*Help* 168). His orderly life is comically inconvenienced by the presence of Cyril the cat, whom he despises. Cyril loves to plump himself in Racer's swivel chair and causes as much disruption as he can, knocking over Christmas presents, emptying the contents of Racer's desk drawers, and disturbing the glasses in his liquor cabinet.

The third regular member of the office personnel is the exotically named Fiona Clingmore, Racer's secretary. She always dresses in black. "Maybe she wanted to be sure she was ready for Racer's funeral" (*Help* 166), and as usual "her neckline was down and her skirt was up. Fiona always seemed to wear her clothes at half-mast; perhaps she was mourning chastity, thought Jury" (*The Man* 24). She makes an indelible impression on Jury whenever he enters the office:

> Fiona Clingmore was dressed today in what should have been a negligee, but was apparently a summer dress. It was black and layered with ruffles all down the front, the layers being the only thing that kept Fiona from absolutely showing through. She stood now, one hand leaning on the desk, the other on her outslung hip, scarlet fingernails drumming, and giving them all the benefit of her décolletage. Fiona had topped forty a couple of years ago, Jury knew, but she was going down fighting [*Dirty* 136].

On another occasion, the narrator describes her applying eyeliner with the solemnity of one taking the veil, but jokingly observes that the prayerful pose she strikes and the black scarf she wears "were about as close as Fiona would ever get to a nunnery" (*I Am* 53).

Jury's neighbors also add to the humor. The actions of his downstairs neighbor Mrs. Wasserman might be considered comic if they weren't so tragic: she suffers from extreme paranoia as a result of her experiences in a concentration camp. But her constant fearfulness is lightened considerably by the eventual arrival of a free-spirited new neighbor named Carole-anne Palutski, a twenty-something former topless dancer who now works as a Covent Garden fortune-teller named Madame Zostra. A whirlwind of activity, she's often either doing exercises or painting her nails while talking with Jury. Dressed in pink shorts and sporting hair dyed several shades of bright red that inspires Jury to liken her to "a Tijuana sunset" (*I Am* 258), she also boasts the kind of figure "that could send all the traffic in Piccadilly Circus running counterclockwise" (*Rainbow's* 89). She often volunteers as Jury's informal answering service, which leads to humorous exchanges between the two, as for example when Jury has to painstakingly coax from her what she really meant when she simply wrote "Zilch" to sum up one phone conversation.

The Crippses of Catchcoach Street, first introduced in *The Anodyne Necklace* (1983), provide plenty of laughs, and Grimes manages to find a way to bring them back from time to time for pure comic relief. Their shabby home and dusty yard are filled with toys and a half-dozen rambunctious, pasty-faced urchins with names like Robespierre and Piddlin' Pete who, like his father, pees wherever he likes, including into the birdbath and on visitors' feet. The parents who oversee the unruly mob with benign indifference are the shiftless Ashley (nicknamed Ash the Flash for his habit of exposing himself) and obese Elephant (called White Ellie because of her elephantine size and apparent uselessness). Visitors to the chaotic Cripps home do so at their own risk; readers are able to enjoy the craziness from a safe distance.

It isn't only the characters that provide laughs. The voice of the narrator contributes wry and witty descriptions like these: "The black gown had a slit back, a front cut to the waist, and a slash up the side, all like arrows pointing danger" (*Jerusalem* 110); "The incredible thing about St. Jude's was the way in which it had maintained its reputation for scholarship, when everyone knew that its graduates were only smart enough to count the money in their wallets" (*Jerusalem* 122); the Three Kings in a nativity scene in an upscale department store window display "were dressed in flowing robes of gold lamé and silky stuff, as if they had come, not to pay homage to the child in the manger, but to call on the girls next door" (*Jerusalem* 78); Aunt Agatha and the local vicar are "dependent on one another in the mindless way of two gibbons dedicated to picking fleas off one another's fur" (*The Man* 13).

The crimes committed in the novels are realistic and often brutal, and Richard Jury is deadly serious about solving them. The humor, which usually arises during breaks from the criminal investigation, is an add-on delight. As Richard C. Carpenter noted, "Like Charles Dickens before her, Grimes rejoices in her characters, quirky or down-to-earth; even when the plot falters, the characters entice the reader to persevere to the end, providing their own reward" (462).

Sue Grafton (1940–)

Any writer brave (or foolish) enough to begin a series that promises to extend to twenty-six entries, as Sue Grafton did when she published her first alphabetically titled Kinsey Millhone mystery, *"A" is for Alibi,* in 1982, had better ensure that the character of the private detective she created is one neither she nor the reader will tire of easily. Now well over three decades later it is obvious she has accomplished this feat, thanks in no small part to Kinsey's plain-spoken, common-sense, down-to-earth personality and the engaging voice of her first-person narration.

One clue to her character is her background. Her parents were killed in an automobile accident when she was five, leaving her to be raised in a series of trailer parks by a no-nonsense maiden aunt who instilled in her the values of independence and self-sufficiency. Now in her thirties and twice-divorced, she earned her license as a private investigator after a two-year stint with the Santa Teresa Police Department. She occupies one small corner of a large suite of offices in a building that houses the insurance company for whom she once worked and now still does occasional investigations for in return for the office space. She drives a VW bug with all her essentials—law books, file boxes, a tool kit, a briefcase with a gun in it, an old pair of pantyhose, a pair of black spike heels, and an all-purpose dress—piled in the back seat.

Kinsey isn't a Sam Spade or Philip Marlowe in skirts. She engages in no macho posturing, no mine-is-bigger-than-yours pissing contests. She avoids activities like engaging in fisticuffs with a male opponent that wouldn't be entirely credible for a woman like herself. Her battles are more the silent, subtle kind; for example, when a woman digs her ring, which she has turned around, into Kinsey's finger while they are shaking hands, Kinsey counters by standing on the woman's toe. She's also not the lonely, alienated figure so many male private eyes are. After two failed marriages she's perfectly content to be alone. Nor is she chronically depressed like many of her male counterparts; her sunny disposition adds a welcome breeziness to her first-person narratives.

Unlike Robert B. Parker's Spenser, who delights in good food and regularly serves up tasty descriptions of one appetizing meal after another, Kinsey hates to cook and proudly boasts that aside from McDonald's Quarter Pounders with Cheese, she has no strong food preferences. Spenser also enjoys showing off his sophistication by frequently making literary allusions, such as when he approaches a restaurant called "The Wings of the Dove" and asks, "Do you suppose they serve the food in a golden bowl?" but then has to explain the obscure references to two Henry James novels (*Mortal* 89). Kinsey never makes a reference that needs explaining; hers are all dawn from the ordinary world we all inhabit.

Kinsey's a blue-collar Everywoman who is great company on the page. Unlike some female detectives like Dana Stabenow's Alaskan private eye Kate Shugak, whose heroic exploits are legendary throughout the state, Kinsey is ordinary in the best sense of the word. She's no superhero with a brilliant mind gifted with flashes of great insight. "I don't want her to be larger than life," Grafton says of Kinsey. "I don't want her to be idealized or in any way perfect" (Herbert 34). She's simply a hard-working, well-organized woman who systematically tacks index cards onto a bulletin board above her desk to keep track of the details of a case. She insists that the fundamental qualities of a good investigator are "a plodding nature and infinite patience," then adds pointedly, "Society has inadvertently been grooming women to this end for years" (*"A"* 30).

Unlike many of her male counterparts she's not much given to wise-cracks or tough talk. Instead of deflecting a threat with a smart remark, she creates pictures in her mind: "I stared at him impassively and warded off his withering assessment by picturing him on the toilet with his knickers down around his ankles" (*"D"* 115). Or she wishes bad things on those she dislikes. For example, after describing one man as "a horse's ass and a jerk," she adds, "I hoped he had itchy hemorrhoids" (*"K"* 174). An unhelpful clerk at the sheriff's department prompts this imaginary attack: "Situations like this bring up an ancient and fundamental desire to bite. I could envision a half-moon of my teeth marks on the flesh of her forearm, which would swell and turn all colors of the rainbow. She'd have to have tetanus and rabies shots. Maybe her owner would elect to put her to sleep" (*"H"* 31).

Her humor resembles that of many stand-up comedians in that it arises out of close observation of life's everyday absurdities and incongruities. Allison Fraiberg's analysis of Ellen DeGeneres's stand-up style of comedy could have been written about Kinsey:

> The content of her work relies on acknowledging common experiences: that is, audience members are positioned to identify with her narratives. For the most part, she talks about situations to which audience members can relate ... she tries to focus on the mannerisms and tendencies of as many listeners as she can, while, at the same time, grounding her observations in extended first-person narratives. Quite simply, she tells what seem to be embarrassing stories about herself, but then sutures audiences into a mass position of identification with her [321].

A healthy sense of humor helps keep Kinsey grounded and her down-to-earth attitude reveals a person at ease in her own skin. She's comfortable poking fun at her physical appearance, beginning with her hair; her practice of cutting it with nail scissors sometimes, she admits, leaves it looking "like something I'd swept up from under the bed" ("G" 93). Her unshaved legs "looked as if I had taken to wearing angora knee socks" ("J" 166). She puts on a dress only when she has to, but then complains that wearing pantyhose makes her feel, "like I was walking around with a hot, moist hand in my crotch" ("D" 132).

She is equally modest about her work, entertaining no fancy romanticized Galahad notions about what she does: "I'm like a little terrier when it comes to the truth," she insists. "I have to stick my nose down the hole and dig until I find out what's in there" ("L" 48). Nor does she harbor any social pretensions. Class to her simply means drinking wine "from a bottle instead of a cardboard box" ("D" 20).

Kinsey also maintains a healthy skepticism when it comes to all kinds of hypocrisy, pretense, and ostentatious behavior. In an extended comic scene in *"D" is for Deadbeat,* Kinsey attends the funeral of an ex-con named John Daggett, a man she describes as "a totally worthless human being" (121). Hearing thumping electronic organ music "better suited to a skating rink than a house of God" (139) coming from a yellow stucco church just off the freeway gets her sarcastic juices flowing. As the effusive service continues with "hosannas ... being called out on all sides, accompanied by amens, huzzahs, and much rending and tearing of clothes," she quips that everything "was beginning to feel like soul-aerobics" (141). The service drags on, its phoniness all filtered through Kinsey's gimlet-eyed perspective, though she gives the final word to Daggett's wife, who stands up, shouts "Buulllshiit!" and reminds the gathered mourners that the deceased "was the biggest asshole who ever lived" (144).

Normal everyday objects and occurrences are comic grist for her. Spotting a Van Gogh reproduction on a hospital wall gets her thinking about what a curious choice that artist is for the psycho ward. She worries after checking the label that the cheap wine she's drinking might be "from one of those wineries the grape pickers are always striking and I pondered the possibility that they'd peed on the crop to retaliate for unfair labor practices" ("C" 53). A five-dollar bill inspires her to pull out a ballpoint pen and draw a mustache on Lincoln's face to make his nose look smaller: "I'd never paid attention to what a hooter he had," she explains ("L" 110). The night sky even gets her ruminating: "I could identify the Big Dipper, even the Little Dipper sometimes, but I'd never seen anything that looked even remotely like a bear, a belt, or a scuttling crab. Maybe those guys smoked dope back then, lying on their backs near the Parthenon, pointing at the stars and bullshitting the night away" (*"G"* 29).

Her entertaining similes also evoke the comedy of the commonplace. Rather than reaching for extravagant comparisons or smart literary allusions, she finds appropriately ordinary connections with a comic edge, as this sampling illustrates: "Along the wide hallway ahead, I could see a row of six elderly people in wheelchairs arranged against the wall like drooping houseplants" (*"P"* 75); "Her fingers were as cold and rubbery as cold rigatoni" (*"F"* 21): "She looked like a bulldog and John looked like he was suppressing a fart" (*"D"* 25); "He had one normal arm and one that ended at the elbow in a twist of flesh like the curled top of a Mr. Softee ice cream cone" (*"D"* 154); "His face was as lined as a crumpled grocery bag pressed into service again" (*"D"* 109): "She wore a pale-yellow sweater about the hue of certain urine samples I've seen where the prognosis isn't keen" (*"E"* 44).

Kinsey's habit of employing such everyday images does, however, on occasion give her pause. After comparing the cold feel of a corpse in the morgue to "a package of raw chicken breasts just out of the fridge," she adds, "God ... why do I plague myself with these domestic images? I'd never be motivated to learn to cook at this rate" (*"C"* 232).

"It's never a good idea to leave me in a room by myself," Kinsey cautions. "I'm an incurable snoop and I search automatically (*"C"* 90). Her nosiness, however, sometimes places her in awkward situations that are more smile-inducing than life-threatening. In *"C" is for Corpse*, for example, she takes refuge in a bathroom shower when the woman whose house she is searching unexpectedly returns home. Hearing the woman enter the room, she can only pray, "Please God ... don't let her decide to take an impromptu shower or a dump" (134).

In *"G" is for Gumshoe* she finds herself in a motel with paper-thin walls next to a room where a couple is engaged in noisy lovemaking. She describes the bed frame thumping against the wall, the woman encouraging her partner—"Get that old bald-headed thing over here"—and finally a yelp of astonishment that leaves her wondering whether "she came or fell off the bed" (68). To block the noise out, she resorts to stuffing a sock in each cup of her bra and tying it across her head like earmuffs, with the ends knotted under her chin. But to no avail.

Along with Marcia Muller and Sara Paretsky, Grafton played a pivotal role in opening up the previously all-male private-eye genre to women. Not only did she show that a female could be a convincing private detective, she also put a new twist on many of the genre's standard features, especially the use of humor. Hers is a comic sensibility that, as Rachel Schaffer has noted, grows out of a *woman's* psyche and sensibilities, so it is understandable that she would employ "traditionally female areas of interest (food, household objects, etc.) as the source of the contrast and surprise needed to create humor." She adds that Grafton's juxtaposition "of homey topics with life-and-death matters" serves to make the contrast between "the traditional role of a woman as homemaker and nurturer and Kinsey's role as tough, independent private investigator all the stronger—and more humorous" (322).

Kinky Friedman (1944–)

Creating a detective hero involves some important decisions. Some authors, like Raymond Chandler, choose to invent romanticized versions of themselves. Others go in the opposite direction and come up with characters completely unlike themselves: female French writer Fred Vargas, a scientist, created a male police detective who solved crimes not by reason but by following hunches and intuition; Scottish law professor Alexander McCall Smith created a female private detective who lived in Africa. And then there's Kinky Friedman, who simply made himself the hero in a series of hilarious novels about a New York private eye.

Some authors of crime fiction are also able to draw upon their previous experiences in the creation of their detective heroes. Dashiell Hammett was a Pinkerton detective, Joseph Wambaugh an L.A. cop. But few writers have put their former occupation to better use than Friedman, who was once a famous country singer and leader of a group with the unforgettable name of Kinky Friedman and the Texas Jewboys.

Richard "Kinky" Friedman (the nickname refers to his hair, not his lifestyle) was born in Chicago but grew up in Texas. After graduating from the University of Texas in 1966, he joined the Peace Corps and spent the next two years working in Borneo. In 1971, he formed his band and quickly became known for irreverent and politically incorrect songs like "They Ain't Makin' Jews like Jesus Anymore" and "Get Your Biscuits in the Oven and Your Buns in Bed." The latter song earned him the Male Chauvinist Pig of the Year Award from the National Organization of Women. He often toured with Bob Dylan and was one of the few musicians to perform both at the Grand Ole Opry and on *Saturday Night Live*. He's also the only country singer/mystery writer to have run for governor of Texas, which he did in 2006.

Friedman turned to crime fiction after his music stalled in the mid–1980s with the publication of *A Greenwich Killing Time* (1986), but instead of leaving his previous career behind, he capitalized on it. He named his private eye hero after himself and brought his sense of humor, irreverence, and even many of the actual people he worked with, both in music and the Peace Corps, into his books. "There's a fine line between fiction and nonfiction," Kinky once observed, "and I think I snorted it in 1979" (*Mile* 118).

Friedman's novels are a comic mixture of Sherlock Holmes and Philip Marlowe. Kinky lives at 119B Vandam Street in Greenwich Village, his address echoing that of Holmes's famous 221B Baker Street. Like Holmes, he has plenty of eccentricities: he keeps two phones on his desk, both connected to the same line, so when one rings, the other does too, giving him a choice as to which one to answer; he stores his cigars in a porcelain bust of Sherlock Holmes and drinks his Jameson Irish Whiskey out of an old bull's horn; he sleeps in a purple sarong from Borneo; and he owns an espresso machine that can whistle and hum various tunes like "The Little Drummer Boy" and "Happy Talk" from *South Pacific*.

Visitors to his fourth-floor loft have to shout up at him and wait until he tosses down the key which is lodged in the mouth of a black puppet head attached to a parachute. Also like Holmes, who had a group of street-urchin assistants known as the Baker Street Irregulars, Kinky is often assisted by a trio of associates he calls the Village Irregulars: Randam, a fellow New York private investigator, McGovern, a reporter for the *Daily News*, and the flamboyantly dressed Ratso, a former editor of the *National Lampoon* whom he considers his Dr. Watson.

Kinky's musings about being a detective like Sherlock Holmes come fully wrapped in his goofy humor:

> Being Sherlock is like being the dog that didn't bark at the Red Headed League that didn't exist. If you're Sherlock, you're lonelier than Sergeant Pepper. You're old enough to realize; young enough to know. You're weak enough to be afraid; strong enough to let it show. But you're weary because sooner or later you get tired of suspecting everybody. Then you grow hideously disillusioned. Then you become totally paranoid. Then men come and take you away to wig city, where you wind up masturbating like a monkey in the same cell with Napoleon and a man from Uranus [*Spanking* 117].

Though he's touted on the dust jacket of his books as "a hip hybrid of Groucho Marx and Sam Spade," Kinky resembles Philip Marlowe much more than Spade, most notably in his wisecracking first-person narration. The spirit of Chandler is also evident in such mood-setting lines as this: "It was a cold night in a cold world, I thought, as I walked the misty, muffled streets in the definite direction of nowhere" (*Roadkill* 149). At other times, however, Kinky sounds more like a sleep-deprived Marlowe:

> Then one day you find yourself standing with a paper suitcase on the track of time, smoking your old pipe upside down in the rain, like a knight born out of your time, wondering not who you are or how you got there in the first place, but why people have been drinking ginger ale on airplanes for over two thousand years and if women really fake orgasms because they think men care. The next thing you know you're wandering around lost and looking for your locker at Coconut University [*Roadkill* 94].

Kinky's sense of humor is a goofball concoction of the hilarious, the silly, the clever, the sophomoric, the fun-loving, the potty-mouthed, the puerile, the absurd, and the offensive. Though he's one of those guys who simply can't pass up an opportunity for a joke, even for the most infantile groaners, he does possess an impressive array of comic techniques.

Let's begin with puns. It takes a very clever mind to come up with a pun like this one: staring out of a kitchen window that is yellowed with grime, Kinky observes that, "Whether this phenomenon manifests itself as Flemish or merely phlegmish is arguable. Beauty, as they say, is strictly in the eye of the beer holder" (*Roadkill* 16). When a neighbor complains after a break-in at her apartment, "I don't even know why we have locks in New York," Kinky quips, "To put on bagels" (*Spanking* 166). He also takes a childlike pleasure in playing around with the sound of famous names: he turns the Texas Book Depository into the "Texas Cookbook Suppository," *The Wall Street Journal* into the *Wall Street Gerbil*, and a Chrysler car into a "Jesus Christler convertible." He also humorously riffs on Chappaquiddick, turning the name of the town into Chappaquitdick, where Nixon resigned the presidency, and Chappaquidproquo, a watering-hole for corporate attorneys.

Friedman's not the only author with a gift for comic similes, but few can match the outrageousness of some of his: "He attacked the food like a frenzied priest going after an altar boy" (*God* 29); "I kissed her tentatively at first, like a guy somewhere in Alabama making love for the first time with his cousin" (*Frequent* 232). Not every writer would stop to describe a glob of dried cat vomit, but if it inspires a comparison to the "distinct shape of General Augusto Pinochet's mustache" (*Spanking* 30), then why not. Other similes are funny simply because of their comic unpredictability: a loud squawking noise sounds "like Jerry Lewis was going down on the Titanic" (*Spanking* 155); the aroma of weed on Willie Nelson's tour bus "would make you high enough to sing castrato in the Vienna Boys Choir" (*Roadkill* 135); after realizing his listener isn't fully understanding what he's saying, he writes, "I felt like Marco Polo trying to introduce the noodle to a crowd of irritated Italians" (*Roadkill* 129).

Though he makes jokes guaranteed to offend just about every ethnic and religious group, e.g., "the only thing wrong with Southern Baptists is they don't hold them under long enough" (*Spanking* 142), he also includes himself among those he makes fun of: "My caseload as an amateur private investigator had been rather light lately and my social life had been a bit sluggish as well, possibly because the architecture of my personality was so repellent that most people never got past my first three minutes of superficial charm" (*Spanking* 20).

Kinky's exchanges with the other characters are also funny. There's the predictable Holmes/Watson style banter—Kinky to Ratso: "Maybe you're just a weak Watson." Ratso: "Maybe you're just an unpleasant Sherlock" (*Frequent* 92). There are the frequent comic putdowns from female characters like this one from a woman named Khadija he's trying to impress. He asks her if her name has any special meaning. "It means 'Woman Who Understands Why You Have Trouble Meeting Chicks On Airplanes,'" she replies (*Mile* 17). Some of the best putdowns come from Kinky's cat, who like Carstairs, the Great Dane in Norbert Davis's novels, may not be able to talk ("The cat, of course, said nothing" is a recurring refrain throughout the series), but she can nevertheless communicate very well, as in this example: "the cat looked at me the way you look at a person you've just discovered is a former mental patient" (*Spanking* 28).

Friedman also capitalizes on one other comic technique, one also put to good use by Stuart Kaminsky in his Toby Peters mystery series, that of mixing real characters with fictional ones. This is especially effective when the real characters are colorful personalities, as they certainly are in Kaminsky's *You Bet Your Life* (1978), where private eye Toby Peters is hired by the Marx Brothers. Groucho Marx even makes a brief appearance in Friedman's *Spanking Watson* (1999) just long enough to make a joke shortly after meeting Kinky while standing next to him at a urinal. In *Roadkill* (1997), Kinky is hired by longtime friend Willie Nelson to find out who might be trying to kill him, which gives Friedman an opportunity to include several funny stories about Willie as well as a generous sampling of Willie's own jokes and comments.

Friedman never allows the mystery elements to get in the way of a joke or a funny line; plots, he insists, "are for cemeteries. If you get a plot in a Kinky book, you can consider it gravy" (Pettengell 387). His raucous, raunchy, and ribald sense of humor isn't for everyone, but if you're the kind of reader who loves to laugh even at humor that hasn't been sanitized, then Kinky's your man.

Carl Hiaasen (1953–)

No one writes funnier crime novels than Carl Hiaasen. He can be as hilarious as the best stand-up comics, but he's also as effective as comedians like George Carlin, Jon Stewart, Stephen Colbert, and Lewis Black in using humor as a way of addressing serious issues.

Hiaasen, who began reading the newspaper at age four and got his first typewriter two years later, always knew he wanted to be a writer. In high school, he published an underground newsletter that poked fun at the school's teachers and administrators. While a student at Emory University he wrote for the campus satirical magazine and helped a med-school friend write an autobiographical novel. After two years at Emory, he transferred to the University of Florida to study journalism. Within days after graduation he started working as a newspaper reporter and later joined the *Miami Herald,* first as a feature writer and then a member of a team of investigative reporters. In 1985, he began writing a regular column for the paper, which he still continues to write. In the early 1980s he also co-authored three crime thrillers with fellow *Herald* journalist William Montalbano.

A self-described smart-aleck in school, he also learned at an early age that humor could win him friends, impress the cool kids, and fend off bullies. In 1986, he drew upon his journalism background and previous novelistic experiences, then unleashed his absurdist sense of humor to write his first solo crime novel, *Tourist Season,* an outrageously funny book that was at the same time a deadly serious commentary on what he saw as the damage the tourist industry had done to his beloved state of Florida.

Florida is the single most defining influence on Hiaasen's work. As one who describes his own sense of humor as "sick," Hiaasen considers himself fortunate to live in a state which he describes as "a magnet for wackos" (Brunet). Although he possesses a delightfully warped imagination, some of the craziest stuff in his novels is simply lifted from a file of newspaper accounts he collects about bizarre examples of human behavior in his native state. Stories about a U.S. Congressman's drunken behavior at a seedy strip club and a young woman who crashes her car while shaving her bikini area were the initial inspiration for his novels *Strip Tease* (1993) and *Razor Girl* (2016). Typically, he simply cranks up the humor a few more notches into pure comic absurdity, but he insists, "I don't put anything into my books that couldn't actually happen" (Booth).

The state has also influenced him in a much more serious way. Growing up on the edge of the Everglades where he and his friends played every day when they were kids and then watching it being bulldozed to make way for condominiums and shopping malls made a lasting impression on him. Nothing angers him more than those responsible for the crime of transforming Florida's stunning natural beauty into what one of his characters calls "Newark with palm trees." That anger has inspired both his newspaper columns as well as some of the most uproariously satirical assaults in his fiction.

As a novelist, Hiaasen considers it his primary responsibility to entertain the reader, which he does by filling his books with hilarious dialogue, farcical action, and plenty of comic examples of human folly and cultural absurdity. In *Star Island* (2010), for example, he creates a South Beach nightclub called Pubes where the bartenders and wait staff wear V-cut vinyl pants that "exposed tufts of their short-and-curlies, dyed luminescently" and where the dance floor features "nine hundred square feet of synthetic bush, black shag pile that mapped a heart-shaped pattern upon a sculpted mound of flashing flesh-tone fiberglass" (*Star* 320). He also has the kind of comic sensibility that finds humor in the absurdly perfect detail, as in this report of a talentless celebrity who overdoses on "an unwise mix of vodka, Red Bull, hydrocodone, birdseed and stool softener" (*Star* 3).

But his greatest gift is the creation of truly memorable comic characters. Sometimes, he simply has fun with a character. For example, Chemo, first introduced in *Skin Tight* (1989) is a fugitive wanted by the police for the robbery-at-pitchfork of a bank in Pennsylvania and the murder of his dermatologist, who accidentally incinerated every pore on his face after suffering a stroke while performing electrolysis. He now looks like "somebody had glued Rice Krispies to every square centimeter of his face" (52), which he tries to cover up with Wite-Out. After his hand is bitten off by a barracuda, he replaces it with a Weed Whacker, which he then wields as a weapon. When he's finally sent to prison for his crimes, he discovers a more constructive use for it when he's assigned to the gardening crew.

Earl Edward O'Toole (better known as Tool) in *Skinny Dip* (2004) is another absurdly funny character. Getting shot isn't funny; getting shot by a hunter who mistakes you for a bear because of your thick pelt of hair is, especially when the bullet still remains lodged in your butt crack. Tool also has an unusual hobby: he collects wooden crosses used along the highway to mark the locations of fatal automobile accidents and plants them in his garden. "They look real nice in the ground," he says, "plus you don't gotta prune 'em like you do trees and shrubs" (179). This leads to a humorous encounter with a police detective named Rolvaag who stops by one day to question him about a case he's working on. Rolvaag bends over to read the inscription on a cross Tool is pounding into the ground that memorializes a forty-five-year-old man who was killed by a drunk driver:

> "Friend of yours?" Rolvaag asked.
> "My dog," said Earl Edward O'Toole, avoiding eye contact.
> "That's quite a name for a dog. Randolph Claude Gunther."
> "We called him 'Rex' for short."
> "I never heard of one living forty-five years," the detective remarked. "Parrots can. Tortoises can. But I'm not so sure about dogs."
> Earl Edward O'Toole took another hard swing with the hammer. "Well, he come from good stock" [178].

The conversation continues with Tool coming up with increasingly ridiculous answers to questions put to him. After he tells Rolvaag that Rex died in a plane crash, Rolvaag asks why the memorial reads, "Please Don't Drink and Drive." The pilot was drunk, explains Tool. What about all the other crosses lying on the ground? "Rex's puppies," Tool replies, "They was all on the same plane."

Humor, however, can be more than purely entertaining; it can also be a powerful weapon which Hiaasen uses to give many of his comic characterizations a stinging satiric edge. Reynaldo Flemm (clearly inspired by Geraldo Rivera) in *Skin Tight* is a television reporter notorious for his sensationalist approach to the news. His main claim to fame is getting beat up on camera. (Sometimes he has to resort to smacking himself in the face with a sock filled with parking tokens so it will at least appear he's been beaten up). In truth, he's lazy, vain, and woefully incompetent. All the serious behind-the-camera work is done by his talented producer who conducts his research, writes his lines, and even has to tell him what questions to ask. Despite her best efforts, he still comes across as a pompous airhead. Unfortunately, when he decides to go it alone and attempt to trap a murderous plastic surgeon on camera, the surgeon employs the instrument he's been using to suction fat from Flemm's belly to kill him. Ironically, his body ends up in a medical school in Guadeloupe, where students use it in their study of anatomy.

Hiaasen's most venomous portraits are those of the corrupt, money-grubbing, soulless individuals who are responsible for the utter despoil-ment of Florida's natural beauty in their pursuit of the Almighty Dollar. Reform-minded candidates often rail against their opponents for being in the pocket of special interests. Hiaasen chooses a different approach: instead of railing, he ridicules. "Politicians don't mind if you get up on a soap box and scream and yell at them," notes Hiaasen. "They can take that—but if you're making fun of them that drives them nuts. And that's what I like to do…. I love to ruin their day. The more I can humiliate them in print the happier I am" (Byrne).

The satiric take-down of nine-term U.S. Congressman David Dilbeck in *Strip Tease* is a good example. Dilbeck's in the pocket of Florida's sugar industry, which relies on him to continue voting for the subsidies that have made the sugar farmers rich, and to continue to ignore the environ-mental damage done as a result of the billions of gallons of water they flush into the Everglades. The problem is that Dilbeck has endangered the continued approval of those subsidies after earning the wrath of his House colleagues by casting the deciding vote against a proposed 22 percent pay raise for them because he was drunk at the time of the vote and acciden-tally pushed the wrong lever. Now his drunken escapades at a strip club have made the situation even worse.

Hiaasen turns this prominent public figure and upstanding deacon in his church into a comic buffoon. Dilbeck has a weakness involving booze and naked women. He falls head-over-heels in love with the dancer to whose defense he gallantly (and drunkenly) rushes at the strip club. Later he has one of his henchmen steal the lint from her clothes dryer so he can make love to it. He subsequently gets his hands on one of her shoes and her pink disposable razor, which he uses to shave his own body. As he explains it, "these little things—they help me get by. It's harmless sport" (207). An interested observer, however, sees it differently: "I'm trying to imagine what Thomas Paine would think of a congressman who has sex with old shoes and laundry lint" (254).

Hiaasen's most inspired comic creation (and his most popular char-acter) is a backwoods hermit named Skink who lives in the mangrove swamps and periodically emerges to make regular appearances throughout the series. A giant of a man, he makes a dramatic first impression: he wears a flowered shower cap over his shaved head, from the sides of which extend a pair of braids adorned with red and green shotgun shells; after losing an eye, he replaces it with one he removed from a stuffed owl, which often pops out; he normally dresses in high-top sneakers and an old trench coat, though he sometimes wears a NASCAR checkered flag around his waist like a kilt. What makes him even more unusual is that he is a former governor of the state of Florida.

His real name is Clinton Tyree and before he became governor he was a star college football player, a decorated Vietnam vet, and a former English professor whose face was featured on the cover of *Time* magazine after his election. A rarity among Florida politicians, he was honest and idealistic, two qualities that have no place in the corrupt corridors of Florida power. Special interests manage to buy off enough officeholders of both parties to stop any of his reforms, allowing his colleagues to step around him "as if he were a small lump of dogshit on an otherwise luxuriant carpet" (*Native* 148). After one particularly painful defeat, he simply walked away and headed for the wilderness, where he has lived, mainly subsisting on roadkill, for over three decades.

Unlike most of Hiaasen's comic characters, Skink is not held up to ridicule. His oddball behavior is put to good use, for he becomes an instrument of comic revenge against the forces he once battled as governor. Like many of Hiaasen's characters, Skink is capable of truly ridiculous behavior, but his actions have a moral purpose behind them. He uses a buzzard's beak to carve the word "SHAME" into the bare buttocks of one of his successors as governor, and shows his contempt for his former lieutenant governor by taking a dump in his washing machine. He is especially creative in devising comically appropriate punishments for land developers who are despoiling his beloved state: he dresses one in a diaper after attaching a spiky sea urchin to his scrotum and then ties him to a poisonwood tree.

A satirist must be optimistic enough to believe satire is worth writing but also realistic enough to know that by itself it rarely produces change. But a satiric *novelist* like Hiaasen at least has the ability to mete out poetic justice on the deserving, which he does with a humorous flair. One bad guy is impaled by a stuffed marlin's beak, another is eaten by a lion. One of the most memorable is the villain who is romanced to death by an overly amorous bottle-nosed dolphin.

Hiaasen's comedy and satire have been compared to a long list of predecessors including Jonathan Swift, Mark Twain, H. L. Mencken, Evelyn Waugh, S. J. Perelman, Joseph Heller, and Woody Allen. While he has much in common with each of them, in the end it is his own distinctive style of raucous humor and biting satire that have made his books so popular, and not just among readers of crime fiction.

Joan Hess (1949–)

Joan Hess was born in Fayetteville, Arkansas, earned a degree in art from the University of Arkansas, and then an MS in early childhood development from Long Island University. While she was teaching art at a preschool, a friend suggested she write a romance novel. Though she had never even read any, she proceeded to write ten unpublishable ones before, as she notes on her Amazon Author page, "I realized I needed a splash of blood and a slather of humor in my prose" and turned to mysteries, which she had been avidly reading all her life.

In 1986, she published the first in a series of mysteries set in the fictional college town of Farberville, Arkansas, that featured amateur detective Claire Malloy, a widowed single mother with a teenaged daughter. Though she owns and operates a bookstore, she still manages to find time to solve several crimes. One year later, Hess began a second series set in the small Arkansas town of Maggody (she hit upon the name after spotting a sign on a shack while vacationing in Jamaica that read Maggotty) about a young woman named Arly Hanks. After a bitter divorce, Arly left the madness of New York where she had been living and moved back to her hometown to lick her wounds. She also ended up being hired as police chief when she was the only qualified applicant for the job.

Arly describes Maggody (pop. 755), a flyspeck of a town located in the northwest corner of the state, as an "oasis of poverty and incest" and a downtrodden "hodgepodge of rusty mobile homes, uninspired tract houses, shacks, a dirty barbershop and a dirtier pool hall, and snotty children playing serial killer in an illegal dump" (*Miracles* 1). This is the same kind of poor backwoods Ozark setting novelist Daniel Woodrell has been exploring in his noir crime fiction which takes the reader deep into the lives of desperately poor people who do whatever they must to survive, even if that means making and selling meth. Hess chose a dramatically different approach: she draws upon all the stereotypes outsiders have of such folk and exploits their comic potential.

Characters are the main source of humor in her series, none more so than the Buchanon clan. Like Faulkner's Snopes family, the Buchanons are scattered across the county like ragweed. Few locals are dumb enough to marry into the clan so they are forced to mate among themselves; one of the unfortunate results of such constant intermarriage is that, according to Arly, "not one of them needs a costume on Halloween" (*Much* 19). The Buchanons aren't very bright—Arly once quips she wants to avoid sticking out "like a high-school graduate at a Buchanon family reunion" (*Moon-beams* 117) and says of one member of the family that "astronomers interested in studying black holes could save billions of the taxpayers' dollars by shining a light in his ear" (*Martians* 153)—but they do have a talent for hilariously inventive names: Cootie, Popeye, Petrol, Moon Pie, Siffalus, Constantinople, Pathetica, Idalupino, Doowadiddy.

Among the many Buchanons who become regulars in the series are Mayor Jim Bob Buchanon and his wife Barbara Anne Buchanon Buchanon (Arly simply calls them Hizzoner and Mizzoner). Jim Bob, owner of the Supersaver Buy 4 Less supermarket, is a lecherous fellow. When sexy young actress Gwenneth D'Amoure comes to Maggody to film a movie, he's excited by the prospect of seeing her in the flesh: "If her honkers were half so luscious as they'd been in *Tanya Makes the Team*, he figured he'd be in hog heaven." His idea of heaven, however, is considerably different than it is for his smug, self-righteous wife: hers is "chock full of harps and angels and that kinda crap. His heaven had honkers" (*Mortal* 66).

Unfortunately for Jim Bob, his sanctimonious wife is vigilant in pointing out the flaws in others, especially his. She's the sort of person who never needs to think things over "since she pretty much always had her mind made up in advance" (*Madness* 208). Her favorite putdown is "common," which she applies to everyone in Maggody but herself. She also takes comfort in the knowledge that, "everybody knew she was the most pious Christian in town and maybe the entire country" (*Miracles* 14).

She has a soulmate in Brother Willard Verber, pastor of the Voice of the Almighty Lord Assembly Hall, where she serves as President of the Missionary Society. The two of them combine forces to fight Satan and his pernicious influence, though they go about it in different ways. Brother Verber is a model of comical hypocrisy. Convinced that one can't fight sin without learning as much as possible about it, he pores over books on witches looking for salacious details (and hoping for photographs) about what they do during bouts of sexual frenzy. He exhorts an unmarried couple accused of sexual activities to describe their lustful behavior to him so that they might escape shoveling coal "into Satan's furnace for all eternity" (*Madness* 117), while he takes his own pleasure at the sordid details. He rationalizes his purchase of pornography by telling himself that "God wanted him to study this depravity, because if God hadn't wanted him to subscribe to *Kittens and Tomcats*, there wouldn't have been enough money in the collection plate" to pay for it (*Madness* 5). He also justifies his purchase of "sacramental moonshine" by telling himself some call it "kill-devil" and "that was the exact reason he had been put on this earth" (*Martians* 56).

Though Arly is the primary crime solver, she is sometimes, to her great annoyance, assisted by a pair of Maggody Miss Marples. Her mother Ruby Bee, owner of Ruby Bee's Bar and Grill, and her best friend Estelle, owner of Estelle's Hair Fantasies, thrive on a steady diet of cop and private detective shows on television. (Estelle once wrote a six-page letter to Tom Selleck pointing out a clue he overlooked on an episode of *Magnum, PI.*) In *Madness in Maggody*, they are clever enough to obtain a list of the long-distance phone numbers a missing person called and use them to snoop out a valuable piece of information that helps Arly solve a case. But they also manage to get themselves into comically sticky situations: e.g., Ruby Bee, who has hidden out in a rat-infested dumpster, is saved in the nick of time just as she and the smelly contents are about to be deposited into a sanitation truck.

Other regular comic characters include dim-witted Kevin Buchanon, who "had cotton for brains and not enough of that to make a tampon for a mouse" (*Much* 74), his 300-pound wife Dahlia O'Neill, whose cheeks "may be the color of peaches, but they're the size of watermelons" (*Much* 52), and Raz Buchanon, a moonshiner whose constant companion is his favorite pig Marjorie, whom he takes for a ride in his truck whenever they can't agree on which television show to watch.

Since there's normally little excitement or crime in Maggody (Arly's main police activity is writing speeding tickets), Hess has to come up with colorful visitors to liven things up and to commit some crimes for Arly to solve. In *Mortal Remains in Maggody* (1992), the cast and crew of Glitter-town Productions descend on the unsuspecting town to shoot a film tiled *Wild Cherry Wine,* which can be more accurately described as "the Clampetts do Romeo and Juliet in the nude" (42). The comedy that arises when several of the locals, including Mrs. Jim Bob and Brother Verber, are given small parts in the movie eventually gives way to Arly's much more serious business of solving the murders of three of the visitors from Hollywood.

In *Martians in Maggody* (1994), one of the best in the series, mysterious crop circles suddenly appear in Maggody, which brings to town a pair of rival UFO "experts" as well as television reporters and tabloid journalists. It isn't long before locals begin seeing flying saucers, aliens, even Bigfoot. And then the body of an assistant to one of the ufologists turns up dead, killed by carbon dioxide poisoning in a clearing in the woods near the apparitions. There's no car at the scene, only a circle of burn marks in the grass around the body. Could he have been murdered by a Martian? Arly has to sort out the real from the phony in order to get to the bottom of all the mysteries.

Hess's one-dimensional characters never rise above hillbilly stereotypes and her comic lines are seldom more sophisticated than the *Hee Haw* variety: "reporters are swarming like flies on a meadow muffin" (*Misery* 7) or "he's busier than an ant at a Sunday School picnic" (*Much* 23). But while Arly goes about the serious business of tracking down murderers, readers will find plenty to laugh about in Maggody.

Janet Evanovich (1943–)

Janet Evanovich wasn't always a famous author (1) whose books routinely debut at the top of *The New York Times* Bestseller List, (2) whose success spawned a corporation (Evanovich, Inc.) that employs her husband, son, daughter, and a small staff to manage her affairs, or (3) who is number six on *Forbes's* list of the world's top-earning authors ($33,000 per page in 2015). She was once a struggling stay-at-home mom who spent ten years trying to get her first novel published.

Born in South River, New Jersey, Evanovich studied art at Douglass College, married her high school sweetheart, gave birth to two children, and in her mid–30s tried to become a writer. Despite filling boxes with rejection letters, she forged ahead, finally selling her first novel in 1987, a romance titled *Hero at Large*. After publishing a dozen romances over the next few years, she began to feel restricted by the form. She jokes that she ran out of sexual positions, but the truth is, she says, "I wanted more action. I had a hard time writing books that were just sheer relationship" (James 51).

She decided to try her hand at writing a mystery novel, so she began reading Robert B. Parker—"I read all the Parker books and decided I wanted to be just like him when I grew up" (Gee)—and Sue Grafton, both of whose influence can be readily seen in her work, especially in the use of a first-person narrator with a strong sense of humor. But instead of making her protagonist a confident private eye like Kinsey Millhone, she got the idea of making her a bounty hunter after watching the film *Midnight Run*, in which Robert De Niro portrayed a character with that job. She was also influenced by the example of the TV sitcom *Seinfeld* in creating a comic series of episodic adventures featuring a regular cast of colorful characters. "I discovered I could be funny, and I could make people laugh," she says. "I thought this is a valuable thing. People need to laugh more. Even for a couple minutes while you're reading my book, if I can make someone feel good, I think that's noble" (Goodreau).

Bounty hunter Stephanie Plum resembles Kinsey Millhone, but with bigger hair, a Jersey accent (and attitude), and a far more complicated romantic life. A third-generation American of Italian-Hungarian heritage, she was born and raised in a duplex in Trenton, New Jersey. She graduated from Douglass College (in the top ninety-eight percent of her class, she jokes), and was married for a year until she caught her best friend riding her husband on her dining room table "like he was Dickie the Wonder Horse" (*Two* 150). She now lives in a small apartment with a hamster named Rex who she insists makes a good companion because he keeps his thoughts to himself, eats cheap food, and his poop is small. Six months after being laid off from her job as a discount lingerie buyer and desperate for money, Stephanie blackmails her cousin Vinnie into giving her a job in his bail-bond business. She becomes a fugitive-apprehension agent, tracking down individuals who fail to appear at their assigned court dates, thus forfeiting the bail that cousin Vinnie had put up for them.

Evanovich's novels are highly formulaic, which helps explain their commercial success. She knows what her readers want and she faithfully delivers the goods. In each novel Stephanie has to locate a missing person, her investigation often reveals other crimes, and along the way either her car or her apartment will likely be blown up. On the personal front, new oddballs will be added to her team, she'll find new messes to get into, and her love life will continue percolating as she juggles her lustful longings for a sexy Italian cop and a super cool Latin bondsman. By combining crime and romance, Evanovich has doubled her audience. Mystery readers might have to tolerate Stephanie's shifting romantic entanglements, and romance fans will have to do the same with Stephanie's adventures tracking down bad guys, but few readers will fail to be entertained by Evanovich's humorous approach to both genres.

Stephanie's a proud product of the Burg, a "blue-collar chunk of Trenton where dysfunctional drunks were still called bums and only pansies went to Jiffy Lube for an oil change" (*Two* 5) and where "houses and minds are proud to be narrow" (*Three* 2). (Trenton is located just three exits on the New Jersey Turnpike away from where Evanovich was born and raised.) Growing up there has taught Stephanie the importance of family and community as well as funeral homes, bakeries, and beauty parlors. It has also forged her strength and tenacity: "Life is about survival of the fittest," she proclaims, "and Jersey is producing the master race" (*Four* 201).

It has also shaped the spunky attitude that spices up her narrative. She has a gift for zingy one-liners: a ninety-two-year-old man "couldn't find his dick if it glowed in the dark" (*Two* 41); a woman's voice "had the rasp of two packs a day, and her breath was hundred proof" (*Four* 12); "if breasts were money, Connie'd be Bill Gates" (*Five* 2); her father "would eat cat shit if it was salted, fried, or frosted, but it took an act of Congress to get him to eat a vegetable" (*Two* 264).

Evanovich surrounds Stephanie with a large cast of comic characters, chief among them her Grandma Mazur, who "was seventy-two and didn't look a day over ninety" (*Two* 25). She lives with Stephanie's parents in the house where Stephanie grew up. Her favorite activity is visiting funeral homes and commenting on the appearance of the deceased. "If people stopped dying the social life of the burg would come to a grinding halt," notes Stephanie (*Two* 12). But unlike Stephanie's mother who is not at all happy about her daughter's chosen line of work, Grandma Mazur is thrilled, especially when Stephanie brings a weapon to dinner. On one occasion, she accidentally shoots the chicken on the dining room table; on another she tasers Stephanie's father while he's quietly enjoying his ham dinner.

It's easy to see who Stephanie gets her sense of humor from. For example, Grandma Mazur tells a friend that the severed penis from a dead man that Stephanie received in the mail reminded her of her own husband. "You talking about size?" asks her friend. "Heck no," Grandma Mazur says. "His part was that dead" (*Two* 261). When Stephanie's father falls over unconscious and farts after she tasers him, she says, "Oops," then quips, "Someone must have stepped on a duck" (*Five* 287). She also loves tagging along on her granddaughter's adventures—"I can only take so much of old people. If I want to see loose skin I can look in the mirror" (*Five* 185)—and gets so pumped up she begins talking like a pulp detective: "So what should I do if I see her again?... You want me to put a hole in her?" (*Four* 266).

Stephanie's sometime partner is a black streetwalker named Lulu whom she met during her first job assignment and who later decides to trade the night life in for a filing job at Stephanie's agency. Lulu stands out in any crowd thanks to her eye-popping ability to cram her 200-plus pounds into clothing that tests the strength of lycra: "Lulu was wearing a canary-yellow spandex miniskirt and a stretchy top that was at least two sizes too small. Her hair was orange. Her lipstick was bright pink. And her eyelids were gold glitter" (*Five* 70). She is pugnacious and a master of the colorful insult: she calls one guy a "slime-faced bag of monkey shit"

(*Five* 145) and tells another, "Drop your gun, you punk-ass old coot.... You don't drop your gun, I'm gonna bust a cap up your ass!" (*Four* 299).

Two other recurring characters serve romantic purposes. Stephanie has known Joe Morelli, a Trenton cop, since they were kids. As a sixteen-year-old she lost her virginity to him on the floor of a bakery behind the eclairs. Now they are professional associates and romantic partners. Though she recognizes the danger of involvement with the hunky guy with "the best ass in Trenton ... maybe the world. Buns you wanted to sink your teeth into" (*Four* 14), the sound of his voice on her answering machine or just seeing his handwriting on a note turns her on. She's even afraid to sit next to him on a couch, fearful that, "I'd go after his leg like a dog in heat" (*Four* 65). Her lusty longings for him and their romantic ups and downs follow the pattern of the romance novels Evanovich once wrote, though she tempers the heat with plenty of humor. For example, after confirming for herself what a girl friend had told her about Morelli, that he had a tongue like a lizard, she crows, "God bless the wild kingdom, I thought with a new appreciation for reptiles" (*Four* 164).

The other hunk in Stephanie's life (and sexual fantasies) is a drop-dead handsome Cuban-American named Ranger, who starts out as a mentor in her new career but soon becomes competition for Morelli in the lust department. Readers who, like Stephanie, can't make up their minds about which one she should choose can purchase a tee-shirt on Evanovich's website with Morelli's name on the front and Rangeman, the name of Ranger's protective services company, on the back.

Slapstick action is another reliable source of humor in the series, especially in the early novels where Stephanie is learning on the job and behaving more like Calamity Jane than Wonder Woman. Chasing down fugitives, she quickly discovers, can be a messy affair: attempting to apprehend a guy who works in a fast-food restaurant dressed as a chicken, she ends up slathered in feathers, mustard, and special sauce; on another occasion, she is covered in mud after being dragged into a mud-wrestling match between two women. Other comic scenes include a car chase during which a body falls off the roof of the car she and Lulu are pursuing and ends up stuck like a bug against her windshield. With Lulu's help, they stuff the body into the trunk and tie a scarf on its foot like a warning flag so they won't get stopped by the police.

Evanovich has become a one-woman publishing industry. In addition to the Plum books which now number nearly two dozen (all numbered so readers can easily keep track of how many they have read), she launched two more series, one with a character named Diesel who first appeared in several of the Plum books, the other about a female engineer and her NASCAR boyfriend. She also co-authors (with Phoef Sutton, Lee Goldberg, and Charlotte Hughes) three other series.

Though the Plum books were partly inspired by *Seinfeld*, Evanovich hasn't followed its example in knowing when to quit before the jokes become stale or episodes get recycled. The later entries in the series often settle for the easy joke and simple variations on comic situations that have previously occurred. None of this, however, has affected the sales of the books, and Evanovich makes no apologies for her success or for her expanding fictional output: "I feel very comfortable to be a commodity that's packaged and sold by my publisher," she insists. "Truth is, my books are product and my readers are consumers. Deal with it" (Gee).

Andrea Camilleri (1925–)

To many outsiders, Italy is a place where one can live *la dolce vita;* the sunlight, the food, the wine, the zest for life—who wouldn't want to live there? But for many of those who do, life is far from that dreamy picture of the sweet life. The reality for them is a daily battle with mindless incompetence, suffocating bureaucracy, corruption, cronyism, and crime. For someone like Salvo Montalbano, an impatient man with a short fuse who is not very good at dealing with frustration to begin with, life as a police inspector in the small town of Vigàta in Sicily is no barrel of laughs. But that doesn't mean the crime series by Andrea Camilleri that features him and his fellow policemen doesn't offer plenty of humor.

After a distinguished career as a theater and television director and longtime teacher at the National Academy of Arts in Rome, Andrea Camilleri at the age of sixty-nine published his first mystery novel, *The Shape of Water* (1994), which introduced Commissario Salvo Montalbano of the Vigàta, Sicily, police department. Since then, the series, twenty volumes of which have thus far been translated into English, has spawned several successful television films, sold millions of copies in translation worldwide, and made Camilleri Italy's most popular writer.

The reasons for the books' popularity are many: they benefit from a strong sense of place; the crimes, often based on actual ones Camilleri reads about, are realistic and explore such important issues as illegal immigration, human trafficking, police brutality, governmental corruption, and of course the ever-present influence of the Mafia. Above all else there is the engaging character of Montalbano and a playful sense of humor that balances the often dark crimes that occur in modern Sicily.

Camilleri draws upon many sources for the humor in the books, but everything starts with the language, which their gifted English translator Stephen Sartarelli describes as a curious pastiche of Sicilian dialect, "normal" Italian, contemporary slang, comic stage dialogue, lofty literary flourishes and "the sort of manglings of proper Italian made by provincials who have never learned it correctly" (8). Though he claims that translating such a mishmash into English is an "impossible task," he nonetheless captures its playfulness brilliantly.

This playfulness begins with the voice of the narrator, whose observations range from the sardonic—"Ingrid's husband was a known ne'er-do-well, so it was only logical that he should turn to politics" (*Potter's* 78)—to the satirical—"In American movies, the policeman had only to tell somebody the license-plate number, and in less that two minutes, he would know the owner's name, how many children he had, the color of his hair, and the number of hairs on his ass" (*Snack* 170). His amusing descriptions have a Chandleresque zing to them: "Her panties were smaller than a G-string. With that in his mouth, a man could still have recited all of Cicero's *Catilinarian Orations* or sung 'Celeste Aida'" (*Paper* 195); "The inspector contemplated his superior's disturbing hairdo, which was very full with a great big tuft in the middle that curled back like certain turds deposited in the open country" (*Voice* 101).

Unlike Donald E. Westlake's John Dortmunder, who is frustrated when his crime capers go awry (as they usually do), Montalbano's frustration is with the everyday world, or what passes for the normal way of doing things in Sicily. Whether it's the daily challenge of negotiating Italy's notoriously inefficient bureaucracy or the insidious, all-pervasive influence of the Mafia in daily affairs, a man like Montalbano won't be happy for long. And it isn't just big things that drive him nuts; clichés, bad food, paperwork, his boss, even his colleague's annoying habit of pouring Parmesan cheese over his plate of pasta with clam sauce make his blood boil.

It is interesting to compare Montalbano with another irascible crime solver, Nero Wolfe. Both are subject to temper tantrums when things irritate or displease them, which is often. In Wolfe's case, the humor arises from the rigid efforts he's made to control his life. He has largely isolated himself from the real world and has organized his routine so completely as to avoid most unpleasantness; as long as he has Archie Goodwin to deal with the messy details of the real world, he doesn't have to. By contrast,

Montalbano lives smack in the middle of a messy world and the humor in his case arises not from his efforts to escape it but from his constant frustration in having to deal with its annoying imperfections.

Camilleri's novels are solid police procedurals. Montalbano is the kind of dogged investigator who, "when he wanted to get to the bottom of something, he did" (*Shape* 11). And even though he sometimes chastises his colleagues for being clowns and idiots, he admires them (especially his two closest, Fazio and Mimì Augello) as honest, hard-working professionals (in a place where many civil servants are neither). Together, they form an effective team dedicated to solving crimes.

Some of the recurring characters in the series, however, exist primarily for comic relief. One such character is Dr. Lattes, the police commissioner's chief. Known as Caffè-Lattes for the cloying warmth of his manner, he always seems to be lingering in the commissioner's waiting room, which prompts Montalbano to complain, "Didn't he have an office of his own? Couldn't he go scratch his balls behind his own desk?" (*Track* 214). Lattes has somehow got the idea into his head that Montalbano is married with children. Nothing can disabuse him of this notion, so Montalbano plays along with him, giving rise to humor. During one conversation with Lattes, he invents an immigrant lover for his imaginary wife. Later, Montalbano is happy to report the good news that she is back under the conjugal roof, which sends Dr. Lattes into raptures: "How wonderful! How very wonderful! Giving thanks to the Blessed Virgin, the home fires are burning again" (*Potter's* 62).

But no character provides more humor than Agatino Catarella, the switchboard operator at the Vigàta police station. Hired only because he's a relative of a powerful political official, he is initially presented as woefully incompetent at his job. However, he later proves to have hidden skills with computers and is also extremely loyal. What makes him so humorous is his unique language, a mélange of garbled syntax, local dialect, mispronunciations, and incomprehensible grammar. Add a healthy dose of malaprops—"doverose" (overdose); "strick flabetical order" (strict alphabetical order); "nickpick" (picnic): "oppocalypso" (apocalypse)—and a delivery that sounds somewhere between Italian Cockney and Brooklynese and his every utterance becomes a challenge to Montalbano (and the reader). Here's a typical example: "'E said, 'e bein' 'im, the beforementioned Mr. C'mish'ner, 'e said 'e wants 'a see yiz immidiotwise straightaways an' oigently oigentwise without a minnit's dillay" (*Angelica's* 199).

Catarella's childlike innocence is endearing. For example, when he informs his boss that a threatening note had been sent to the police station overnight, Montalbano asks him if it was anonymous. "No, Chief," he replies, "it wasn't on nominus, it was onna wall outside" (*Rounding* 6). Camilleri's portrait of the dim-witted character might be considered cruel if it weren't for the way he emphasizes Catarella's computer skills and also for the rare patience Montalbano uncharacteristically displays whenever he deals with the man he clearly has affection for.

Luca Bonetti-Alderighi, Montalbano's imbecilic boss, is a pompous administrator who routinely summons Montalbano to his office to be chastised for some failing or another. The creative excuses Montalbano comes up with for not being able to meet with him (e.g., he has to undergo an imaginary medical procedure he calls a double scrokson that involves a tube being inserted into his anus) and the inventive way he ridicules his boss during their meetings (the man's too dense to realize he's being made fun of) are thoroughly entertaining.

One especially rich source of humor is Montalbano's prickly relationship with longtime girlfriend Livia Burlando, who lives in faraway Genoa, so they are seldom together. Mostly, they talk on the phone, and they can barely complete a few sentences before they start arguing. Things aren't much better when they do get together. For example, in *Angelica's Smile* he and Livia are in bed after an argument that began when a woman's voice on the phone who claims she dialed the wrong number causes Livia to accuse Montalbano of having an affair with the woman. Awakened during the night when Livia begins talking in her sleep, he gets up, grabs a chair, and sits by her bedside for hours hoping she will say something incriminating he can use against her. When he hears her mutter, "No Carlo, not from behind," it drives him nuts wondering who Carlo is. Naturally, every man he comes in contact with the next day is named Carlo. After several days of torment, he is relieved when he learns that Carlo is the name of the tailor who was fitting Livia for a new dress.

Despite their arguments, the two love one another, which is why Montalbano struggles mightily to remain faithful to her. The most challenging test of his resolve comes in the person of a beautiful Swedish woman now living in Vigàta named Ingrid Sjostrom. They first meet during an investigation, and later she helps in another case. She's so completely at ease around him that she's comfortable taking nude swims in the ocean in front of his house, massaging his bruised body while he showers, and when she's had too much to drink, spending the night next to him in bed, which becomes a "torture grill" that turns him into "Saint Salvo, burnt alive by the fires of temptation" (*Treasure* 153). His Herculean efforts to rein in his sexual urges and maintain a fatherly relationship with Ingrid provide ongoing comic relief.

Montalbano also often finds himself in slapstick situations. A botched assault on a house turns into such a comedy-of-errors fiasco that it makes him feel like "a character in an Abbott and Costello movie" (*Terra* 28). Frustration at being unable to open a lock on a door after using everything from a hammer and chisel to a gun has him behaving "like Donald Duck ... kicking and punching the door, screaming like a madman" (*Excursion* 235). On another occasion he's surprised when he opens his door to walk out onto his veranda dressed only in his underwear and bumps into a beautiful woman standing there. Naturally, when he dashes back inside to put on some pants, he slips on the wet tiles and falls on his ass like a buffoon.

Some comic scenes are more satirical than cartoonish. In *The Track of Sand*, Montalbano, sympathizer of the downtrodden, is dragged to a charity horserace among the rich and well-connected. His worst fears that he'll be stuck "in the middle of a sea of assholes" (78) are realized as soon as he arrives: "what kind of loony bin had he stumbled into?" he asks himself (83). When the master of the house claps his hands after being introduced to him, the fish-out-of-water Montalbano becomes confused: "What was he supposed to do? Should he clap his hands, too? Maybe it was a sign these people used on such occasions to express happiness" (84). So he too claps, only to become mortified when he realizes the clap was a signal to a servant to sound the horn. Adding to his discomfort, the horn is only inches from his ears, which are left ringing after the blast. To top it all off, his fussy taste buds are later subjected to a soup that smells like "a cross between beer gone sour and turpentine" (103) and tastes like it was seasoned with hydrochloric acid.

Camilleri never downplays the seriousness of the often violent crimes that occur in the series. But he's not afraid to use humor to ridicule a wide range of subjects, including his main character. Perhaps if Montalbano could develop a sense of humor and learn to laugh more instead of cursing the saints when things don't go his way, he'd save himself plenty of grief. But then he'd make for a far less entertaining character to read about.

Colin Bateman (1962–)

Colin Bateman writes comic crime thrillers whose violence and dark action are seen through the eyes of zany narrators. Terrible things happen but the jokes keep coming, which according to Bateman simply reflects the Northern Ireland style of dark humor: "You laugh about everything that goes on. Maybe it's not unique in that a joke always follows a tragedy, but it's how you deal with things" (Dwyer). The humor in his novels isn't all dark, however; it can also be smart, sophomoric, situational, purely verbal, silly, and sometimes even thought-provoking.

Bateman was born in 1962 in County Down, Northern Ireland. At age seventeen he began a career in journalism, working for the *County Down Spectator*, where he was given freedom to write whatever he wanted, ranging from regular news stories to articles on entertainment, film, and music. He also authored a satiric column where he was able to show off his sense of humor. But thanks to Robert B. Parker, he turned to the life of a crime writer:

> When I was a callow youth and despairing of ever being able to write, I read all the Spenser books and loved them and they absolutely inspired me to start writing: so simply written, yet great fun. *Divorcing Jack* started out just copying Robert B; before very long I developed my own style and went back and started that book again, but he absolutely got me going [Jordan].

A versatile author, Bateman has written stand-alone novels, young adult books, television dramas, screenplays, an opera, and a pair of comic crime series. The more famous and longest-running of the two features Dan Starkey, a former Belfast journalist who made his debut in Bateman's first novel, *Divorcing Jack*, in 1994. His second series, featuring a Belfast bookshop owner who inadvertently becomes a private eye, was launched in 2009 with *Mystery Man*. Both share a Belfast setting and an offbeat sense of humor.

An ex–newspaper reporter and columnist in Belfast known for his satiric attitude, Dan Starkey now takes free-lance assignments which invariably lead to deadly complications. Whether he's asked to investigate the birth of a female messiah on a remote island, follow an Irish boxer to New York where he's scheduled to fight Mike Tyson, or write a book about an actor directing his first film, trouble follows him everywhere, requiring him to figure things out. Eventually, in *Nine Inches* (*2011*), he decides to go into the private-eye business, or as he prefers to describe it, "I offer a boutique, bespoke service for important people with difficult problems" (*Nine* 4).

Starkey is a trouble-magnet. "You can't go out for a pint of milk," his wife Trish complains, "without having an adventure" (*Nine* 325). These escapades are usually filled with violence and littered with victims, many of them Starkey's friends and associates. But because he's also the kind of person who can't pass up an opportunity to make a pun or joke about things, his first-person narratives are hilarious.

He's a wiseacre, which isn't surprising considering his confession that, "I was forty, but I had a mental age of twelve" (*Driving* 93). For example, when a woman finds him passed out on the ground and asks if he's OK, he quips, "I'm fine. I'm a gravel inspector for the Department of Stones" (*Divorcing* 12). Even in the midst of a harrowing experience when the trailer he's in careens down a hill and ends up perched precariously over the sea below and his stunned companion asks where they are, he jokes (quoting Bob Dylan), "the answer my friend ... is blowing in the wind" (*Turbulent* 7). He even channels the spirit of the Marx Brothers when, after a character tells him, "I told her I'd forgotten to lock up and went downstairs and out the door and drove to the airport in my pyjamas," he replies, "There's an airport in your pyjamas?" Some of his funniest wise-cracks, however, are his most inept efforts, as in this feeble attempt at an insult: "Up your hole with a big jam roll" (*Shooting* 219).

He has a knack for puns. (A sampling of Bateman's titles illustrates his love of wordplay: *Running with the Reservoir Pups*; *The Prisoner of Brenda*, *The Seagull Has Landed*, *The Day of the Jack Russell*, *Doctor Yes*.) He salutes his wife just after she has given birth with a raised arm and the salutation, "Hail Caesarean." When a woman tells him her husband flushed all his drugs down the toilet, he quips, "The fish'll be singing tonight then. Salmon chanted evening" (*Shooting* 127). When an attractive young woman nods at a line of guys sitting at the bar and says she knows them all by name—JJ, CJ, DJ, and MJ—he jokes, "Well, they seem okay to me, but that's only an initial impression" (*Driving* 213). Sometimes his humor has a macabre edge: after witnessing a man's finger being cut off, he says to the assailant, "That was a bit out of hand" (*Of* ch. 19).

He also has a flair for colorful descriptions—"The sheets on the bed were thrown back and there was an indentation that, given time, might prove a major attraction in Turin" (*Horse* 132); an older couple looked "to be in their sixties but may not have spoken since their thirties" (*Divorcing* 106)—and witty similes—"I could see the pain and the hurt in her eyes, as if I had laddered the tights of her soul" (*Turbulent* 18); a chair with yellow foam rubber poking out through the seat looks "like an Edam cheese with legs" (*Divorcing* 269). He can even squeeze a laugh out of hilariously bad similes: "The church loomed up out of the fog like a big churchy thing in a fog" (*Turbulent* 165); "They will have you out of this country quicker than a very quick thing" (*Nine* 242).

Starkey is mainly a jokester, but some of the books' humor also grows out of the farcical action. In *Shooting Sean* (2001), for example, he travels to the Cannes film festival where he rubs shoulders with celebrities, air kisses Kate Moss, shouts, "You lookin' at me?" to Robert De Niro, and accidentally breaks Barry Manilow's nose, then follows it up with a deliberate sock to the jaw for being responsible for "I Write the Songs That Make the Whole World Sing." He also manages to get himself in plenty of embarrassing situations. To escape his pursuers who are chasing him along the roof of a speeding train, he scrambles over the side and into the window of a toilet. Unfortunately, an elderly nun is sitting on the toilet, her knickers around her ankles. But here too humor rescues him, as he's quick-witted enough to quip, "Beam me up, Scotty," before exiting.

In a kind of meta-fictional commentary, he even makes humorous remarks about his own narrative style. After a meal of burgers and baked beans, he writes, "It was hardly *nouvelle cuisine,* unless you ate *nouvelle cuisine* all the time, and then it definitely was *nouvelle cuisine.* Whatever the truth was, I'd discovered italics in a big way" (*Shooting* 49). After referring to someone as a "bleached-blond beach bum," he acknowledges that the description reads "like a work-out at the alliteration Olympics" (*Driving* 85).

Bateman is, however, also effective in putting his humor to serious purposes, notably in how he deals with the subject of the Troubles, the three decades of sectarian violence in Northern Ireland that finally ended with the signing of the peace accords on Good Friday in 1998. Like Joseph Heller, whose *Catch-22* he cites as an early influence on his writing, Bateman finds humor in some of the absurdities of the conflict. For example, in *Divorcing Jack* he introduces a Roman Catholic priest in a small Northern Ireland village whose parishioners have all deserted him after he undergoes a heart-transplant operation in London because they suspect he was given a Protestant heart.

Another dependable source of humor comes from Starkey's relationship with his wife Trish. Here too one can see the debt Bateman owes to Robert B. Parker, for Trish is a comic version of Spenser's longtime girlfriend Susan Silverman. Susan serves as an interpreter of Spenser's actions and an enthusiastic cheerleader of his heroic deeds. Trish is never shy about commenting about Starkey's behavior, but to her he's no hero. She's more a scold than a cheerleader. One can't imagine Susan ever telling Spenser that he's a "useless waste of space," as Trish tells her husband, or asking him, "Do you have any idea how much of a wanker you sound like sometimes?" (*Nine* 264).

One feature both relationships do have in common is playful romantic banter, though Starkey's remarks are earthier than Spenser's more romantic ones. For example, after one of their many arguments, he asks Trish if he's forgiven. "I neither forgive nor forget," she advises him. "I merely extend the time in which you're allowed to travel in my exalted circle." "That's one name for it," he quips (*Belfast* 155).

Bateman's Mystery Man novels are more conventional mysteries than the Starkey books in that they focus on the actual search for the solution to a crime. The hero, who is never given a name and is known only as the Mystery Man, is the owner of a Belfast mystery bookstore named No Alibis (a real place). He becomes a private eye entirely by accident when the detective whose office is next door turns up missing and his clients come to the bookstore instead. He figures that a life spent reading and selling crime fiction has given him all the training he needs: "I have the combined wisdom of ten thousand fictional detectives whizzing about in my brain" (*Day* 166), he insists. He doesn't like to put himself out too much, however, preferring "iitty-bitty crimes" over those that might require him to exert himself too much.

Dan Starkey is entertaining because of his non-stop jokiness. Mystery Man is humorous because of who he is: like the Michael Scott character on *The Office*, he's obtuse and self-absorbed, which is fully exposed thanks to his first-person narration. He has an unreasonably high opinion of himself: "I am an important person," he brags, although he has to reluctantly slip in the proviso, "albeit in the shrinking world of independent bookselling" (*Mystery* 170). He credits his girlfriend/partner Alison for sometimes being partially right, but then adds, "She could never be completely right, because then she would be me" (*Day* 207). A comic highlight of the novels is the dramatic gathering-of-suspects scene where Mystery Man intends to publicly expose the identity of the killer, though he ends up resembling Inspector Clouseau more than Perry Mason as he fumbles his way to the big reveal.

His sense of superiority notwithstanding, his crime-solving career is comically hampered by several factors. Among other things, he's the world's worst hypochondriac; a short list of his imagined medical complaints includes vertigo, tinnitus, irritable bowel syndrome, hemophilia, insomnia, psoriasis, rickets, malaria, degenerative myopia, fibromyalgia, and a case of seasonal affective disorder so severe he gets depressed by all four seasons (which inspires his doctor's nurse to call him Frankie Valli). He claims to be allergic to everything from flies and cows to dogs and dead people. He takes sixteen pills a day for his various maladies, which he complains dulls his senses so much that if he were ever caught in a flood, "I would be able to cut off my own arms for use as paddles without flinching, although I wouldn't be able to hold them" (*Dr.* 192).

Some of his cases are also comic. In "The Case of the Missing FA Cup," he's hired by a soccer fan to find a Chinese woman with big ears who stormed out after he, in the midst of sexual excitement while making love with her, grabs her ears and shouts, "I've won the FA cup." In "The Case of the Cock-Headed Man," he's hired by the owner of a no-frills airline to find the culprit who has painted male genitals over his face on a billboard, an image that has gone viral on YouTube.

Bateman clearly has fun using Mystery Man's sarcastic attitude to get in some comic jabs at crime writers like James Patterson and John Grisham. He also has him from time to time adopting the names of famous mystery writers like Lawrence Block, Walter Mosley, Donald Westlake, and even Belfast journalist-turned-crime-solver Dan Starkey. After four books, however, Bateman decided to end the series. "I really don't want the joke to wear too thin," he said, then adds that "living with a headcase like Mystery Man isn't easy for anyone" (Burke).

Few crime writers provoke a wider range of humorous responses than Bateman: groans at clever puns, giggles at smart remarks, guffaws at farcical episodes, embarrassed chuckles at politically incorrect quips, belly laughs at goofy jokes. No matter what the reader's taste, Bateman will likely find a way to tickle his or her funny bone.

Fred Vargas (1957–)

When it comes to the creation of their detective heroes, crime writers often end up with a character who closely resembles themselves. Younger, smarter, and more handsome, perhaps, but similar in temperament and personality. The French writer Fred Vargas (the pseudonym of Frédérique Audouin-Rouzeau) is a notable exception to this practice. Her detective hero, Jean-Baptiste Adamsberg, *commissaire* of the police headquarters in the 5th arrondissement in Paris and later head of the Serious Crime Squad, is about as different from his creator as one can imagine. Fashioning such a character has led Vargas to alter some of the fundamental conventions of the genre, resulting in a series of refreshingly original police procedurals imbued with touch of whimsy and plenty of off-kilter humor.

Vargas shares a pseudonym first used by her twin sister Jo, a painter who was inspired by the name of the character played by Ava Gardner in *The Barefoot Contessa*. Her father was a prominent surrealist who wrote about André Breton and other leading figures in the movement; her mother was a chemist. She ended up following in both their footsteps: she became an archaeologist and medieval historian who spent six years researching and writing an influential study of the Black Plague; like her father she also became something of a surrealist herself when she began writing crime novels.

In 1986, while working as co-director of an archaeological site, she felt the need for an escape from the rigors of her professional activities. "I used to play the accordion in order to relax from the job," she says, "but I wasn't good enough at music, so I decided to write a detective story for fun" (Reisz). Instead of creating a scientifically minded individual like herself, however, she created one who is her exact opposite: she made Adamsberg a detective who "never seemed to be tied down by tedious facts" (*Chalk* 156), a man for whom "inferring, deducting, concluding ... was a complete mystery" (*Chalk* 46). Rather than thinking things through, he relies on instinct and hunches, always ready to "follow some vague scent in the air" (*Chalk* 156), much to the befuddlement of his fellow policemen.

Vargas is no anti-intellectual, as her scientific career amply demonstrates. And while she is an admirer of Sherlock Holmes's brilliance, she also notes that while Conan Doyle "gives the impression of realism," the world he creates in his stories is, like hers, "a mad, almost a surrealist world" (Henley). Writing about a detective like Adamsberg, she felt, would be a whole lot of fun. Besides, as the cases she creates for him prove, there are some mysteries that can't easily be solved by logical methodology or scientific investigation.

Adamsberg grew up in the stony foothills of the Pyrenees, where for twenty years as a local policeman he amazed his fellow cops with his unorthodox methods, solving crimes no one else could. One frustrated colleague complained, "You sit around daydreaming, staring at the wall, or doodling on a bit of paper as if you had all the time and knowledge in the world, and then one day you swan in, cool as a cucumber, and say, 'Arrest the priest. He strangled the child to stop him talking'" (*Chalk* 9). Another policeman tells him, "You make me laugh, Adamsberg. You make me think of the guys who pull rabbits out of hats," to which Adamsberg replies, "The rabbits really do come out of the hats though, don't they" (*Wash* 71)? How does this unimpressive little man (at only five-seven, he barely made the minimum requirement to join the force, making him possibly the shortest policeman in all of France) with a sleepy demeanor and a disheveled appearance that others variously describe as making him look "like a pig's breakfast" (*Have* 33) or "a dandelion on the putting green" (*Have* 153) manage to do it? The answer to that question is one of the many charms of the series.

Much of the humor in Vargas's books comes from the way she plays with the convention of the Great Detective and his sidekick. Instead of making the brainy Adrien Danglard, Adamsberg's second in command, the hero, like Conan Doyle's Dr. Watson he's the one who is in awe of his superior's unusual skills. Danglard is both amazed and frustrated by his boss's unconventional methods. How can a logical person like himself, who "sorted sheep from goats, put things in little boxes, found the missing links, and thereby solved problems," lag behind Adamsberg, who merely "put one thing with another, or turned them upside down, or scattered what had been brought together and threw it up in the air to see where it would fall" (*Seeking* 87)?

Adamsberg is no magician. He conscientiously assigns investigative tasks to his underlings and uses modern technology whenever he can. He even relies on the expertise of an eighty-six-year-old female computer-hacker to solve one case. He also highly values Danglard's intelligence and encyclopedic knowledge. But he knows that some cases can't be solved by "people who think two and two make four" (*Seeking* 196). Such mysteries require the "walking, dreaming, straggly-thinking method" (*Have* 31) of a cloud-shoveller like himself.

The mysteries Vargas dreams up for Adamsberg to solve are also highly unconventional. Dozens of large circles drawn in blue chalk, each containing a single item (e.g., a shoe, an orange, a dog turd, a doll's head, an "I Love Elvis" badge) begin appearing all over Paris; things take an ominous turn when murder victims start appearing in the circles in *The Chalk Circle Man* (1996). A giant wolf, or perhaps a man posing as a werewolf, is terrorizing a small mountain community in the French Alps by killing sheep; when the monster begins killing people, it needs to be stopped before any more die in *Seeking Whom He May Devour* (1999). Eight people in various regions of France were stabbed to death by what appears to be a trident between 1949 and 1983; now some twenty years later, two new victims are found. The problem is that the man Adamsberg is convinced committed the first eight murders has been dead for sixteen years in *Wash This Blood Clean From My Hand* (2004).

The lead-up to the crimes in *Have Mercy on Us All* (2001) is particularly bizarre. A man from the country moves to Paris and, inspired by the ghost of his dead great-great-grandfather, resurrects an old family tradition by becoming a town crier in his neighborhood. A bookish listener recognizes that among the announcements the crier reads are passages in various languages (medieval French, Arabic, even excerpts from Samuel Pepys's 1665 diary) that describe the coming of the Black Plague. At the same time, large backward images of the number 4 begin appearing on the doors of apartment buildings all over Paris. And then bodies covered with flea bites and charcoal patches that mimic death by plague begin turning up. Adamsberg has to determine what's going on before a nationwide panic about the return of the plague sets in.

Eccentrics are not uncommon in crime fiction, especially in those traditional cozy mysteries set in quaint English villages where characters with exaggerated quirks are sometimes presented as objects of gentle satire. Vargas's delightfully loopy oddballs are of a different order. Their eccentricities are endearing rather than off-putting and the humor they generate reinforces the playful tone of the series.

Vargas presents her characters in such a matter-of-fact manner that their actions seem plausible in the world she has created for them. For example, Adamsberg wears two wrist watches, one faster than the other, so he needs to average the two to determine the correct time. No one, however, thinks this is particularly crazy; one colleague offers a simple explanation: "He's got two watches, so he wears two watches" (*This* 108).

Her quirky characters resemble people standing in front of a funhouse mirror: the image is slightly distorted for comic effect, yet it remains recognizably human. A man who becomes blinded in an accident isn't especially unusual; that the blindness was caused when the scalpel he was using to dissect a lioness slipped, squirting something toxic into his eyes, is. A shepherd who talks to his sheep isn't unusual; one who phones his favorite one (whom he has named George Gershwin) every day when he's away to see how he's doing is. A man who quotes poetry isn't unusual; one who regularly speaks in rhyming lines of twelve-syllable alexandrines is.

Vargas's interest in oddball characters can be traced to a trio of mystery novels she wrote beginning in 1995 with *The Three Evangelists* that feature a trio of unemployed historians who live together in a ramshackle house in Paris. Nicknamed "The Three Evangelists" because of their first names—Mathias, Marc, and Lucien—they solve unusual mysteries (e.g., why a beech tree has suddenly appeared overnight in a neighbor's yard) by applying skills from their various disciplines. Thanks to their eccentricities (e.g., Mathias hates to wear clothes and when he has to put on pants, he holds them up with string rather than a belt), when they make cameo appearances in the Adamsberg books, they fit it right in.

Crime writers ordinarily strive to avoid creating improbable actions and coincidences; Vargas embraces them and makes what wouldn't seem credible in other crime novels strike us as quite normal in her off-kilter world. Her aim is not to undermine realism but to re-imagine it: *"J'essaye de le rendre plus réel en le rendant moins réaliste"* ["I try to make it more real by making it less realistic"] is how she puts it (Aussenac). She says she doesn't start out with the intention of creating strange characters, but when they do appear, she simply goes along with it. Once she releases her scholarly mind from its fetters, she isn't afraid to follow whatever imaginative path it chooses to travel.

Vargas's novels may be playful but they are far from frivolous. In her view, mystery novels can be read as "latter-day fairy tales" in which the murderers are the dragons of medieval myths and the detectives the knights who must enter the dark forests after them: "They are the stories we tell ourselves to survive," she insists, "or to live better, or to explain the dangers in life. It's only by facing the threats that we discover how to go on" (France). Since in her opinion detective novels belong to "the great family of tales, legends, myths" (Rosovsky), she doesn't feel bound by the rigid rules of realistic literature. When she's writing she's willing to "let go" and "open the door to the unconscious" (Kerridge).

Vargas's fiction is more likely to produce smiles rather than belly laughs, but her impish sense of humor and playful approach to the mystery novel have earned her widespread critical and popular acclaim: she is one of France's best-selling authors; her work is translated into dozens of languages; and her novels have won the prestigious British CWA International Dagger Award an unprecedented four times since its inception in 2006.

Ken Bruen (1951–)

Humor doesn't always come from a happy place; sometimes a smile has to be coaxed out of dark and painful experiences. This is certainly true in the case of Irish crime writer Ken Bruen. In 1979, while teaching in Rio de Janiero, he and four other Europeans were arrested after a bar fight he wasn't even involved in and imprisoned and brutalized for four months. Surviving such a hellish experience taught him that, "Evil is only a concept to those who've never experienced it. To those who've met it, the term 'concept' dropped from their vocabulary" (*Devil* 27). The dark crime fiction he writes is, not surprisingly, imbued with the presence of evil (Satan himself even makes an appearance in one novel), but being Irish, he can't avoid finding humor in the most unlikely places. His sardonic sense of humor offers no escape from the darkness, though it effectively illustrates the redemptive power of a "laugh-so-you-don't-cry" approach to life.

Bruen's first series began in 1998 with *A White Arrest,* one of seven novels about Detective Sergeant John Brant of the London Metropolitan police force, an Archie Bunker type who goes out of his way to spout racist, sexist, homophobic, and other politically incorrect insults. Only his irreverent and raunchy sense of humor keeps him from becoming a totally obnoxious character. He's the kind of jokester who wears a sweatshirt with the logo "EAT SHIT" on it, gives a woman he's just slept with a t-shirt that reads, "I AM A NATURAL BLOND. PLEASE TALK SLOWLY," and thinks it's funny to goose a nurse while visiting a friend in the hospital just to provoke a reaction. Even his compliments have an insulting edge to them: he tells a black colleague, "You're the first nigger I ever liked" (*White* 152), and praises another, who is gay, for being such a good cop "for a pooftah" (*Blitz* 87).

Even the few friends he has are wary of him: a fellow cop cautions that if you had dealings with Brant, "you needed a great sense of humour or a sawn-off" (*Ammunition* 2); a female colleague concedes, "Brant was the most unpredictable person she'd ever met, and yet, you were knee-deep in shite, he was the guy who would find you a shovel. You'd probably have to do the digging, but he'd keep you company" (*Ammunition* 187); even his best friend on the force has mixed feelings about him: "There were times Roberts truly hated Brant, wanted to put a fist hard in his mouth and beat on him for an hour" (*Calibre* 41).

These are not police procedurals in the usual sense of the word. As crime novelist Joseph Wambaugh, himself a former L.A. cop, has observed, crime novels about cops aren't really about how cops work cases, but how cases work cops. The methods Brant and his fellow London cops employ are often illegal and morally reprehensible. It's as if Bruen is writing not about police procedure in solving crimes but about how those procedures are corrupted by having to deal with criminals. His novels, however, offer no moralistic hand-wringing over such lapses on the part of his cops. It's all just background for his comically anarchic tales of cops at work.

Brant's outrageous sense of humor comes with plenty of attitude. Eyeing a man's stylish apartment, he remarks, "The Japs have a word for this ... this type of bare look, don't they?" The apartment's owner, flattered by

Brant's comment, says, "Yes, minimalist." To which Brant quips, "Shite was the word I'd in mind" (*Blitz* 80). His humor also reflects his cynical attitude toward the bad guys. After yanking a suspect onto the knife he's holding in his hand, forcing it into the man's chest, he jokes, "Whoops, watch yer step" (*McDead* 320). To a guy he's just knocked to the floor, he says, "You gotta be hurting, am I right?... No, no, don't answer 'cos I still have to break your nose ... shshhhhhh, be done before you can shout 'police intimidation'" (*Vixen* 32). While he's celebrating in a pub after shooting a guy in the head, the barman, eyeing his empty glass, asks, "Another shot?" Brant laughs and announces proudly, "Nope, just needed the one" (*Vixen* 195).

He sometimes uses humor to cushion his offensive remarks. Sitting beside a woman wearing a see-through blouse gets him wondering whether he's supposed to look or avert his eyes. So he simply says, "Lady, you are stacked. Is that the wonders of Wonderbra or just you?" (*Calibre* 42). To a woman with strep throat, he helpfully offers a cure: "What's it called?" she asks. "C-men." "C-what?" "C-men. It's got to be delivered orally. I'm off at four, I could come round, let you have it" (*White* 35).

Brant isn't the only jokester in the series: a witness to a crime describes the suspects he saw: "They were in their teens with baseball caps and them hooded tops, like half a million other young thugs. But they used offensive language. Might that be a clue?" (*White* 26); a medical examiner, asked for his opinion at the scene where a body is discovered dangling from a lamppost, declares, "Drowning, I'd say" (*White* 20); at the site of a second hanging body, he pronounces, "This was not a boating accident" (*White* 52); even a woman about to swallow a fatal overdose of pills manages to squeeze a final laugh out of her situation: "Considered very briefly as she popped more pills what the verdict would be. How many times had she heard 'death by misadventure'? Well, she was a Mrs. ... could they put Mrs. Adventure" (*McDead* 318).

Bruen says the Brant books were pure fun to write. The same can't be said about his second series set in Galway, Ireland, that began with *The Guards* in 2001. The books feature fifty-something Jack Taylor, who describes himself as a "broken-down Irish PI, with a limp and a hearing aid" (*Headstone* 6). He might have added that he is also an alcoholic—he was kicked out of the Garda (the Irish police force) for being, as the saying goes, overfond of the jar—with drug and anger-management issues. He's also a man with an overactive conscience who struggles to do the right thing, then lacerates himself when he fails, which is often. Unlike Brant, who "knew his strengths and ignored his failings" (*Calibre* 81), the deeply introspective Taylor is haunted by guilt and recrimination over his actions. "When God was bestowing 'Lighten Up' on babies," he confesses, "he skipped me" (*Magdalen* 154). Brant was kept at a safe distance from the reader by Bruen's use of third-person narration; thanks to the intimacy of Taylor's first-person narration, his tormented soul is put on full display.

Irish poet William Butler Yeats is reputed to have once said, "Being Irish, he had an abiding sense of tragedy, which sustained him through temporary periods of joy." This mixture of sorrow and smiles certainly applies to Taylor, a modern-day Job who endures a multitude of trials and tribulations. Readers familiar with Al Capp's popular *Li'l Abner* cartoon strip might be reminded of Joe Btfsplk, the jinxed character who walks around with a dark cloud circling above his head as misfortune follows him wherever he goes. Private eyes have an unfortunate habit of getting beaten up from time to time. Taylor endures more than his fair share of physical assaults, but few of his fellow detectives have ever had to endure the kind of emotional and psychological beatings he routinely experiences, including the loss of many of those closest to him, whose deaths he often feels responsible for.

Make no mistake about it: these are not primarily comic novels. They are extremely violent and address deadly serious subjects beginning with Jack Taylor's alcoholism, which he terms Ireland's "own weapon of mass destruction" (*Priest* 47). Having lost his own brother to the disease, Bruen refuses to glamorize drinking. Other painful issues include the harrowing revelations about the notorious Magdalen Laundries (institutions for unwed mothers and disobedient daughters run by the Catholic Church) and the disturbing scandals involving the sexual abuse of young children (and its subsequent cover up) by Catholic priests. Much of Bruen's anger is directed at the consequences of the Celtic Tiger, the decade-long economic boom that transformed the economy of Ireland but brought with it a whole new attitude of what he calls "mercenary yahooism" (*Killing* 186).

Subjects like these might be too unremittingly grim and difficult to read about were it not for Bruen's redemptive sense of humor. For example, the painful recession and economic suffering that followed in the wake of the collapse of the Celtic Tiger at least gave birth to a caustic joke: "St. Patrick's Day was looming and the government, in the midst of the worst crisis we had faced in twenty years, awarded themselves a twelve-day holiday. St. Patrick had obviously seriously screwed up the ridding-of-snakes gig" (*Devil* 229).

Bruen employed humor in the Brant series to make the outrageous cop at least semi-likable. In the case of Taylor, humor is used more to ease suffering, both his and the reader who experiences it vicariously. Taylor's sardonic attitude is his primary defense against the darkness. Though haunted by guilt, remorse, despair, bad luck, alcoholism, etc., he still manages to cling to a sense of humor. He has a quick mind always ready with a wisecrack. A friend, shocked to see he's armed when he greets her at the door, asks, "Who were you expecting?" "Jehovah's Witnesses or Mormons," he replies, "I'm never sure which is which" (*Priest* 250). When Taylor asks a priest whether he's ever encountered a truly evil person, the priest responds that no one is beyond redemption. To which he counters, "You're not getting out much, I'd say" (*Priest* 255).

His descriptions also testify to his edgy comic sensibility: "He had that half-insane expression of a patient newly released from a mental hospital or a recent convert to vegan. Which is much of the same thing" (*Purgatory* 269). He can turn a man wearing a cravat into a joke with a political zinger at the end: "Nobody—and I mean nobody—other than Roger Moore and the stray mason wears them. Even Edward Heath had managed to forgo them. John Major had wanted to wear them but lacked the balls" (*Priest* 116). Even his similes have a sharp Irish edge to them: he describes poteen (Irish moonshine) as having a kick "like a nun whose polished floor has been walked on" (*Devil* 90).

He's also a master of self-mockery. "The Irish are superlative mockers," Terry Eagleton observed in his book, *The Truth About the Irish,* "not least of themselves.... A lot of Irish speech is aimed at deflating rather than affirming. Few nations have such a keen sense of the ridiculous, not least when it comes to themselves" (53). Waking up one morning with a vicious hangover, Taylor says, "I came to with paranoia screaming at me. My neck was cramped, I'd been sick on my leather coat and my nose howled. Muttered, 'Could be worse'" (*Killing* 89). After another rough night, he throws up, then lacerates his finger trying to open a can of beer. "Thank, you, God" (*Killing* 232), he quips. He's so experienced in dealing with the morning after that he's able to boast, "If they ever have an Olympic event for hangovers, I'm gold" (*Sanctuary* 107). He employs the same gallows humor when it comes to other misfortunes: in the hospital where he's being treated after an assailant sliced off two of his fingers, he somehow manages to joke, quoting from *The Rubaiyat of Omar Khayyam,* "The moving finger, having writ, moves on" (*Headstone* 117).

He also finds plenty of other subjects to mock, beginning with his mother, a stern, cold, self-absorbed woman who's so skilled at sighing dramatically over his failings, he jokes, "They ever put together an Olympic sport for that, she's a shoo-in" (*Killing* 73). He's also adept at combining self-mockery with a jab at popular entertainers he doesn't like: "I was going to say that I put on my best suit but I only have one. Bought in Oxfam two years ago. It's dark blue with narrow lapels. Makes me look like a wide boy. Remember the Phil Collins video where there's three of him. That's the suit. I can only pray it doesn't make me look like Phil Collins" (*Guards* 53); another time, after looking at himself in the mirror, he asks, "How frigging old was I getting? Not old enough to ever like George Michael" (*Killing* 69).

Like John Brant, Jack Taylor isn't an easy man to like. He too can be boorish, abrasive, impulsive, and brutally violent. He's no saint, which is what Bruen intended: "I've no interest in people with no baggage," he declares. "God bless 'em and long may they be so lucky." He adds that he has no interest in what makes saints, but he'd like to know "what makes saints human" (Ruttan). Bruen does an excellent job of humanizing Taylor, balancing the bad with the good by revealing Taylor's charming, generous, thoughtful, and self-reflective side. As Bernice Harrison observed about this complicated Irishman with an acerbic sense of humor, "You don't want to meet Jack Taylor in person, ever, but if you're a big crime fan, you want to read every book he features in."

Alexander McCall Smith (1948–)

Alexander McCall Smith's No. 1 Ladies' Detective Agency novels about Precious Ramotswe, owner and operator of Botswana's first private-eye business, had a modest beginning. Though McCall Smith was born in Southern Rhodesia (now Zimbabwe) and lived for a while in neighboring Botswana (where he taught law at the University of Botswana and assisted in writing the country's criminal code), he has spent most of his adult life in Scotland, where until recently he was a professor of medical law and ethics at the University of Edinburgh. Though he had previously published many books, it wasn't until he was approaching fifty that he decided to write a mystery novel, *The Ladies' No. 1 Detective Agency* (1998), set in Africa. The first few books in the series were published by a small press (Polygon, the fiction imprint of Edinburgh University Press), but word of mouth gradually propelled these quiet and gentle novels about a modest and good woman in Africa into an international publishing phenomenon:

now translated into dozens of languages, the series boasts a global audience of devoted readers.

Despite their worldwide popularity, the series isn't for everyone. Readers who prefer tough, realistic mystery novels may not find the easygoing Mma Ramotswe books to their liking. (Mma is the honorific term used for women; for men it's Rra.) Nor will those who don't want anything getting in the way of a suspenseful mystery plot. But those looking for a temporary escape from the hard-boiled to the good-hearted and have the patience to allow the mystery elements to unfold at a pace as unhurried as the way life is lived in this part of Africa will find much to enjoy in these entertaining stories about good and decent people in a faraway land.

The Precious Ramotswe mysteries don't follow the classic form in which a murder is committed, there are several suspects, and the detective eliminates them one by one until the guilty party is exposed and order restored to society. Although Botswana faces serious problems—young children are still sometimes stolen and killed for *muti* or medicine and the country suffers from one of the highest rates of AIDS in the world—McCall Smith has chosen to paint an idyllic picture: "I am sometimes accused of not writing enough about grim social reality," he says. "I can see why people say that but, as it happens, I am not that sort of author. I would hope that my books might help to counteract bleakness" (Kellaway). He prefers to think of his mystery novels as fables, as "optimistic books about the world as we'd like it to be; we want to believe that there are people who are kind and decent—and are happy to see such a world exist" (Nayar).

Given that Botswana is a peaceful country with very little crime, the small mysteries Mma Ramotswe is hired to solve are far more mundane and far less dangerous than those a Sam Spade or Philip Marlowe might encounter. "I am not a lady who deals with criminal business," she declares. "That is the job of the Botswana police force." Instead, she says, "I just do the things which we ladies know how to do—I talk to people and find out what has happened. Then I try to solve the problems in people's lives. That is all I do" (*Miracle* 71). Her rare involvement in actual crime fighting sometimes has comic results: while sipping a cup of tea at her favorite cafe in *In The Company of Cheerful Ladies* (2004), she spots a jewelry theft in progress. When she dashes out to stop the thief, a waitress accuses her of running off without paying her bill, and demands money or she will summon the police.

McCall Smith says he wants to make people "smile while they read the books" (Weinman), and notes that the main source of his humor can be found "in the small events of everyday life" (Moore). His gentle, understated comedy has its source in the good people of Botswana who may be simple, but are never simple-minded and who are celebrated rather than ridiculed. While its main purpose is entertainment, the humor also helps to keep the novels from becoming too saccharine in their emphasis on goodness and human decency; at times it is also used for a gentle satiric chiding of certain types of human behavior.

Rather than employ the kind of cynical observations and snarky wisecracks that are associated with disillusioned private eyes and disgruntled cops, McCall Smith prefers a kinder, gentler humor that grows out of his characters' innocence, as in this example in which Mma Ramotswe muses about the value of asking questions:

> Time and again she had proved the proposition that if one wanted the answer to anything, then one should simply ask. It was simple, and she wondered whether the police were sufficiently aware of the attractions of such an approach. If they were investigating a crime they should simply stop and ask, "Who did this?" and they would surely be given the answer—perhaps even from the criminal himself, who might just stand up and say, "I did it, Rra" [*Miracle* 183].

When it comes to liars, she has an equally simple method: look into their eyes. It's easy to detect a liar, Mma Ramotswe insists, and she "could not understand why everybody could not tell when another person was lying. In her eyes, it was so obvious" (*Tears* 190).

Mma Ramotswe may not use wisecracks, but she does have a talent for the quick rejoinder. For example, when a man warns her to be careful where she parks her van so she won't hit a tree, she replies that she has never hit a tree in her life. "But I have known many men who have hit trees," she says. "It may not have been their fault," the man insists. "Yes," she quips, "It could have been the fault of the trees. That is always possible" (*Full* 127). When another man makes the mistake of saying that women like to talk a lot, she corrects him: "There is a lot of talking that goes on in this country, and most of it, in my opinion, is done by men. The women are usually too busy to talk" (*Morality* 52).

Mma Ramotswe is justifiably proud of many things—Africa, the old values, her ability to help others, and for being what she calls a woman of "traditional build." She considers it one of the very worst features of modern society "that people should be ashamed to be of traditional build, cultivating instead a look that was bony and positively uncomfortable. Everybody knows, she thought, that we have a skeleton underneath our skin; there's no reason to show it" (*Miracle* 10). But her defensiveness about her weight also has a comic ring to it:

She did not have to worry about dress size, unlike those poor neurotic people who were always looking in mirrors and thinking that they were too big. What was too big, anyway? Who was to tell another person what size they should be? It was a form of dictatorship, by the thin, and she was not having any of it. If these thin people became any more insistent, then the more generously sized people would just have to sit on them. Yes, that would teach them [*Morality* 215]!

Her generous girth also leads to some comic situations. In *In the Company of Cheerful Ladies,* her afternoon nap is interrupted by a strange noise every time she shifts her weight. It turns out that what she hears are moans coming from a man who is being crushed underneath her bed. He's so desperate to escape that he wriggles out of his pants which are snagged on a spring and runs out of the house half naked.

Mma Ramotswe's trusted sidekick is her secretary Grace P. Makutsi, a woman whose proudest achievement is the unprecedented score of 97 percent she earned on her final exam at the Botswana Secretarial College. A plain woman from a poor rural family, her skin is dark-hued and splotched, and her hair is unruly. Her most distinctive feature is the pair of large round eyeglasses she wears. But she's a hard worker and extremely proud of her small successes as she has steadily climbed the ladder from senior secretary to assistant detective and finally associate detective.

But her often cranky attitude, especially when it comes to the subject of glamorous, empty-headed girls like those classmates of hers who always seemed to get the jobs that hard-working girls like herself couldn't, is the source of some humorous moments. She frequently spars with Charlie, the older of the two feckless apprentices who work at Speedy Motors, over his attitude toward women. When Charlie tells her that it is not good for women to think too much, she shoots back, "It is not good for men if women think too much.... If women start thinking about how useless some men are, then it is bad for men in general." Then she adds, "You did not know what you were saying because your tongue is out of control. It is always walking away on its own and leaving your head behind. Perhaps there is some medicine for that. Maybe there is an operation that can fix it for you" (*Full* 76). When he describes a woman as "a very pretty woman. Big bottom too," she counters, "You think of nothing but bottoms.... You are like a little boy." Charlie fires back, "So there are lots of bottoms about. So that's my fault, is it?" (*Miracle* 166).

Ironically, it is Charlie's obsession with women that helps Mma Makutsi solve two cases. In one instance, his discerning eye identifies a female suspect for her by recognizing the woman's shapely bottom when he spots it at the supermarket. On another occasion she is given the task of determining which of the four finalists in the Miss Beauty and Integrity contest is a person of good character who won't do anything that might discredit the award. Who is better qualified than Charlie to help her identify the bad girls?

Mr. J. L. B. Matekoni, "the kindest man in Botswana" (*Tears* 171), is proprietor of Tlokweng Road Speedy Motors and, after a prolonged engagement, Mma Ramotswe's husband. Though not a comic character, his kind heart does cause him to become entangled in some sticky humorous situations. If this were a sitcom, he'd get laughs by playing the role of the befuddled husband at the mercy of the women in his life, though he's never made to look foolish. For example, he is incapable of saying no to Mma Potokwane, the pushy matron of the local orphanage. All she has to do is offer him a slice of her famous fruitcake and he's putty in her hands, willing to repair her vehicles or fix a balky pump. After agreeing to adopt two orphans without first consulting Mma Ramotswe and also to participate in a parachute jump to raise money for the orphanage, his fear of telling his future wife about the children and his dread at the thought of jumping out of an airplane cause him no end of worry, though his discomfort will likely bring smiles to the reader's face.

McCall Smith's wry humor occasionally has a gentle satiric edge to it. One target is politicians. For example, after encountering a young boy with a habit of telling lies, Mma Ramotswe notes wryly, "That boy will grow up to be a politician.... That will be the best job for him" (*Full* 28). She even has a deadpan way of linking politicians with people who suffer from constipation: "There were probably enough of them to form a political party—with a chance of government perhaps—but what would such a party do if it was in power? Nothing, she imagined. It would try to pass legislation, but would fail" (*No. 1* 195).

McCall Smith's genial satire is aimed at readers in the West who might be tempted to feel superior to these "primitive" folks in "backwards" Botswana. These simple folk have a way of putting things in perspective for their more sophisticated Western readers. For example, Mma Ramotswe feels sorry for people who have money but no time to enjoy the simple things in life: "What use was it having all that money if you could never sit still or just watch your cattle eating grass? None, in her view; none at all." Then she adds the pointed observation that there were some white people who did understand this, but "other white people often treated them with suspicion" (*No. 1* 162). She is also is horrified to read about people being described as consumers: "That was a horrible, horrible word, which sounded rather too like cucumber, a vegetable for which she had little time.

People were not just greedy consumers, grabbing everything that came their way, nor were they cucumbers for that matter; they were *Batswana*, they were *people!*" (*Company* 163).

While smiling at her naiveté, readers might also pause a moment to think about the serious message McCall Smith is sending in his gently humorous way.

Ben Rehder (1965–)

Ben Rehder's Blanco County mysteries are often compared with those of Carl Hiaasen, whom Rehder credits with being the main inspiration on his writing. Both feature humorous characters and absurd plot developments, and both employ comedy for satiric purposes. Hiaasen's satire, however, is broader, angrier, and more barbed than Rehder's. Hiaasen skewers evil, usually the result of man's insatiable greed, wherever he sees it. Rehder is amused rather than outraged by man's folly. The human behavior he pokes fun at mostly involves what game warden John Marlin, his central character, describes as "stupidity, ignorance, drunkenness, or folks just plain being weird" (*Gun* 20).

Rehder is more benevolent and forgiving towards his characters than Hiaasen is. For example, in *Holy Moly* (2008), Pastor Peter Booth, a "media-savvy clergyman with a trophy wife and more material possessions than a Saudi prince" (43), is a ripe subject for skewering. But once Rehder is finished poking fun at him, he lets him off the hook by having him pay a visit to a terminally ill child in a hospital that inspires him to give away all his ill-gotten millions anonymously to good causes.

Born in Austin, Rehder is a lifelong Texan with a tattoo of the state on his left ankle. But that doesn't prevent him from ridiculing the attitudes, customs, and behavior of his fellow Texans, many of whom fit one out-of-state visitor's putdown of them as "an astounding assortment of hicks, hayseeds, bumpkins, yokels, rednecks, and rubes," dressed "as if they were auditioning for *Hee Haw*" (*Holy* 137). One can get a sample of Rehder's sense of humor by looking at the biographical profile on his website, where he admits to wanting to become a writer ever since he was dropped on his head as a toddler. He goes on to say he was inspired to try his hand at writing his first mystery when his father-in-law tossed him a copy of a Carl Hiaasen novel: "And then it hit him. It literally hit him, right in the forehead" ("Ben").

Unlike Hiaasen, who introduces new characters and new Florida locations in each novel, Rehder writes about a small cast of recurring characters who live and work in Blanco County, located in the Texas Hill Country west of Austin. The central figure in the series, which fits comfortably into the category of the police procedural, is John Marlin, a game warden with the Texas Parks and Wildlife Department who has worked in Blanco County for twenty years. He followed in the footsteps of his father, who served in the same position for twenty-two years until he was killed by a poacher. Marlin's primary duty is enforcing hunting and fishing laws, which mostly involves checking licenses and making small talk with men he has known all his life. But because Texas game wardens are also certified as real police officers with the power to enforce any state law, he often joins up with his good friend county sheriff Bobby Garza in investigating local crimes. The crimes they must solve are serious, but their investigation is balanced by bright splashes of humor.

The series began with *Buck Fever* (2002), which was nominated for an Edgar Award as Best First Novel. It opens with a pair of late-night deer poachers looking to shoot a prize white-tailed buck. One of them fires at the buck but instead hits the doe he is mounting. When they hear the doe call out, "Help me," they run off in a panic. It turns out the shooting victim is a wildlife biologist who was wearing a deer costume to get close enough to study the whitetail's nocturnal behavior. But the real crime is revealed to be something far more serious than deer poaching; the attempted shooting of the buck leads to the exposure of a lucrative smuggling operation involving deer with their stomachs packed with drug-filled balloons being imported into Texas from Mexico. Things turn deadly when a Colombian drug lord and his gang arrive in Blanco County to find out what has happened to their drugs.

One of the primary sources of humor in the series is a pair of dimwitted rednecks, Red O'Brien and his 300-pound friend and trailer-mate Billy Don Craddock. "If being a redneck was against the law," one observer quips, "those guys would get a life sentence" (*Bone* 122). Red considers himself to be brighter than his dimwitted friend, but it's a close contest: "He [Billy Don] wasn't a big-picture kind of guy like Red was. You had to work up to important stuff one step at a time. Hell, half the battle was just getting the man's attention, getting him to focus for even just a few minutes. It was like he had that attention-defecate disorder or something" (*Bone* 187). Another example of Red's chronic malapropism comes in the assurance he gives Billy Don that if they get caught engaging in one of their criminal activities, "we could ask for a flea bargain" (*Gun* 276).

On the other hand, he has big dreams and an inflated sense of his own worth:

> Granted, he was already what most people would consider an American success story. He owned his own Palm Harbor mobile home, complete with satellite TV. His 1977 Ford Truck was nearly paid for. And just last month, he'd bought his own washer and dryer on revolving credit. The rate was only eighteen percent, and they don't offer those kinds of terms to lowlifes [*Flat* 173].

Red also considers himself something of a ladies man. He's especially proud of his expertise when it comes to satisfying a woman in the sack: "He figured he'd done a pretty good job. They'd had the radio on, and Red had made it through a George Strait song and most of a Faith Hill" (*Guilt* 208). Later on, he does even better, pleased that he makes it through "a Merle Haggard, a Pam Tillis, and most of a Kevin Fowler song" (*Guilt* 265).

Rehder gets great satiric mileage by using Red as a spokesperson for redneck opinions. Whether it's Canadian singer Shania Twain—"Red shuddered to think about the future of our great country when something as sacred as country music was being taken over by foreigners" (*Buck* 15)— or gays—"Red honestly didn't have a problem with homos, as long as they had the common courtesy to keep it to themselves.... But Armando was just so open about it. Like he expected people to just accept it and treat him like a normal person" (*Hog* 76)—he, fortunately for the reader, can't keep his opinions to himself. He's even eager to weigh in on the thorny issue of gun control:

> See, they had what they called the "desirable" people, which was the Nazis themselves, and the "undesirable" people, which was the Jews, the Gypsies, the Po-locks, and such. They wouldn't let the undesirables have guns. Now, say what you want about the Jews, but I'd say that ain't right, taking their weapons like that. Besides, where's the threat, because I imagine your average Jew is about as handy with a handgun as he is with a hockey stick. Anyway, point is, if you're gonna make it okay to have guns, then you can't just say one particular group should be excluded. 'Cept maybe the towelheads. Ever'body hates them nowadays [*Gun* 28].

Good-natured ribbing between friends is a reliable source of humor in many series, but what passes for witty banter between Red and Billy Don never reaches the level of that, say, between Archie Goodwin and Nero Wolfe or Spenser and Hawk, to name but two classic combos. Red and Billy Don sound like not-too-smart kids:

> "He's just funnin' with you," Billy Don said. "You been skipping your AA meetings, Red?"
> "That's hilarious, Billy Don, but I'm afraid your medication ain't doing its job."
> "Speaking of medication," Billy Don said, "how's that Viagra working out?"
> "Whyn't you call your mama and ask her?"
> "I think I'd have to call your mama too for a full report" [*Guilt* 117].

Rehder fashions clever plots that allow him to interject fresh new odd-ball characters into the action in each novel. In *Holy Moly* (2008), for example, a man who discovered a dinosaur fossil on land owned by a famous televangelist who is building a massive religious complex on it is murdered. Was he killed by someone in the evangelist's circle who wanted to silence him because such a discovery might prove embarrassing to a person preaching strict interpretation of the Bible? Or did someone simply want the bone, potentially worth millions, for his own profit? One interested party, the aptly named Darwin Parker, is a rich man with an obsession with dinosaurs: he has his own private museum filled with several fossils as well as a collection of every dinosaur film ever made. His fascination with prehistoric creatures even extends to his lovemaking: ever since a Halloween party where, dressed as Barney the Dinosaur, he got laid by a sorority girl dressed as Dino from *The Flintstones,* he's only interested in partners who agree to roar like a mating tyrannosaur while engaged in sex with him.

"Two Chinese dwarves were having sex in front of Marty Hoffenhauser, and he definitely didn't like what he was seeing" (48) is the attention-grabbing introduction to a producer of porn films who has come to Blanco County in *Flat Crazy* (2005) looking for the largest deer antlers he can find. Hoffenhauser's films feature a trio of Chinese dwarves named Wanda Ho, Willie Wang, and Mike Hung, his star performer who has come down with a bad case of performance anxiety. Marty hopes the crushed-up deer antlers will provide the aphrodisiac boost Hung needs to allow him to resume his performance in his latest film, *Fortune Nookie.*

Rehder also uses plenty of comic similes—"You're nuttier than a squirrel's morning crap" (*Buck* 125); "Mitch was sweating like a whore in church" (*Gun* 225); "He'll stand out like a turd in a fruit salad" (*Gun* 226)—and humorous descriptions—"Betty Jean Farley wouldn't win any beauty pageants, though she might earn a blue ribbon at a livestock show (*Holy* 138); "The truth was, Bonita was nearly the perfect woman—except for the penis" (*Gun* 179). And of course there are jokes with a distinctive Texas flavor: e.g., "You know why it's so hard to solve a murder in a small Texas town?" "Why?" "All the DNA is the same.... And there're no dental records" (*Flat* 121).

Rehder juggles multiple subplots, deftly switching from one to another to keep the action moving at a fast pace. He doesn't allow his comic characters and farcical situations to overwhelm the mystery plots. Eliminate the comedy and Rehder's novels would still be effective police procedurals. Adding the humor, however, results in a riotous mixture of mystery and mirth.

Christopher Fowler (1953–)

British author Christopher Fowler achieved success in a variety of fields by the time he reached fifty. He started out as an advertising copywriter (including a stint at J. Walter Thompson), then co-founded a film marketing company called The Creative Partnership that promoted such films as *Reservoir Dogs, Trainspotting,* and *Goldeneye* (and where he reportedly came up with the famous line used to promote *Alien*: "In space no one can hear you scream"). He also had a second career as a popular writer, turning out comedies and drama for the BBC, several collections of short stories, and novels in a number of genres—science fiction, fantasy, horror.

Then in 2003, his writing took a new direction. A firm believer that "there is nothing more satisfying than showing that something is impossible, then proving how it can be done," he decided to write a mystery novel in the John Dickson Carr tradition of the impossible crime (Rosh). He resurrected a pair of London detectives named Arthur Bryant and John May whom he had used as minor characters in some of his previous fiction and made them the main characters in *Full Dark House* (2004). Set mostly during the London Blitz in 1942, the novel describes how the two of them began working together in what is known as The Peculiar Crimes Unit (PCU). The novel was planned as a stand-alone, but the characters interested Fowler so much that he has since written a dozen more, and the Bryant and May books have become the most inventive and entertaining series in recent British crime fiction.

The PCU was charged with solving crimes of a politically sensitive nature or those of high risk to public morale, ones that might cause social panic or general public malaise. It would be misleading to describe the novels as classic police procedurals as the PCU's investigative methods are anything but approved textbook procedure. As in Fred Vargas's police novels, strange crimes demand unorthodox methods. While John May and the rest of the PCU busy themselves reviewing surveillance tapes, gathering forensic evidence, and interviewing witnesses, Arthur Bryant pores over obscure books and consults with an oddball assortment of psychics, fortune tellers, necromancers, shamans, and spiritualists. His primary "occult consultant" is Maggie Armitage, a white witch with a fiery red perm who wears chiming incense balls and a necklace of little plastic babies around her neck and sports miniature bunches of bananas dangling from her ears. She is a delightfully loopy character whose presence enlivens the novels each time she appears.

Although the Bryant and May partnership began in 1942 when they were young men, Fowler came up with the brilliant idea of jumping forward some sixty years to the present, where the detective duo is still solving crimes, but now they are in their eighties. Unlike the creators of the BBC Shakespeare films, who magically brought a young Holmes and Watson to contemporary London, Fowler, who readily confesses, "it's impossible for me to keep a sense of fun out of what I write" (Mathew), exploits the comic effects of placing a pair of octogenarian detectives in a city that is nothing like the one they began working in six decades earlier.

Bryant and May are a classic Odd Couple, both personally and professionally. Bryant has an unusual mind and employs unorthodox methods: "Bryant had no interest in the common grounds of detection. He refused to be swayed by plausibility or likelihood. Human beings, he knew, were capable of acting in extraordinary ways for reasons that extended into the realms of the bizarre, and the best way to uncover their confidences was to match the strangeness of their thinking" (*Memory* 86). As the narrator warns the reader in *Bryant & May and the Bleeding Heart* (2014), "If you're looking for the steely grip of deductive logic, you may wish to find some other narrative that doesn't involve Mr. Arthur Bryant" (20). The much more logical May, by contrast, is "the healing voice of reason, a counterbalance to the maddening pandemonium of Bryant's mind" (*Victoria* 34). To Bryant, he's more than just a friend, he's "the other half of my brain" (*Invisible* 27).

On the personal level, Bryant is a careless dresser (May says he looks like somebody who hasn't looked in a mirror since the year of the Coronation), a loner with few social graces who is watched over by a loyal landlady/housekeeper, who calls him "a stubborn old mumpsimus"(*On* 26), and drives a beat-up Mini Minor. May, three years younger, is always impeccably dressed, is charming and diplomatic with those he meets, is still something of a ladies' man, and drives a silver BMW. After sixty years together, it's not surprising that the two of them can occasionally get on one another's nerves. For example, when at one point Bryant asks his partner, "You see what I'm getting at?" May fires back, "No. Your every utterance is a mystery to me" (*On* 248). Then there's this exchange:

> "I wanted to make a particular point, and I find that sometimes, if I just talk to you, you sort of tune out."
> "That's because you have a habit of lecturing me," said May.
> "I most certainly do not. I try to direct your attention toward topics of interest."
> "Yes, and you used to tap me with a pointing stick until I broke the damned thing in half."
> "That was you, was it?" [*Victoria* 106]

Although the two of them are theoretically equal partners, it is Bryant who is the primary source of humor, thanks to his many eccentricities, odd habits, codger ways, and devilish sense of humor. Let's begin with this description of him:

> Arthur Bryant; Have you met him before? If not, imagine a tortoise minus its shell, thrust upright and stuffed into a dreadful suit. Give it glasses, false teeth and a hearing aid, and a wispy band of white hair arranged in a straggling tonsure. Fill its pockets with rubbish: old pennies and scribbled notes, boiled sweets and leaky pens, a glass model of a Ford Prefect filled with Isle of Wight sand, yards of string, a stuffed mouse, some dried peas. And fill its head with a mad scramble of ideas: the height of the steeple at St. Clement Danes, the tide table of the Thames, the dimensions of Waterloo Station, and the MOs of murderers. On top of all this, add the enquiring wonder of a ten-year-old boy [*Off* 19].

His unusual habits (he keeps a marijuana plant under his office desk), love of practical jokes (he once replaced his boss's foot cream with super-glue, causing him to spend hours trying to get his shoes off), cluttered collection of odd objects (a Tibetan skull that still reeks, a moulting championship perch in a glass case, a miniature model of the port of Gdansk made entirely out of painted bread), and the bizarre books he owns (*Phrenology for Beginners*; *Mortar and Mortality: Who Died in Your House*; *A User's Guide to Norwegian Sewing Machines*; *The Complete Compendium of Lice*; *How to Cook Bats*; *Re-Creating Renaissance Masterpieces with Cheese*) all contribute to the humorous portrait Fowler paints.

Bryant may be a bit doddering, but he's no fool. He has a quick wit, especially about his advanced age, e.g., examining his image in a mirror causes him to complain, "If I get any wrinklier, I'll be mistaken for a shar-pei" (*On* 21). When told he can't park in a restricted zone, he shoots back, "What are you talking about? I'm elderly, I can do whatever I want" (*Memory* 117). When his doctor warns him he needs to start acting his age, he counters with, "If I did that, I'd be dead" (*Invisible* 16). Advised that his smoking will kill him, he quips, "Doesn't matter. I'm ninety-five percent dead anyway" (*Memory* 315).

Along the same lines, here's a funny conversation Bryant has with a young boy who asks:

> "Are you more than a hundred years old?" he demanded, as if interviewing an Egyptian mummy.
> "I feel like it most days," Bryant admitted. He did not like children because he had always been an adult.
> "Then how do you stay alive?"
> "I eat small boys."
> "Yeah, right."
> "You don't believe me."

The boy looked disgusted. "Duh. Get real."
Bryant removed his false teeth and nipped the child hard on the arm with them.
The boy screamed and burst into tears [*On* 204].

Bryant is also a rich source of humorous observations, comments, and descriptions. Asked by a young boy if he knows a lot of weird stuff about London, he cracks, "Do I—? Is Kim Jong Un having a bad hair day?" (*Burning* 289). After seeing all the fat people with red faces at the beach, he jokes, "The seaside is full of people who look like they've been carved out of Spam" (*Memory* 155). He also has a jaundiced eye when it comes to people he doesn't like: he describes one man as looking "like Christopher Lee with irritable bowel syndrome" (*Invisible* 51) and refers to a female newspaper editor as "That awful Botox-faced woman who could put a frost on a cappuccino from twenty paces" (*Off* 91). Though he's often insulting, he knows how to soften a barb by adding a bit of humor, as when he says to his ineffectual boss, "I know I can always count on you for an unbiased opinion because you're not really involved in anything important that goes on here" (*Burning* 150).

Sometimes, however, the joke's on him. The elderly are often portrayed as being hopelessly incompetent when it comes to modern electronic or digital instruments. Unlike the BBC's Sherlock Holmes, who is completely at ease in the digital age (he has a web site, uses Skype to observe the details of a crime scene from afar, and views a YouTube video to learn how to fold napkins), Bryant is a Luddite who doesn't have a clue what "the bookface thing and that tweety thing" (*Burning* 253) are all about. He manages to infect virtually every electronic device he touches: he causes part of the air control system at Heathrow to crash and somehow manages to disrupt the police transmitter frequency so that it can only receive selections from Gilbert and Sullivan's *The Pirates of Penzance*. When he tries to take credit for fixing May's toaster, his friend reminds him that, "It's not supposed to fire bread that far. And it took out the lights" (*Off* 17).

The narrative voice Fowler adopts for the novels accentuates their comic tone. It's especially effective when it comes to similes: "Helena Parole had a handshake like a pair of mole grips and a smile so false she could have stood for Parliament" (*Full* 67); a sour-faced man with an annoying sniff and a hiking stick "looked like he harboured thoughts of attacking kittens with a hammer" (*Off* 86); loud music bellowing from a speaker "sounded like a busload of pensioners going into a ravine" (*Burning* 201); a PCU colleague drives "like Ayrton Senna needing to find a bathroom" (*Invisible* 336).

Mystery fans will enjoy Fowler's knack for coming up with strange and unusual crimes that challenge the PCU (and grab the reader's attention): a sleeping baby is thrown to his death out of a locked room and the only suspect is a Mr. Punch puppet lying on the floor (*The Memory of Blood*); a woman is found dead in front of a nineteenth-century London pub that vanishes the next day, replaced by a supermarket (*The Victoria Vanishes*); a man who had committed suicide is seen rising from his grave and stumbling forward before dying again, and then one of the young witnesses to the scene is killed the following day in a suspicious car crash (*Bryant & May and the Bleeding Heart*).

Lovers of London will appreciate the detailed portrait Fowler paints of the city. Though he has been called "the post-modern bard of contemporary London" (Zafon), he is equally adept at bringing the city's past to life. Over the course of the series, he explores such subjects as life during the Blitz, the city's hidden underground rivers, and the history of many of its classic pubs, theaters, and churches. Readers are served up a steady diet of fascinating details about the city and its places that few today know anything about.

But above all else, it is the towering presence of Arthur Bryant that will keep readers of the series charmed and entertained. In the words of John May, "Arthur Bryant was the most annoying man he had ever met, but at least he was fun to be around" (*Full* 299).

Craig Johnson (1961–)

Thanks to a helpful assist from the successful TV series *Longmire*, Craig Johnson's novels about Sheriff Walt Longmire of fictional Absaroka County, Wyoming, have become one of the most popular contemporary American crime series. The reasons for this are many: believable characters and compelling stories; a clever melding of a contemporary police story with elements of the classic western tale; and a remote setting known for its stunning natural beauty and harsh demands. But one cannot overlook the role humor plays in the success of his series.

Some writers use humor sparingly, others are unable to pass up an opportunity to joke or make a wisecrack. Few, however, manage to employ it as seamlessly and as naturally as Craig Johnson. Walt Longmire, his first-person narrator, is an easy-going fellow with a gentle sense of humor which arises naturally out of his personality. The same is true of the characters around him, many of whom also contribute to the humor in the series.

Johnson follows the example set by other popular crime writers who employed first-person narration like Raymond Chandler, Robert B. Parker, and Sue Grafton in striving to ensure his narrator is someone the reader would enjoy spending time with. One sure-fire way of doing this is giving your protagonist a healthy sense of humor. Humor is important to Johnson personally: "I think it's my own defense mechanism against the abyss of a chaotic and anarchistic universe" (Montgomery). It is also, he insists, "one of the finest weapons we have in tough situations, and one of the things that keeps us human.... Being funny can save your life" ("Penguin..., *Hell*" 4). It's not surprising then that it is also an important tool to him as a writer: "I think it's my job, to engage the reader with every tool I have. So, I think that I can do both—leave 'em laughing and crying" (Padilla). Without humor, he confesses, "the writing can get pretty pedantic, and then I'd find myself insufferable" ("Penguin..., *Death*" 6).

Walt made his debut in 2005 in *The Cold Dish*. After playing college football at Southern Cal, he spent several years as a Marine policeman in Vietnam before returning to his hometown of Durant, Wyoming. He has been sheriff of Absaroka County for twenty-four years and a widower for four, following the death of his wife Martha, to whom he had been married for twenty-five years. His has one daughter, Cady, who lives in Philadelphia where she works at a prestigious law firm.

At first glance, Walt might strike the casual observer as a simple John Wayne type macho hero. At six and a half feet tall and weighing 250 pounds or so, he looks like the menacing offensive lineman he once was. But the tall cop in the cowboy hat proves to be more than the stereotypical strong silent hero. In addition to playing football in college, he also majored in English, which is reflected in his knowing references to writers like Shakespeare, Cervantes, Balzac, Faulkner, etc. He also displays more than a passing knowledge of philosophy, opera, art, and history, especially Roman history.

Although Johnson and his wife live in a ranch house he built himself in the tiny Wyoming town of Ucross (population 25), he too defies easy stereotyping: though his love of Wyoming can be traced back to his first visit there as a young man, he has an undergraduate degree from Marshall University in West Virginia (the state where he was born in 1961), a graduate degree in playwriting from Temple University in Philadelphia, and two years experience working as a security policeman at the Metropolitan Museum of Art in New York.

Like Raymond Chandler, he has a marked talent for colorful and entertaining similes: "I was starting to feel like a baby seal in a Louisville Slugger factory" (*Junkyard* 88); "he had grown loopy as a barn swallow in late elderberry season" (*Death* 158); a swig of water from an old canteen tastes "like a Civil War mud puddle" (*Dark* 236); men scattered "like Wyoming wild turkeys on the third Thursday of November" (*Another* 257); a woman wearing an apron and with her hair up "looked like an Amish centerfold" (*Cold* 40).

He is also a master of clever lines—"She looked at me as if I'd just fallen off the official sheriff's-only turnip truck" (*As* 238)—and self-deprecating humor—"I put on my serious face which, I'm told by some, makes me look like I am mildly constipated" (*Death* 130).

Unlike some first-person narrators, Walt doesn't hoard all the funny lines for himself. Johnson surrounds him with a gallery of colorful characters each with his or her own distinctive style of humor. Walt's oldest friend is Henry Standing Bear, a Northern Cheyenne, whom he has known since grade school when they got into a fight at the water fountain. Henry gives Johnson an opportunity to showcase the Indian sense of humor: "I don't think there's ever been a group of individuals more maligned than the American Indian as having no sense of humor," he observes. "Now that's not the Natives I know. The Indians I know work on about seventeen different layers of irony, and if you're not aware of that irony, you get to be the butt of it" (Ambrose). Observing the body of a man hanging from a rope, Henry quips, "It appears he has received a suspended sentence." (*Another* 218). On another occasion he announces to Walt that there are two things he knows beyond any shadow of a doubt: one is that the future is uncertain; the other, he says, is the most important thing about a rain dance. What is it, asks Walt. "Timing," cracks Henry in characteristic deadpan fashion (*Serpent's* 121).

The verbal jousting between the two old friends is, like that between Spenser and Hawk, reflective of the deep mutual respect that allows them to make fun of racial stereotypes. For example, as they are checking out at a convenience store, Walt says to Henry, "Gina here says she has to keep an eye on you Indians because you steal." Henry nods, then says, "We do, but only small stuff, unlike you whites" (*Junkyard* 104).

Walt's deputy Victoria Moretti, whom he describes as "a beautiful, intelligent woman with a body like Salome and a mouth like a saltwater crocodile" (*Death* 151), is a spunky, foul-mouthed firebrand. A transplant from South Philadelphia whose father, uncles, and brothers are all cops, she brings a wised-up urban attitude to the wide open spaces of Wyoming.

With her no-nonsense perspective on the world, she often acts like a pro-
fane Greek chorus, commenting on situations and characters in a few choice
words, one of which is usually "fuck": upon entering a truck stop/cowboy
bar with sawdust on the floor, saddles instead of bar stools, and country
music playing, she stares in disbelief and quips, "Happy fuckin' trails" (*Junkyard* 219); examining the naked body of a dead ex-con whose tattoos
suggest that he might have been a founding member of the Aryan Brotherhood, she remarks, "Wow, the George Washington of Nazi fuckheads"
(*Junkyard* 261). She can also sum up the essence of a character with
raunchy wit: "That was one fucker from strange" (*Serpent's* 58) and "The
voices in that fucker's head are singing barbershop" (*Hell* 37).

Lucian Connelly, Walt's predecessor as sheriff, is a politically incorrect, crusty old one-legged curmudgeon with an ample supply of funny
lines: "He couldn't find his pecker in a pickle jar" (*Dark* 98) and "What's
that got to do with horseshit and hat sizes" (*Dark* 99)? Johnson also gets
comic mileage out of Walt's regular visits to the Busy Bee Cafe, where he
and owner Dorothy Caldwell engage in an ongoing verbal dance each time
he orders breakfast that recalls Abbott and Costello's comic masterpiece,
"Who's On First?" It begins like this: "Do you want the usual?" "I didn't
even know I had a usual." "Everybody's got a usual." "I'll have the usual"
(*Cold* 82). Later on: "The usual?" "Yes, please." "What's the usual?" "I haven't
decided yet" (*Junkyard* 81). Or, "This the usual?" "Usually" (*Another* 167).

Johnson also manages to have comic fun with his hero without either
demeaning him or diminishing the serious nature of what he ordinarily
does. For example, Walt often becomes trapped in harrowing situations,
but one of the scariest involves a classroom full of schoolchildren to whom
he's reading a book in *Kindness Goes Unpunished* (2007):

> "Where's your gun?"
> My thought exactly. "I didn't think I was going to need it." They all nodded, but I
> wasn't particularly sure they agreed.
> "How long have you been a sheriff?"
> "Twenty-three years." It just seemed like a million.
> "Do you know Buffalo Bill?"
> Maybe it was a million. "No, he was a little before my time."
> "My daddy says you're a butt hole" [1].

In *As the Crow Flies* (2012), Walt is invited to participate in a peyote
ceremony. At first he feels little effect of the hallucinogenic cactus, but
then he stumbles upon a talking bear. Several comic moments follow. For
example, Walt, unsure of his whereabouts, asks the bear if they are in
Powder River country. "How should I know," the bear growls. "I am a bear"
(125). When Walt tries to get the bear to clarify exactly what he meant

when he told him he shouldn't let go of the twine he has wrapped around his hand, the bear only shrugs, which leads the frustrated Walt to complain, "Well, what use is a talking bear if you're not going to carry on the conversation?" (127). He later encounters another talking animal, this one a foul-mouthed female crow whose profanely funny language sounds suspiciously like Vic Moretti's.

In explaining why it was important to make his first-person narrator an interesting character, Johnson asked, "Would you want to spend three hundred pages in the head of a dullard?("Penguin..., *Another*" 4). Thanks to Walt's lively mind and nimble sense of humor, he's anything but a dullard, as countless readers have discovered to their delight.

Lisa Lutz (1970–)

One effective way of achieving humor in a crime novel is to fiddle with a convention. For example, the private-eye hero was originally a lone-wolf male who often acted in the knightly tradition of rescuing damsels in distress. Over the years, significant modifications have been made to this profile of the hero. Thanks to Marcia Muller, Sue Grafton, and Sara Paretsky, the hero no longer has to be male. Modifications have also been made to the hero's lonely lifestyle. Roger Simon's 1970s private eye Moses Wine is divorced but has custody of his two young sons on Saturdays, which sometimes has him scrambling to find a babysitter so he can go about his detective work. And Robert B. Parker's Spenser is only one of many private eyes who have a wife or girlfriend. But no one, not even Janet Evanovich, has turned the private eye's domestic life into a richer source of humor than Lisa Lutz, beginning with the debut appearance of Isabel "Izzy" Spellman in *The Spellman Files* in 2007.

Oh, how the life of a San Francisco private eye has changed since the days when Sam Spade walked the fog-shrouded streets. Twenty-eight-year-old "Izzy" Spellman is no solitary private eye; she lives and works with an entire family of them. Her mother, father, sister, and for a while even her grandmother and an uncle are all employees of Spellman Investigations located in a four-level Victorian home in the lower Nob Hill district of San Francisco. To make matters worse (but more humorous), they also all live together there too. Family and work are so intertwined that all manner of comic situations complicate their lives, especially Izzy's.

The novels are narrated by Izzy, who is caught in the middle of everything. Her older brother David, a Stanford law school graduate and now a successful San Francisco attorney, is the only one to have escaped the business. Unfortunately for Izzy he was the model child to whom she was always being compared: "it seemed the only two sentences spoken in our household were *Well done, David* and *What were you thinking, Isabel?*" (*Spellman* 19). To the dismay of her parents, she has now become the role model for her fourteen-year-old sister Rae, who began training to be a private eye even before she knew how to read.

The Spellmans are far from a typical American family. They love one another but, as Izzy notes, "Love in my family has a bite to it and sometimes you get tired of icing all those tooth marks" (*Spellman* 275). They all also *really* take their work home with them. Every aspect of their domestic lives is affected by their profession. Deception, suspicion, and snooping are built into the Spellman DNA. Mothers often worry about the men their daughters date. Izzy's mother secretly conducts in-depth investigations of Izzy's dates aimed at turning up any incriminating details that might be harmful to her daughter. In a normal household, an item missing from the refrigerator might lead to questions, but as Izzy notes, "In my family, we don't ask questions; we investigate" (*Revenge* 33). (How many other American homes have an interrogation room in the basement?) Rooms are bugged. Car taillights are routinely smashed in order to make following that car much easier. The whole home environment may be suffocating to Izzy, but it is a rich source of humor for Lutz.

Rarely do we see private eyes in their formative years. Izzy's little sister Rae Spellman fills in that gap by showing how growing up in such a family can affect a child. She becomes so in love with surveillance that her parents have to lay down strict rules about how much time she can spend doing it the way others might have to restrict TV watching. For her eighth-grade "What I Did on My Summer Vacation" essay assignment, she submits a full surveillance report. Like many in her profession, this pint-sized adult goes to her favorite bar to drown her sorrows, though she only drinks ginger ale. Rae proves to be almost as smart as her brother. She secretly parlays $5000 in savings into $50,000 by investing in Apple and Google at the right time and despite her best efforts, she is still accepted at Yale. So she sends them a rejection letter, forsaking a healthy escape from the family, choosing instead to attend nearby Berkeley so she can live at home and continue to make life interesting for her family (and the reader).

Izzy's search for an appropriate boyfriend is a rich source of comic mishaps. At one point she prepares of list of parting remarks from ex-boyfriends that paints a hilarious picture of the way her professional life has undermined her romantic prospects: e.g., "You ran a credit check on my brother?" (*Spellman* 31) and "If I have to answer one more fucking question, I'm going to kill myself" (*Spellman* 32). Before dating one promising prospect, a dentist she meets during a surveillance, she dispatches a friend to pose as a patient and secretly tape the man's answers to a list of questions she has prepared. The relationship is inevitably doomed, however, because Izzy lies and tells him she's a school teacher like her parents. Despite wearing pencil skirts and sweater sets for several months, she is eventually exposed and the relationship ends.

Izzy is far from perfect and often makes mistakes in her investigations. But few private eyes can match her sassy, smart-alecky narration. One feature that immediately distinguishes her from most first-person narrators is that like Lawrence Block's Bernie Rhodenbarr she speaks directly to the reader, to whom she confides more than to anyone else. She also employs footnotes, which include everything from her commentary on what she has just written to a justification of her actions (e.g., Slipping out of her bedroom window one night prompts this footnoted defense: "There is absolutely *no* logical reason why this exit should be used exclusively in case of fire" [*Curse* 73]). Some notes offer helpful advice: after mentioning that a couple was married by a person who became a minister of the Universal Life Church, she helpfully provides the web address where one can get a free online ordination. On the other hand, she refuses to divulge the address of a favorite French bakery because it's already too crowded. And whenever she mentions a previous case, she always makes sure to remind the reader that that book is now available in a paperback edition.

The novels race along at breakneck speed thanks to short paragraphs with catchy titles (e.g., "The Case of the Disappearing Doorknobs" and "Two Car Chases and a Buddhist Temple") and plenty of snappy dialogue. Izzy's narratives also feature case reports (under such titles as "Suspicious Behavior Reports" and "Ex-Boyfriend #9"), e-mails, text messages, and transcripts of conversations she or some other member of her family has recorded. Since much of the novel's dialogue is reported in such transcripts, there is no "he said" or "she said" to interrupt the brisk flow of real talk. Some of the funniest conversations involve Izzy and her mother. Here's a sample of a typical phone conversation:

"Hello."
"Isabel, it's Mom."

"Who?"

"I'm not in the mood for this today."

"Not ringing a bell. When did we meet" [*Curse* 12]?

On another occasion, after her mother tries to offer her some parental advice, Izzy asks, "What business is this of yours?" "I'm your mother," her mother insists, to which Izzy retorts, "It's my life. You're just a member of the audience." But then her mother proves she can dish out the snarkiness just as well as her daughter: "Well," she says, "I want my money back!... Because this show sucks" (*Revenge* 71)!

Some mystery fans might complain that there are few real crimes to solve in the series, that no one gets murdered or kidnapped. This is in keeping with Lutz's intention to depict the real nature of a private eye's job. She says that her own experience working for a private detective agency taught her that the kinds of mysteries represented in most detective novels have "absolutely NOTHING to do with very real PI work. Cases aren't solved with all loose ends neatly tied up." She also notes that, "Surveillance is seriously dull work—you're usually sitting in a car for hours at a time. I have yet to read a novel about a PI that expresses that very real sentiment" (Rentilly).

Because there are few serious crimes in the books and the Spellman firm appears to have few paying clients, Izzy's family ends up mainly investigating one another. Lutz does, however, manage to come up with enough mysteries to satisfy her readers. For example, in *Curse of the Spellmans* (2008) Izzy becomes curious about her new next-door neighbor, based upon his suspicious behavior involving women and the presence of a locked room in his house that despite her best snooping efforts she can't get into. She also has mysteries to solve involving her mother (why does she secretly drive off in the middle of the night to vandalize a motorbike?), her brother (why has her childhood friend Petra, now her brother's wife, gone off to Arizona turning her brother into a depressed wreck?), and her father (why is he secretly going to a gym to work out?). Also, who is the culprit who is reenacting the exact way she and Petra vandalized Mrs. Chandler's holiday tableaux when they were kids? And then there's the Mucous Mystery Rae is trying to solve: why has her teacher filled his desk with used snot-filled tissues?

Lutz tries to keep things fresh by introducing new characters (Granny Spellman, "the Mussolini of grandmas," moves in for a while in *Trail of the Spellmans* (2012) to make everyone's life even more miserable) and allowing for changes as the characters age: Rae goes off to college and discovers there's more to life than surveillance; brother David and his wife have a baby; and Izzy takes over the family business. *The Last Word* (2013) appears to suggest that the series might be coming to an end, but a change in title for the paperback edition to *Spellman Six: The Next Generation* hints that perhaps only a switch in narrator from Izzy to sister Rae might be in the works.

Although she lists Jim Thompson, Patricia Highsmith, George Pelecanos, Dashiell Hammett, Richard Price, David Foster Wallace, and Vladimir Nabokov among her favorite authors, Lutz confesses that comedians were more influential in shaping her as a writer. "When I was child I was always drawn to comedy and comedians, and I continue to obsess over whatever impossible formula it is that ends with a laugh" ("5"). The ones she singles out as the most important to her—Mel Brooks, Don Rickles, Bob Newhart, The Smothers Brothers, and Sarah Silverman—provide a pretty good picture of the comic sensibilities she brings to the Spellman books.

Among the blurbs and reviews quoted on the dust jackets of Lutz's novels are several colorful attempts to describe Izzy: "The love child of Dirty Harry and Harriet the Spy" (*People*); "Part Bridget Jones, part Columbo" (*USA Today*); "Nancy Drew after a bottle of Jack Daniels" (Lutz's favorite). Izzy may not be the world's greatest detective, but there's one thing everyone can agree on: she never fails to deliver the laughs.

Timothy Hallinan (1949–)

Like many authors, Timothy Hallinan had several interesting jobs before becoming a writer. In the late 1960s he was a singer/songwriter whose group, The Pleasure Fair, released an album in 1967. (One member of the band later teamed up with David Gates, the album's producer, to form Bread, one of the most popular musical groups of the 1970s.) He later started a television consulting business that advised major corporations as well as public television stations. Then he became a writer of a pair of crime series: the first, which debuted in 1989, features an L. A. college-professor-turned-private eye named Simeon Grist; the second, launched in 2007, is a series of thrillers set in Bangkok, Thailand, with a travel writer named Poke Rafferty as protagonist.

But during the writing of a Rafferty novel Hallinan says he "kept hearing this voice in my ear, trying to tell me a story in the first person, and every time I listened, it entertained me" (Mead). Having also found in his previous novels that he sometimes had to work to keep the bad guys and gals from taking over, he decided to solve both problems by writing *Crashed* (2010), a humorous novel about an L. A. burglar named Junior Bender who would narrate his own story. "I laugh out loud all the time when I write Junior," he confesses. "It's such a liberating experience, writing first-person narrative by someone with a really, really skewed perspective" (Neubauer).

Junior Bender committed his first crime at age fourteen when he broke into his nasty next-door neighbor's house and switched all the spices and herbs into new bottles, put some plastic-wrapped dog poop in the refrigerator, and then superglued in place every thing he could. Now a divorced father of a teen-aged daughter named Rina, whom he deeply loves, he lives out of a suitcase in a variety of cheap hotels with names like the Snor-Mor, the Valentine Shmalentine, and Bitsy's Bird's Nest. He's brighter than your average crook, which is why he's never been caught by the police. He's so good at his job that he is often pressured to work for others in his profession who can't go to the cops for help. Reluctantly, he becomes the "go-to-guy for crooks with problems" (*Little* 10).

Junior may be a crook, but he's also a good man, a loving father, and with a few notable exceptions a law-abiding citizen. He never misses an alimony or child-support payment, donates to good causes like tutoring in inner-city schools, and even confesses he voted for Obama. The challenge Hallinan faces is how to make a thief sympathetic without turning him into what he calls a "Hallmark Burglar, a sort of criminal unicorn who steals from the bad and leaves sparkly hand-wrapped gifts for the kiddies" (DeSilva). The outlaw code of justice Junior and his criminal associates follow is not the knightly one that defined Marlowe; in *Crashed* (2012), for example, he decides to kill a person he believes deserves to die.

Aside from his criminal profession, Junior is in many ways a contemporary version of Chandler's private eye. Like Marlowe he is the narrator of his adventures, which is one of the primary sources of comedy in the books. He also has a healthy sense of humor about himself and the world around him, and his amusing narrative voice balances the seriousness of the cases he gets involved in. Like Marlowe he also lives and works in L. A., though the City of Angels has lost much of the glamour it had in Chandler's day. Hallinan includes frequent reminders of the fabled town down whose mean streets Marlowe walked three-quarters of a century earlier. Like a visitor to Rome, one can still stumble upon relics that call to mind the glory of the past.

Our introduction to Junior in *Crashed* is a comic one. He's hired to steal a Paul Klee painting from a mansion protected by a quartet of Rottweilers. Things go well until the dogs break into the house, forcing Junior to scramble to escape the clutches of the angry foursome. He ends up swinging from a crystal chandelier high above the ferocious dogs who gaze up at him like he was "a squirrel whose time was up" (*Crashed* 23). He manages to escape when the chandelier crashes to the ground and scatters the dogs, but then his troubles only get worse. He learns that he has been set up by a guy named Wattles, who now has a security tape clearly showing Junior stealing the painting. Wattles threatens to give it to the painting's owner unless Junior agrees to work for the daughter of a mob boss who wants him to ensure that a porno film she is making starring Thistle Downing, a young actress who was once the most beloved child star in America, gets made.

Private eyes are normally registered with the state and work for clients who hire them to do a job. Like Lawrence Block's crime-solving burglar Bernie Rhodenbarr, Junior gets his cases in unorthodox ways. For example, in *Little Elvises* (2013), a cop threatens to frame him for the armed robbery of a judge and the beating of his wife unless he agrees to look into a murder his uncle, a mobster from Philadelphia who once promoted a small army of teen-aged Elvis Presley impersonators, is suspected of committing.

Junior lives in a world of burglars, con men, loan sharks, fences, gangsters, and hit men (and women) whose colorful monikers like Rabbits Stennet, Stinky Tetweiler. Louie the Lost, Burt the Gut, Dippy Thurston, and Handkerchief Henderson might lead one to assume they are lovable rogues. They aren't. Though Junior ends up working for many of them, they can't always be trusted. And the threat of deadly consequences is omnipresent. A man in his precarious position needs eyes in the back of his head and a healthy sense of humor to get through the day.

Though Hallinan is a very humorous writer who confesses that writing about Junior is "almost illegally enjoyable" (*Fame* 323), he's not primarily a jokester. Unlike Lisa Lutz's series about the Spellman family of private eyes where the mysteries are secondary to the comedy, the Junior Bender novels are mysteries first, and the novels involve serious matters: in *The Fame Thief* (2013), for example, four murders are committed over the course of one night alone. The humor arises naturally from Junior's personality and attitude and Hallinan knows when to put it to good use, but never at inappropriate times.

Some of the humor comes from the action, as in the aforementioned chandelier episode or in a scene in which Junior struggles to fold up a life-sized, blow-up naked female doll into a box while decorously taking care to avoid touching any of her "sensitive" parts. But the primary source of humor is Junior's narrative voice. He's a master of comic description: "At first glance, Pinky Pinkerton was the size of a ventriloquist's dummy. He wore his clothes as though they'd been buttoned on him thirty years ago, when he was normal-size; he seemed to be sinking into them to the point where it was easy to envision his clothes sitting here empty in another five or ten years, long after Pinky slid out, probably down a pants leg" (*Fame* 88); a former Hollywood director who was a very good-looking young man is now "doing everything money, medical science, and a high pain threshold could accomplish to make him a very good-looking old man. His skin had the fraudulent flawlessness of a wall that's just had graffiti sandblasted off it" (*Fame* 75).

He's particularly effective in employing comic details to capture the look of an object or the sound of a character: a knit shirt is a shade of green "so vile that people would have thrown rocks at it even in Ireland" (*Herbie* 310); a yellow silk business suit "would have turned heads at a Braille convention" (*Crashed* 83); a black garment "looked like something that might be worn to a *Star Trek* funeral" (*Crashed* 102); a voice sounds like "Tom Waits probably has when he's just woken up and he's got the flu" (*Crashed* 30).

His robust verbal humor echoes Chandler, especially in his use of exaggeration—A woman "had piled her hair into a beehive high enough to conceal a highway safety cone" (*Little* 284); "Guy's got a nose he could vacuum a cruise ship with" (*King* 121); "We were in a sunken living room, long enough to have goalposts" (*Little* 124)—strikingly visual images— "He was draped in a loose, flowing white gown that looked like something Lawrence of Arabia might have worn to his prom" (*Herbie's* 48)—and freshly minted similes: a man sports a tiny soul patch that "clung uncertainly to his lower lip, like a misplaced comma" (*Little* 22).

Hallinan is a versatile writer and an eclectic reader whose favorite authors range from nineteenth-century notables like Jane Austen and Anthony Trollope (whose six Palliser novels he has read several times) to contemporaries like David Mitchell and Haruki Murakami. Like Junior Bender, he is especially fond of William Gaddis's 1955 900-page cult classic, *The Recognitions*. But it was Raymond Chandler's *The Big Sleep* that made him want to become a writer; furthermore, he says that Chandler's letters, "provide more good writing advice than any other single source I know of" (Godwin). He's also a big fan of Rex Stout, who like Chandler taught him the value of humorous first-person narration, and P. G. Wodehouse's Jeeves novels about whose narrator he says, "I wish I'd invented Bertie Wooster, the owner of the most sublime first-person voice I know of" (Thompson).

Junior's offbeat humor combined with an inventive twist on the classic private-eye tale has resulted in an entertaining and critically acclaimed series. (Hallinan won the 2015 Lefty Award for *Herbie's Game* as Best Humorous Mystery of the Year.) Few would argue with fellow mystery writer Julia Spencer-Fleming's comment prominently displayed on the dust jacket of the Junior Bender novels: "If Carl Hiaasen and Donald Westlake had a literary love child, he would be Timothy Hallinan."

Part II: Crime Films

Killers, Crooks, Kidnappers

Movies love bad guys. Some of the greatest films ever made feature lawbreakers of one kind or another. Sometimes they earn our sympathy, sometimes our disgust. Often, however, they make us laugh, as in the following films.

Arsenic and Old Lace (1944)

Arsenic and Old Lace (directed by Frank Capra, screenplay by Julius J. and Philip G. Epstein) is a crime comedy based on a popular Broadway hit of the same name written by Joseph Kesselring. The movie features two of the sweetest and two of the creepiest serial killers in film history. Add to the mix the dashing figure of Cary Grant and a deluded character who thinks he's Teddy Roosevelt and the result is a hilarious madcap farce built upon murder and madness.

Newlywed Mortimer Brewster (Cary Grant) and his bride stop by for a visit at the Brooklyn home where Mortimer's elderly aunts Abby (Josephine Hull) and Martha (Jean Adair), "two of the dearest, sweetest, kindest old ladies that ever walked the earth," live with his brother Teddy, who thinks he's Teddy Roosevelt (each time he climbs the stairs he shouts "Charge!" like Roosevelt going up San Juan Hill). Mortimer is shocked when he learns that the kindly old ladies have poisoned a dozen lonely old men with arsenic-laced elderberry wine, then had them buried in the basement by Teddy, who believed he was digging the Panama Canal and burying victims of yellow fever.

147

Things become truly scary when Mortimer's older brother Jonathan (Raymond Massey, made up to resemble Boris Karloff, who played the role on Broadway) and his assistant Dr. Einstein (Peter Lorre at his creepiest best) arrive with a dead body they intend to bury in the basement. Darkly comic misadventures follow, with bodies being switched and arguments arising between Jonathan and his aunts over who has killed more: currently they are tied at the number twelve. Meanwhile, Cary Grant is at his wit's end trying to get his brother safely off to a mental institution while keeping the local police out of the basement.

The laughs keep coming despite all the dead bodies thanks to the breakneck pace of the action and the comic performances of the entire cast. Grant's frenzied dashing about and over-the-top mugging (especially when he's gagged and tied to a chair) work as a comic contrast to the serene demeanor of his dotty aunts and the icy reserve of his brother Jonathan. Humor is also a regular feature of the clever dialogue, as in this conversation between Mortimer and Aunt Abby: "Aunt Abby, how can I believe you? There are twelve bodies in the cellar and you admit you poisoned them." "Yes, I did. But you don't think I'd stoop to telling a fib." The film's funniest line is spoken by Mortimer, who explains to his fiancée, "Insanity runs in my family.... It practically gallops."

Frank Capra, known for directing heart-warming stories with a strong social message, decided to make a movie that was pure comic entertainment. Ranked #30 on the American Film Institute's List of the 100 Funniest American Movies of All Time, *Arsenic and Old Lace* continues some seventy years after its release to entertain audiences with its blend of homicide and hilarity.

Too Many Crooks (1959)

The British comedy *Too Many Crooks* (directed by Mario Zampi, screenplay by Christiane Rochefort, Jean Nery, and Michael Pertwee) is mistitled; the problem isn't the number of crooks but their sheer incompetence. The film's zany humor is what one might get if Laurel and Hardy, The Three Stooges, and the Marx Brothers got together to make a crime movie.

The quartet of crooks is led by Fingers (George Cole), who has a habit of fouling up every one of their criminal efforts: e.g., he crashes his car too far into the window of the jewelry store they plan to rob; when they find the door to the safe they intend to rob in the home of wealthy businessman Billy Gordon wide open, they are delighted until Fingers stumbles against the door, slamming it shut. They then decide to try to change their luck by kidnapping Gordon's daughter but instead mistakenly grab his wife Lucy (Brenda de Banzie). Unfortunately for them, the lecherous Gordon is delighted to be rid of his wife, and refuses to pay anything for her return. Angered at her husband, she in turn enlists the gang's help in stealing his fortune, which is hidden under the floorboards in his home. They manage to get the cash, but in the process accidentally burn his house down. The film ends with them driving off with a suitcase full of cash, happily singing, "We're in the money," unaware that the suitcase has opened, scattering a fortune to the winds.

Besides the non-stop farcical action, the film also derives much of its comedy from its absurd dialogue, puns ("I thought you were coming by hearse." "We changed hearses in midstream"), spoonerisms ("One move and I'll shoot you to Comedom King"), and slightly naughty remarks (when a buxom woman explains to Billy Gordon that she's wearing a veil to conceal her identity, he quips, "Take my advice. Next time wear a cape").

Too Many Crooks makes no pretense at being anything more than what it is: a rollicking comedy about a bunch of bumblers who learn over and over again that crime does not pay.

Take the Money and Run (1969)

Virgil Starkwell, the poor loser in *Take the Money and Run*, the first film Woody Allen wrote (with Mickey Rose), directed, and starred in, is another totally inept criminal. Allen employs the serious tone of a news documentary (voiced by famed radio announcer Jackson Beck) to tell the life story of a hardened criminal. Virgil's criminal biography, however, is simply the framework for a barrage of verbal and visual jokes, beginning with this introduction: "Before he is twenty-five years old, he will be wanted by police in six states for assault, armed robbery, and illegal possession of a wart."

Whatever he tries to do is doomed to failure either because of his utter incompetence or bad luck. His first attempt at crime as a young boy goes awry when his hand gets stuck in the gum machine he's trying to rob. He later ends up in prison after attempting to rob an armed car with a gun-shaped cigarette lighter. To escape from prison he carves a gun out of soap and paints it with black shoe polish. Unfortunately, it begins to rain and his gun turns into a handful of soap suds.

In the most famous scene in the film, Virgil hands a bank teller a note demanding money. Things quickly turn comic when two bank employees begin arguing over whether the note reads, "I am pointing a gun at you" or "I am pointing a gub at you." Once they determine that Virgil does indeed intend to rob the bank, they inform him that the note must first be approved by a vice president. In the end a dozen or more bank employees animatedly debate the meaning of the note, leaving poor Virgil, who insists he's in a rush, standing by helplessly.

Some of the film's humor is purely visual. For example, Virgil plays the cello (poorly) in his high school marching band. Watching him struggling to keep up with his bandmates while he has to keep moving his chair forward is a scene Buster Keaton would have been proud of. In another episode, he and five other escapees from a chain gang try to act casually so as not to be noticed, though they are still chained together at the leg. When one needs to use the bathroom, all six must shuffle in together. Attempting to smooth things over with his wife is another challenge for Virgil, as the five guys attached to him act like a Greek chorus offering a commentary on his efforts.

Humor also arises from the interviews with the various experts in the documentary who speak seriously and, in the case of one who explains the sexual implications of his choice of the cello, pedantically about Virgil's character. Particularly funny are the conversations with Virgil's parents, who wear fake noses, eyeglasses, and bushy eyebrows to disguise their appearance.

Take the Money and Run lacks the comic sophistication of Allen's later films; instead it reflects his previous career as a stand-up comic whose routines are a steady stream of absurdist jokes. Virgil's story can't be taken seriously; the object of the film, Allen told film historian Richard Schickel, "was for every inch of it to be a laugh" (92). In this effort he has succeeded thanks to the comic misadventures of one of the most hilariously incompetent criminal in film history.

Raising Arizona (1987)

Raising Arizona (directed by Joel Coen, screenplay by Joel and Ethan Coen) combines elements of Elmore Leonard's and Donald E. Westlake's crime fiction with a hearty dose of cartoon looniness to create a classic screwball crime film. H. I. ("Call me Hi") McDunnough (Nicolas Cage) is a small-time criminal who falls madly in love with Edwina (Holly Hunter), the police photographer who handles each of his many arrest bookings. They eventually marry and settle down in a cozy trailer in the Arizona desert. However, their life feels incomplete without a child, and Hi is disheartened to learn that Ed's insides "were a rocky place where my seed could find no purchase." Reading a newspaper account of the birth of quintuplets to Florence and Nathan Arizona gives them an idea; feeling that it was "unfair that some should have so many while others should have so few" and convinced that the new parents will have their hands so full with five babies they won't miss losing one of them, they decide to take a baby for themselves. But as in one of Donald E. Westlake's Dortmunder novels, things quickly go awry for Hi and Ed.

The complications begin when two of Hi's prison buddies, Gale and Evelle Snoats (John Goodman and William Forsythe), show up unexpectedly at his trailer home after breaking out of prison. They decide to steal the baby from Hi and Ed in hopes of claiming the $20,000 ransom the distraught parents are offering for its safe return. Also interested in the child is Leonard Smalls, an evil bounty hunter who aims to use the baby to squeeze an even higher ransom from the parents by threatening to sell him to another bidder if they don't cough up more dough.

The events depicted in the film—kidnapping, armed robbery, extortion—are serious, but the tone is pure comedy. Right from the beginning, visual clues like the shaggy haircut Nicolas Cage wears, one of the goofiest in film history, as well as the Woody Woodpecker tattoo he gets prepare us for the slapstick action that resembles a Chuck Jones *Roadrunner* cartoon. A rollicking musical score further adds to the film's comic tone. There's also a zany Mack Sennett–like chase scene that ensues after Hi decides to rob a convenience store while he's picking up some diapers for the baby. Another comic misadventure features Gale and Evelle who not once but twice drive off with the baby in its car seat perched on the roof of their car. In each instance, true to the rambunctious cartoon spirit of the film, they eventually find the infant sitting safely in the middle of the road enjoying the scenery around him.

The Coen brothers also exploit Hi's voice-over narration, and the incongruity between the sunny language of his account and the events he's describing, for comic effect. For example, while proclaiming that in prison, "there's a spirit of camaraderie that exists between the men, like you find only in combat maybe, or on a pro ball club in the heat of a pennant drive," the film shows him being escorted down a dark corridor past a scary inmate who hisses at him. When he later returns to jail to serve another sentence and passes by the same menacing inmate, he remarks, "I can't say I was happy to be back inside, but the flood of familiar sights, sounds, and faces almost made it feel like a homecoming."

His two prison buddies also speak in an overly florid language, and like Elmore Leonard's small-time crooks, don't realize that their deadpan delivery is humorous. For example, Gale justifies their prison escape this way: "We released ourselves on our own recognizance." To which Evelle adds, "we felt the institution no longer had anything to offer us." Their hope is that their planned bank robbery will be just the beginning of a spree across the entire Southwest. "We keep goin' till we can retire—or we get caught," Gale says. "Either way we're fixed for life," Evelle adds.

Everything ends on a rosy note. Hi and Ed decide to return the infant to his parents, no harm done. They even refuse the reward the father offers to pay them for his safe return. The film concludes with Hi, ever the optimist, dreaming of a future Thanksgiving gathering surrounded by children and a dozen grandchildren. "It *seemed* real. It *seemed* like us," he says. "It seemed like ... well ... our home.... If not Arizona, then a land, not *too* far away, where all parents are strong and wise and capable, and all children are happy and beloved.... I dunno, maybe it was Utah."

A Fish Called Wanda (1988)

Thirty-seven years after directing the classic comic caper film *The Lavender Hill Mob*, Charles Crichton teamed up with Monty Python–alum John Cleese (who wrote the screenplay) to create *A Fish Called Wanda,* one of the funniest crime films ever made. Unlike the droll comedy found in the earlier film, the latter film is a hilarious blend of British and American humor and zaniness.

The film is more about the aftermath of a jewelry heist than the caper itself, and more about the characters than the crime. Two Americans, a sexy manipulator named Wanda Gershwitz (Jamie Lee Curtis) and her volatile, not-so-bright "brother" Otto West (actually her lover, played by Kevin Kline, whose performance earned him an Academy Award for Best Supporting Actor), join up with two London gangsters, George (Tom Georgeson) and Ken (another Monty Python alum, Michael Palin, saddled with a severe stutter and an obsessive love for animals, especially the fish in his tank) to steal twenty million dollars worth of diamonds. Almost immediately after the successful theft, they begin double crossing one another to get the diamonds for themselves, which leads to increasingly farcical complications.

What follows is a series of side-splitting situations. John Cleese plays stuffy, henpecked British barrister Archie Leach. Having fallen under

Wanda's spell, he strips naked in anticipation of an exciting sexual romp with her. Unfortunately, the family that has just rented the apartment he's in unexpectedly shows up at the front door, forcing him to grab a picture of the shocked wife off the table to cover up his genitals and maintain his British dignity.

A running gag in the film involves Ken, who sets out to kill an elderly woman who was the sole witness to the gang's getaway. The animal-loving Ken manages to accidentally kill one of her beloved Yorkshire terriers in each of his three bungled efforts to bump her off. He's the only one with any reason to celebrate when the old woman collapses and dies of a heart attack after the third dog's demise.

A comic highlight of the film is a scene in which Otto ties Ken to a chair and begins asking him questions about Nietzsche. Each time he is unable to answer them, Otto sticks a french fry up one of Ken's nostrils. Otto then tries to force Ken into revealing the location of the missing diamonds by removing his beloved fish out of the tank one by one and eating them. (After downing one of the fish he cautions Ken to avoid the green fish because they aren't ripe yet.) The questioning ends with Ken's favorite fish (named Wanda) wiggling in Otto's mouth just before he swallows it. (The scene gives new meaning to the term drop-dead funny: it has been widely reported that a Danish audiologist laughed so hard watching it that it triggered a fatal heart attack.)

In addition to inspired visual humor, the film also provides plenty of verbal jokes, including a few in Italian. For example, Wanda becomes sexually aroused by the sound of foreign languages, so Otto often speaks to her in nonsense Italian (e.g., *"La fontana di Trevi ... mozarella ... parmigiana ... gorgonzola"*). At one point while gazing down between her legs while separating them, he jokes in perfect Italian, *"Dov'e il Vaticano?"* ("Where is the Vatican?").

A Fish Called Wanda is the highest ranking comic crime film (#21) on the American Film Institute's list of the 100 Funniest American Movies of All Time. A follow-up film featuring the same cast (*Fierce Creatures*) was released in 1997, but as is often the case with sequels it failed to recapture the inspired comic magic of the original.

Miami Blues (1990)

Miami Blues (written and directed by George Armitage) is, like the Charles Willeford novel it's based on, a mixture of brutal violence and offbeat humor. The first thing violent ex-con Junior Frenger (Alec Baldwin) does after landing in Miami is steal a woman's suitcase. Then he breaks the finger of a Hare Krishna who is harassing him on his way out of the airport. But what might have been a serious study of a violent psychopath on the loose changes tone when the Hare Krishna dies from the shock of a broken finger. The absurdity of his death gives grizzled homicide detective Hoke Moseley (Fred Ward) and his partner plenty to joke about, concluding with the partner's insistence that it's not his turn to inform the victim's family of his unfortunate death: "I did the fat lady who sat on that kid," he explains, "That's good for two."

Moseley's false teeth also play a comic role. Thanks to some discomfort with his dentures, he frequently takes them out of his mouth for relief (even in the middle of an interview). Once he tracks Junior's location down, the two begin a kind of cat-and-mouse game over a home-cooked dinner (for which he puts his teeth back in). Later, Junior violently ambushes Moseley and steals his gun, badge, and dentures. Junior's childish delight in playing cop, breaking up robberies in progress and then pocketing the loot for himself, all while being pursued by the now toothless Moseley wearing a neck brace, provides plenty of offbeat humor right up to the violent climax.

One other source of humor is Susie (Jennifer Jason Leigh), arguably the sweetest and most clueless hooker in the entire state of Florida. A small-town girl in the big city, she takes classes at the local community college and dreams of one day owning a Burger World franchise, buying a nice little house with a white picket fence, and living happily ever after. Her relentlessly sunny outlook blinds her to Junior whom she marries and cooks for, unaware that he's out all day long committing violent crimes. Even after learning about all the horrible things he has done, she still vouches for his good qualities, such as always eating whatever dish she prepared for him.

Pulp Fiction (1994)

In *Pulp Fiction*, which he wrote and directed, Quentin Tarantino assembled the kind of crime stories he called "the oldest chestnuts in the world," filtered them through his love of old movies and popular culture, added a quirky comic sensibility, and crafted a brilliantly funny crime film. The movie cleverly weaves together separate stories like those found in the classic pulp magazines of the 1920s and 30s—an armed robbery, a pair of hit men on the job, a boxer who disobeys orders to take a dive, a man who is given the job of entertaining his gangster boss's wife—into a tale that marries bloody violence with humor in a wildly original way.

The tone of the film and the director's knack for toying with the viewer's expectations are established even before the opening titles. A young man (Tim Roth) and woman (Amanda Plummer) are sitting in an L. A. coffee shop early one morning. The couple, who endearingly call one another "Pumpkin" and "Honey Bunny," are quietly discussing their future. The man tells his companion that he no longer wants to rob liquor stores and suggests that perhaps robbing restaurants might be a safer bet. The woman thinks about it for a moment and agrees he's right. They suddenly pull out their guns, kiss sweetly, and declare their love for one another. Then Honey Bunny stands up and shrieks, "Any of you fucking pricks move and I'll execute every motherfucking last one of you."

The scene then switches to Vincent (John Travolta) and Jules (Samuel L. Jackson), both dressed in black suits and narrow ties, riding in a car. Vincent is describing to Jules some of the things he learned during a recent trip to Europe, such as in France beer is served at McDonald's and a Quarter Pounder with Cheese is called a Royale with Cheese. After this extended bit of inconsequential to and fro, the two open the trunk of their car and pull out guns. Then they resume their conversation while walking, this time getting into a discussion about the differences between giving a woman a foot massage and oral sex. Finally arriving at their destination, they knock at the door, enter, and point their guns at a trio of young men. We now learn that these guys are hit men on assignment for their boss, a man named Marsellus (Ving Rhames). After sampling a bite of hamburger from one of the men, Jules says, "Uuummmm, that's a tasty burger," then calmly turns and shoots the man's partner lying on a couch. Moments later, Jules recites a passage from the Bible and then he and Vincent empty their guns at the other man. The next sound we hear is Al Green's soothing voice crooning his romantic classic, "Let's Stay Together."

This mixture of the violent and the mundane is both shocking in its unexpectedness and comic in the disparity between bloody action and everyday talk. Tarantino is a master of the incongruous, what he calls "unexpected dissonances" (Peary 58), which he often achieves by placing violent criminals into situations of ordinary life.

Some of the film's humor is situational. Some is verbal, as Tarantino's characters are all great talkers who are allowed to rattle on at much greater length (and with intense comic effect) than most directors would allow. Some humor is purely visual: Vincent slowly walking though Jackrabbit

Slim's, a fifties-style diner staffed by impersonators of famous celebrities like Ed Sullivan, Buddy Holly, James Dean, Mamie Van Doren, and Marilyn Monroe; or Butch the boxer (Bruce Willis) silently rummaging around in a pawnshop for a weapon he can use to attack the men assaulting a friend: he first grabs a hammer, drops it in favor of a baseball bat, then spots a chainsaw. And then his eyes fall on the perfect weapon: a samurai sword.

One of the finest sequences in the film effectively draws upon all three types of humor. As Jules and Vincent drive away from the apartment where they have just executed two men, Vincent's gun accidentally discharges, blowing the head off a passenger sitting in the back seat. Covered now with blood and gore, they rush to the nearby home of a friend (played by Tarantino himself) who warns them they have only an hour and a half to clean things up before his wife returns. The situation pushes a classic Laurel-and-Hardy "fine mess" situation to its bloody extreme, prompting Jules to update Hardy's usual lament, "Well, here's another nice mess you've gotten me into" to "I will never forgive your ass for this shit. This is some fucked-up repugnant shit!"

Under the watchful eye of Winston Wolf (Harvey Keitel), nattily dressed in a tuxedo, they race against the clock to get the job done. Meanwhile the characters continue to jabber about matters seemingly inappropriate to the situation like the quality of the coffee they drink, "This is some serious gourmet shit," and the beauty of oak bedroom furniture. Even Winston's parting words to Vincent and Jules—"stay outta trouble, you crazy kids"—are uttered in the same deadpan comic spirit.

Tarantino has variously described *Pulp Fiction* as an opera, a modern-day spaghetti western, and a kitchen-sink movie. The latter term may be the most accurate in the sense that he throws so many disparate things together—pulp crime stories, echoes of movies of every genre from gangster and dance films to kung-fu and blaxploitation flicks, and all kinds of music (soul, rock classics, surf guitar)—into a narrative that at first seems disconnected as it jumps around in time and place. Assisted by an eye-catching visual style and uniformly outstanding performances, he pulls everything together into one of the most original comic crime films ever made.

Get Shorty (1995)

Few writers have seen more of their novels and stories made into movies than Elmore Leonard. But despite his longtime success in selling his works to Hollywood, (beginning in 1957 with *3:10 to Yuma,* based on an early western story), few of those movies have lived up to the standard of the original source. Most have missed the mark either because they focused too much on the story, which in Leonard's novels is always secondary to the characters, or failed to capture the distinctive comic tone and sound of the characters, which is so integral to Leonard's writing. Only three films have managed to make an effective transition from novel to the big screen: Barry Sonnenfeld's *Get Shorty* (1995), the most faithful adaptation and among the best comic crime films of its kind; Quentin Tarantino's *Jackie Brown* (1997), based on *Rum Punch* (1992); and Steven Soderbergh's *Out of Sight* (1998), from the novel of the same name.

Get Shorty features Chili Palmer (John Travolta, the personification of Leonard's cool, in his first movie after *Pulp Fiction*), a Miami-based loan shark who ends up in Los Angeles where he is asked to convince Harry Zimm (a very funny Gene Hackman), producer of schlock films with titles like *Slime Creatures* and *Grotesque,* to pay off a $150,000 gambling debt to a Vegas casino. Before long, Chili, a devoted movie fan, ends up pitching a film idea based on one of his cases to Harry. Harry offers to partner with Chili on the film if Chili can get Bo Catlett (Delroy Lindo), who has invested $150,000 in Harry's latest project, off his back. Unfortunately for Harry, it was Catlett's money he gambled away in Vegas.

Though it involves mobsters, South American drug dealers, loan sharks, a couple of murders, and a duffel bag stuffed with hundreds of thousands of ill-gotten dollars stashed in an airport locker that everyone wants to get their hands on, *Get Shorty* is ultimately about the film industry. It makes the point that both the crime business and the business of making films have much in common: both rely on fear, intimidation, cons, and double crosses. Putting shady characters alongside film stars and then blurring the line between them is a recipe for great fun; e.g., the loan shark wants to get into the movie business while pint-sized Hollywood star Martin Weir (Danny DeVito), who makes up in ego what he lacks in height, becomes excited at the prospect of becoming a gangster (at least on film): "It scares me how well I know him. I could do this one tomorrow, no further preparation."

Much of the humor arises from the satirical portrayal of Hollywood. Whether it's Martin Weir babbling about his acting—"All I had to do was find the character's center, the stem I'd use to wind him up and he'd play, man, he'd play"—or drug dealer/limo owner Bo Catlett, who asks, "What's the point of living in L.A. if you're not in the movie business?," explaining how to write a screenplay—"You write down what you wanna say. Then you get somebody to add the commas and shit where they belong ... you come to the last page you write 'Fade Out' and that's the end, you're done"—phoniness is exploited for pure comic effect.

Get Shorty succeeds where so many other adaptations have failed because director Sonnenfeld and screenwriter Scott Frank (who also wrote the screenplay for *Out of Sight*) remain faithful to the spirit of Leonard's novel. Frank's screenplay preserves much of Leonard's original dialogue and what he adds to it fits in seamlessly. Even more importantly, the actors play it straight, never milking a line for its humor or even being aware that what they are saying might be funny. This is the exact opposite of what happened with the film version of Leonard's *Stick* (1985), starring Burt Reynolds, for which Leonard wrote the screenplay. The actors mugged and smirked their way through the film, prompting Leonard to make one correction in the line that appeared on the poster for the film that he hung on his wall: "The only thing he couldn't do was stick by the rules." He replaced "rules" with "script."

Leonard liked the movie version of *Get Shorty* so much he wrote a sequel to the novel entitled *Be Cool* (1999), which deals with Chili Palmer's adventures in the music business. A film adaptation, directed by F. Gary Gray, was released in 2005, but despite the return of John Travolta as Chili Palmer, it lacked the energy, style, and smart humor of its predecessor.

Jackie Brown (1997)

Although Quentin Tarantino's influences are primarily cinematic, there is one writer he singles out as a major inspiration: Elmore Leonard. "He was the first novelist I read as a kid who really spoke to me" (Peary 107), he has said. The two share a similar comic sensibility, an interest in criminal characters, and a knack for dialogue that both reveals character and is funny in itself. "He showed me that characters can go off on tangents, and those tangents are just as valid as anything else" (Peary 113). Despite the obvious influence of Leonard on *Pulp Fiction*, the screenplay for that film was an original written by Tarantino. But his very next film, *Jackie Brown*, would in fact be an adaptation of one of Leonard's novels, *Rum Punch.*

Though Tarantino changes the setting from Miami to Los Angeles, the name of the main character from Jackie Burke to Jackie Brown, and her race from white to African American, his film is second only to *Get Shorty* in faithfully capturing the tone and spirit of Leonard's fiction.

The film's dialogue contains half from Leonard's novel, half written by Tarantino, but the sound of both meshes seamlessly. Admirers of Leonard's brand of character-driven humor will find much to enjoy in the film. A perfect example is the scene where bank robber (Robert DeNiro), just days out of prison, can't take any more of the incessant nagging of his young companion Melanie (Bridget Fonda) and shoots her dead in the parking lot of a shopping mall. His explanation to his partner Ordell (Samuel L. Jackson) for why he had to shoot her is Leonard/Tarantino comic deadpan dialogue at its best.

Lock, Stock and Two Smoking Barrels (1998) and *Snatch* (2000)

Lock, Stock and Two Smoking Barrels and *Snatch* are a pair of British comic gangster films written and directed by Guy Ritchie that show the obvious influence of *Pulp Fiction*. Noisier, more cartoonish, and far less verbally inventive than Tarantino's film, they are more an exercise in style over substance. Ritchie brings a fresh new visual look and a slapdash energy to the genre.

Both films are constructed around intersecting plots and subplots that exist mainly to highlight some funny bits. In *Lock, Stock and Two Smoking Barrels,* a quartet of in-out-of-their depth young men scrape together 100,000 pounds to bet in a private poker game. Of course the game is rigged and they end up owing 500,000 pounds to a violent mobster named Harry Hatchet. The film follows their efforts to raise the money to save their lives. In *Snatch*, the main event is a bare-knuckled boxing match in which an Irish gypsy fighter played by Brad Pitt, who speaks in an almost unintelligible accent, is ordered to take a dive by another violent gangster boss. Will he take the fall or double cross the gangster, and if he does what will the consequences be?

The bad guys in both films are outlandish figures with Dick Tracy–like names.(Besides Harry Hatchet, there's Barry the Baptist, Nick the Bubble, Boris the Blade, and Franky Four Fingers.) The over-the top violence (one crime boss is shown beating a man to death with a rubber penis, another is fond of feeding his victims to the pigs) and pulp-style gangster talk are equally cartoonish. There are also several funny bits, including some comic business with a pair of ancient muskets that come to play a key role in *Lock, Stock and Two Smoking Barrels*, especially in setting up the very funny ending. *Snatch* also contains some extended scenes of slapstick humor involving a pair of bumbling armed robbers and their incompetent getaway driver, some over-the-top gangster talk, and a dog that swallows a toy that squeaks whenever he's squeezed.

Both films have a comic exuberance generated by a sprightly visual style (a result of Ritchie's background as a director of commercials) accompanied by the sound of throbbing rock music in the background. Employing imaginative camera angles and unusual lighting effects (e.g., *Lock, Stock and Two Smoking Barrels* is shot in sepia tones), each film has a distinctive look. A prime example of Ritchie's visual style can be seen in the extended bare-knuckle fight scene in *Snatch* where boxer Brad Pitt is ordered to take a dive in the fourth round. The film switches back and forth from fast-motion to stop-action to extreme slow-motion. The use of the latter to show Pitt's character being launched into the air by a punch and floating slowly backwards before landing gently on the canvas is particularly eye-catching.

Ritchie apparently liked the scene so much he uses it again in *Sherlock Holmes* (2009), the first of two movies he directed based on Conan Doyle's famous detective, the other being *Sherlock Holmes: A Game of Shadows* (2011). Holmes, played by Robert Downey, Jr., engages in a bare-knuckle fight filmed in the same fast-stop-slow-motion style Ritchie employed in *Snatch*. Though the action is set in the 1890s, Ritchie turns Conan Doyle's brilliant crime-solving genius into a modern big-screen action hero and animates his films with foot chases (filmed upside down), fistfights, exploding fireballs, and the like. Those looking for a more creative reimagining of the Holmes character with a far more humorous slant may find the recent BBC adaptations starring Benedict Cumberbatch and Martin Freeman more to their liking.

Bandits (2001)

Bandits (directed by Barry Levinson, screenplay by Harley Peyton) mixes together several genres—bank robbers on the run, buddy movies, noir, and romantic comedy—to create a screwball crime film that also pays tribute to such classics as *Butch Cassidy and the Sundance Kid, Take the Money and Run*, and *Bonnie and Clyde*. Joe (Bruce Willis) and Terry (Billy Bob Thornton) use a cement mixer to bust out of prison and then begin robbing banks, quickly earning notoriety as the "Sleepover Bandits" for their habit of holding a bank manager's family hostage overnight and forcing him to open the vault first thing in the morning. But their crime spree becomes complicated when a bored housewife with flaming red hair named Kate (Cate Blanchett) ends up in their custody. Both men are attracted to her, leading to what at first appears to be yet another variation on the familiar noir triangle among thieves. Instead the story takes a comic turn in the direction of romantic comedy.

Everyone mistakenly believes Kate has been kidnapped, but she is energized by the thrill of being with a pair of outlaws on the run. However, instead of pitting them against each other for her affections, she loves both and can't choose between the strong sexy one or the brainy sensitive one. "Together," she tells them, "You're the perfect man." She confesses that she may have bit off a bit more than she can chew, but she breezily makes the most of the love triangle she has created.

What gives the film its comic energy are the performances of the three main actors. Willis summons up all his grinning charm as the romantic hero and plays it off against nerdy Thornton's numerous neuroses. The humor is visually underscored by the goofy hats, wigs, and facial hair the duo wears as disguises at various times during the film. Cate Blanchett is especially fun to watch playing the daffy femme fatale who gets laughs from the unlikeliest places including an opportunity to display one of the worst singing voices in film history.

Bandits may lack the suspense and slick pace of a true crime thriller and it devotes more time to the romance plot than necessary, but it also provides plenty of laughs with the comic antics of its odd-couple bank robbers and their red-headed moll.

In Bruges (2008)

The opening line of *In Bruges* (written and directed by Irish playwright Martin McDonagh)—"After I killed them, I dropped the gun in the Thames, washed the residue off my hands in the bathroom of a Burger King, and walked home to await instructions"—alerts the viewer that the film is about serious matters. Ray (Colin Farrell), the speaker of that line, and his partner Ken (Brendan Gleeson) are a pair of Irish hit men who have been dispatched to the picturesque medieval town of Bruges, Belgium, to await further instructions, perhaps even orders to carry out a killing in that city.

The film is a prime example of how a good crime story is really more about characters than crime. The relationship between Ray and Ken makes the film much more interesting than a story about hit men on the run; it's about the personalities behind the stereotyped image of the hired killer and reveals their human side thanks in large part to the humorous byplay between them.

The two guys are a classic odd couple, which is made clear once they set foot in Bruges. Ken, the older and calmer of the two, decides to take full advantage of the beautiful city, buying a guidebook and visiting local churches and museums. Ray, a bundle of nervous energy, decides even before seeing the town that, "Bruges is a shithole." Walking down cobbled streets past picturesque canals, quaint shops, a 12th century hospital, and the town's landmark 300-foot bell-tower fails to impress the stubborn Ray: "I grew up in Dublin. I love Dublin. If I'd grown up on a farm, and was retarded, Bruges might impress me, but I didn't, so it doesn't." When Ken drags him to an art museum, he declares that with the notable exception of Bosch's "Last Judgment," everything else is "rubbish by spastics."

But amidst the humorous dialogue darker matters begin to emerge. The reason for the trip to Bruges turns out to have been a botched killing in which Ray, on his first assignment, accidentally killed a young boy when he shot at a priest he was hired to kill. His negative attitude toward everything around him appears to be related to his guilt over having killed an innocent child, and as the film progresses we see even more evidence of how that incident is tearing him apart inside.

Events take a decidedly tragic turn when Ken's boss Harry (Ralph Fiennes) calls him with his new assignment: he is ordered to kill Ray for having killed the child. Sending Ray to Bruges was Harry's idea of providing Ray with one last happy experience before he's executed. The scene where a very reluctant Ken approaches Ray from behind to shoot him contains a good example of McDonagh's darkly comic dialogue. Ray has been watching a mother play with her child, who bears a strong resemblance to the boy he shot. As soon as they leave, Ray pulls out a gun and raises it to his head. Ken shouts at him to stop, but when Ray sees Ken with a gun in his hand, he realizes what he was intending to do.

"Oh my God! You were gonna kill me."
"No I w—You were gonna kill.yourself!"
"Well.... I'm *allowed* to."
"No you're not."
"What? I'm *not* allowed to and you *are*? How's that fair?"

Ken convinces Ray to flee Bruges, but warns him not to return to London or he'll be a dead man. To which Ray replies "Ken, I *wanna* be a dead man! Have you been missing something?"

Ken's refusal to kill his partner forces Harry to come to Bruges to settle the score with him. Ironically, in the end it is Ken not Ray who is the one who has enjoyed a final happy experience in Bruges before he dies. But in an even bigger irony, Harry also chooses to kill himself after he re-enacts Ray's error by accidentally killing an innocent child when he shoots Ray, though he's unaware that the child is actually a dwarf actor dressed as a child for a re-make of Nicholas Roeg's classic *Don't Look Now* being filmed in Bruges. Ray, carried away after being shot by Harry and likely mortally wounded, gets the last laugh, spoken in voiceover: "Fuck, man, maybe that's what Hell is. The entire rest of eternity spent in fucking Bruges."

Few crime films have mixed comedy and tragedy more effectively than *In Bruges*. The humor never detracts from the tragic elements of the story; instead it serves to reveal the human side of its two hired killers and makes us care about them as they meet the fate that awaits them.

Heist/Caper Films

The heist or caper film dates back to the earliest days of the medium. *The Great Train Robbery* (1903), an eleven-minute film about the hold-up of a train, is generally regarded as both the first Western and the first caper movie. Since then there have been countless film versions of the big heist including such classics as *The Asphalt Jungle* (1950), *Rififi* (1955), *The Killing* (1956), *The Thomas Crown Affair* (1968), and *Heat* (1995).

The big caper lends itself to filmmaking. Some crimes take little time to commit and need very little planning. A heist, on the other hand, requires careful planning beforehand and adequate time to carry out a complex operation, all of which can be shown on screen. One reason for the popularity of these films is the pleasure that comes from identifying with criminals engaged in a kind of artful performance. According to Kirsten Moana Thompson, heist films provide "escapism and voyeurism" by offering characters and stories "that dramatise transgressive behaviours that may appeal to our fantasies and desires" (4).

John Huston's *The Asphalt Jungle*, generally considered the first of the big heist films, appeared in 1950; one year later saw the release of director Charles Crichton's *The Lavender Hill Mob*, the first comic caper film. Since then heist films have generally followed one of two paths: one takes a seriously dramatic approach to the elaborate planning and systematic execution of a complicated heist; the other opts for a humorous treatment of the same subject. These films aren't really parodies of the serious caper film; instead they offer an alternative version by focusing on what might go wrong, either through simple bad luck or the laughable incompetence of the perpetrators.

The Lavender Hill Mob (1951)

The Lavender Hill Mob (directed by Charles Crichton, screenplay by T. E. B. Clarke) is about the heist of a truckload of gold bullion worth one million British pounds. The mastermind of the plan is a meek bank employee named Henry Holland (Alec Guinness), whose formal attire and derby hat make him look like Stan Laurel. Holland has spent the previous twenty years overseeing the delivery of gold bullion bars from the refinery to the bank where he works as a clerk. No one would expect the man whom his boss calls "unimaginative" and "without initiative" to come up with such a bold plan: i.e., to steal the gold bars and with the help of Alfred Pendlebury (Stanley Holloway), a manufacturer of travel souvenirs he has just met, melt the gold into Eiffel Tower paperweights at Pendlebury's factory, and then have them shipped safely out of the country to Paris. After inevitably hitting several comic snags, the plan amazingly succeeds with the gold booty safely waiting at a tourist shop at the Eiffel Tower.

Things then begin to go awry in antic fashion. Six of the gold paperweights have just been mistakenly sold to British schoolgirls on vacation. Holland and Pendlebury race down the winding staircase of the Eiffel Tower in a mad dash to stop the girls. Their hot pursuit continues back across the English Channel and doesn't end until they finally catch up with them in their London classroom. More comic bedlam ensues, involving a Keystone Kops-style chase of the pair of gold robbers on foot and then by car through the London streets, culminating in a crash involving three of the pursuing police vehicles.

The film opened with a scene set in a Rio de Janerio nightclub where Holland is apparently enjoying the fruits of his enterprise and generously sharing a pile of cash with those around him. Only in the last shot of the movie do we see that he is handcuffed and about to be led away by the police. Justice is served, but not before Holland has had a year to enjoy his new life. His misadventures have also provided plenty of comic enjoyment to the audience.

The Ladykillers (1956)

Alec Guinness starred in another classic comic caper film from the famous Ealing Studios, *The Ladykillers* (directed by Alexander MacKendrick, screenplay by William Rose). A delightful combination of light and dark humor, the film features outstanding performances, especially by Guinness and seventy-seven-year-old Katie Johnson as a lovable widow who unwittingly outfoxes a gang of robbers. In 2010, *The Guardian* named it 5th best comedy film of all time.

Alec Guinness plays Professor Marcus, the leader of a gang of London thieves. Two of his accomplices are portrayed by Peter Sellers and Herbert Lom, who would later go on to achieve fame in the Pink Panther movies playing Inspector Clouseau and his frustrated boss. Marcus rents a room in the home of an elderly widow named Mrs. Wilberforce that he intends to use as a base of operations for his gang. He tells Mrs. Wilberforce that his associates are fellow members of a string quintet that will be visiting him often for practice sessions. Their arrival leads to several humorous scenes as they are repeatedly forced to scramble to shut off the turntable playing the music they are supposedly playing and grab their instruments every time kindly Mrs. Wilberforce knocks on the door to offer them tea or coffee. Her request for help in administering medicine to her pet parrot triggers another slapstick episode when the bird escapes.

Despite the comic interruptions, the planned robbery of a security van goes off without a hitch thanks in part to Mrs. Wilberforce, who unknowingly becomes an accomplice when she agrees to pick up a trunk for the men, unaware that it is filled with stolen loot. But things begin to unravel when Mrs. Wilberforce happens to see the banknotes and becomes suspicious. Professor Marcus decides she must be killed before she can go to the police, as she has threatened to do. The comedy now turns much darker as repeated efforts to bump off the old lady eventually result in the gruesome deaths of all five gang members. A macabre visual joke is repeated several times as one by one the bodies of the dead are dangled from atop a tunnel before being tossed onto a train passing below.

The film ends on a note of supreme comic irony. After the gang members all mysteriously disappear, Mrs. Wilberforce dutifully marches to the local police station and asks what she should do "with all the lolly" she has back at her house. They of course think the old woman is a bit dotty, and tell her to keep it. Things turn out just fine in the end for sweet Mrs. Wilberforce.

The Coen brothers released a remake of the film starring Tom Hanks in 2004, with the action moved from London to a Mississippi town where a riverboat casino is the robbery target. Not surprisingly, the film lacks the droll charm of the original, leading film critic Roger Ebert to conclude, "The old and new *Ladykillers* play like a contest between Buster Keaton and Soupy Sales" ("Ladykillers").

Big Deal on Madonna Street (1958)

Still one of the best comic heist movies of all time is the Italian classic, *Big Deal on Madonna Street* (directed by Mario Monicelli, screenplay by Mario Monicelli, Furio Scarpelli, Suso Cecchi d'Amico, and Agenore Incrocci). Blessed with an outstanding cast (including Marcello Mastroianni, Vittorio Gassman, and Claudia Cardinale, all of whom would later became well known to American audiences) and a clever script filled with hilarious twists and turns, the film has become the model for all comic caper films that have come after it.

The film opens on a dark night on a shadowy street in a poor neighborhood of Rome, but any thought that what follows will be a typical noir tragedy is quickly countered by the breezy jazz music playing on the soundtrack. This will be a light comedy, and what a rollicking comedy it turns out to be. The film spoofs *Rififi*, the 1955 French film about an elaborate jewel heist carried out by a quartet of pros, by introducing a motley crew of petty criminals who encounter a series of hilarious setbacks in their half-baked plan to break into a pawnshop to rob a safe full of jewels. Their doomed efforts never seem to dampen their spirits, however, despite one calamitous mishap after another.

The film is a clever mix of subtle wit and laugh-out-loud farce, an amusing grab-bag of sight gags, verbal jokes, goofy characters, and plenty of frustration. The elaborate planning leading up to the heist, a usual convention in such films, is a classic illustration of the motto, "If Anything Can Go Wrong, It Will." One comic setback after another undermines the efforts of these hapless bumblers, whose never-say-die attitude in the face of their incompetence and bad luck endears them to the audience. In the end, having to settle for a plate of pasta and beans rather than the precious jewels they had hoped for is sadly what they have come to expect out of life.

The movie inspired a Broadway musical directed by Bob Fosse (*Big Deal*, 1986) and a pair of film remakes that sought to recapture the goofy charm of the original, with mixed results. *Crackers* (1984), directed by Louis

Malle and featuring Donald Sutherland as the leader of the gang, was a comic misfire. Steven Soderbergh and George Clooney, one year after their highly successful remake of *Ocean's Eleven*, joined forces again to produce *Welcome to Collinwood* (2002; written and directed by Anthony and Joe Russo), whose characters, closely modeled on the original team of amateur thieves, plot to carry out their ill-fated jewel heist in suburban Cleveland. Despite its comic energy and faithfulness to the wacky spirit of *Big Deal on Madonna Street*, the film was a box-office dud.

Topkapi (1964)

American film director Jules Dassin, who moved to France after being blacklisted during the Communist witch hunts in the 1950s, made two heist movies. *Rififi*, about a jewel robbery on the Rue de Rivoli in Paris, was hailed as a classic and became the model for subsequent films in the genre. For his second effort, *Topkapi* (screenplay by Monja Danischewsky), he filmed another exciting heist, that of a priceless dagger encrusted with diamonds and emeralds from the Treasury at the famed Topkapi Palace in Istanbul. This time, however, he also added humor, proving that a caper film with a comic touch could be both suspenseful as well as exhilaratingly entertaining.

The film opens with Elizabeth Lipp (Melina Mercouri) talking directly to the audience as she leads them on a tour that ends at the display of the dagger she intends to steal. "I'm a thief," she confesses. "Honest." She recruits a former lover, criminal mastermind Walter Harper (Maximilian Schell), who at first declines because the job's too difficult. But he finally agrees if he can hire only amateurs with no prison record. The motley crew he assembles includes a British toymaker (Robert Morley), a mute acrobat known as "The Human Fly," and a strongman. He also needs a sucker to drive a car containing guns and grenades to Istanbul and finds the perfect "schmo" in Arthur Simpson (Peter Ustinov), a disheveled would-be hustler and travel guide who ends up being pressed into duty as a key player in the heist when the strongman is injured.

Most of the humor comes from the characters, especially Ustinov's Mr. Simpson, a performance that earned him an Academy Award for Best Supporting Actor. He's a visual joke dressed in a wrinkled, ill-fitting suit (even funnier are the scenes where he's dressed only in his underwear); his expressive face also finds highly amusing ways of registering emotions ranging from fear and confusion to pleasure and triumph. Among the film's comic highlights is a scene in which Elizabeth employs her sultry charms to convince Simpson he's strong enough to carry out his assigned task followed by the hilarious sight of the poor man, who is deathly afraid of heights, nervously scuttling across the rooftops of Topkapi Palace.

The final joke in the film at first appears to be on the thieves themselves when their successful heist is sabotaged at the last moment by a bird. However, when we next see the intrepid gang now housed in a Turkish prison, Elizabeth whispers to her associates through the bars that separate them, "I have an idea. There's a secret stairway in the Kremlin ...The Romanov Jewels." The film ends with the entire gang frolicking in the snow in front of the Kremlin in Moscow's Red Square.

Topkapi takes full advantage of the picturesque Istanbul setting, showcasing the exotic city's many visual delights. The detailed presentation of the actual heist, which is executed with acrobatic precision, is done with great flair. But it is Dassin's integration of humor into the heist formula that elevates the film to a new level of entertainment.

How to Steal a Million (1966)

Director William Wyler came up with a novel approach to the caper film in *How to Steal a Million* (screenplay by Harry Kurnitz): the object of the heist isn't cash secured in a bank vault or a fortune in jewelry stashed in a safe but a statue on public display in a museum. And the motivation isn't profit: the statue is worthless. Nor does the heist involve a crack crew of criminals or con men. It's carried out by a pair of amateur thieves, a man and a woman who have just met. In the end, the payoff isn't really the statue but the flowering of the romantic relationship that develops between the couple.

Nicole Bonnet (Audrey Hepburn, enchanting as usual) is worried that her father Charles (Hugh Griffith), a skilled art forger, will sooner or later get caught, especially after he loans a statue of Venus by Cellini (in reality, a fake made by his father) to be displayed in a Paris museum. Then, in the "meeting cute" tradition of romantic comedies, Nicole is introduced to Simon Dermott (a very suave Peter O'Toole) when she accidentally shoots him in the arm when she interrupts him as he's about to steal one of her father's fake Van Goghs from the home she shares with him. When she later learns that the Venus statue is going to be authenticated for insurance purposes, she comes up with the idea of convincing

Dermott to steal it. He, of course, agrees to help. Who could resist Audrey Hepburn?

Once the caper story gets under way, the movie deftly combines thievery with romance and comedy. Instead of using any of the sophisticated techniques that are a staple in many such films, Dermott pulls off the theft with the help of a pair of pliers, a piece of chalk, a magnet, and a boomerang. The film gets plenty of comic mileage out of the frantic museum guards, assisted by a dozen French policemen, who dash around the museum after Dermott repeatedly sets off the alarm system. Comic pratfalls and cops running around helter skelter are played for laughs (as is the animated mustache of a French actor named Moustache). Meanwhile, in a quieter and more intimate scene in the tiny broom closet where they are scrunched together, Nicole and Dermott banter humorously while they not surprisingly realize they are in love. In the end, the very elegant Hepburn (ordinarily dressed for the film in high fashion by Givenchy) disguises herself as a scrubwoman and begins cleaning the floors of the museum until she is able to grab the fake Venus statue and hide it in her bucket.

In a final twist, it turns out that Dermott is also a fake. He's no burglar, but a private detective whose specialty is art fraud. But his first outing as a thief is a smashing success as he gets the girl and saves the reputation of her father.

The Italian Job (1969 and 2003)

The Italian Job (directed by Peter Collinson, screenplay by Troy Kennedy Martin) is a moderately entertaining caper film, though much of its humor is more of the add-on variety than organic to the story. Ex-con Charlie Croker (Michael Caine) inherits plans from a criminal mastermind for the heist of a lifetime: stealing four million dollars of gold bullion being transported from the Turin, Italy, airport to a local bank; the success of the plan hinges on the ability of a trio of Mini Cooper cars to cause a massive traffic jam in the center of the city.

The lead-up to the robbery isn't particularly funny, except for the scene where one of Corker's henchmen accidentally blows a van to smithereens, prompting Corker to reprimand him with the famous line, "You were only supposed to blow the bloody doors off." (The line was chosen in a 2003 survey as British moviegoers' favorite line, beating out Clark Gable's "Frankly my dear, I don't give a damn"). To heighten the humor, the filmmakers added a jaunty musical score by Quincy Jones and a group of comics whose sole purpose is comedy, with mixed results. For example, famed English comedian Benny Hill plays a computer genius, but his main job is to milk humor out of his character's unhealthy obsession with overweight women. A more successful comic performance comes from urbane British playwright Noel Coward (the director's godfather) as Mr. Bridger, the financial backer of the scheme who runs his crime empire from the prison he also appears to run.

The visual highlight of the film is the now-famous car chase involving the Mini Coopers as they climb up and down stairs, hurtle alongside crowded sidewalk cafes, drive up and over roofs, race across buildings, and dash through the sewers, all with the local police in hot pursuit like an Italian version of the Keystone Kops. Unfortunately for the film, the cars have more comic personality than Charlie's henchmen.

The film ends on a genuine cliffhanger: as the robbers and their gold are balanced precariously on the side of a mountain, Charlie utters the movie's final line, "Hang on, lads, I've got a great idea." The ending certainly seems to promise a sequel, which never happened. The film, however, did inspire a remake in 2003, written by Wayne and Donna Powers and directed by F. Gary Gray, that gives viewers two heists for the price of one.

The film opens with the nifty robbery of a safe containing thirty-five million dollars worth of gold bars from a palazzo in Venice followed by a stunning chase sequence through the city's picturesque canals. The heist was carried out by of a team of experts led by Charlie Coker (Mark Wahlberg) and John Bridger (Donald Sutherland), playing a far more active role than the character portrayed by Noel Coward in the earlier film. But things take an unexpected twist when one member of the team (Edward Norton) double crosses his partners and grabs all the gold for himself, killing John Bridger in the process. The movie now becomes a revenge thriller with Charlie and his team, joined by Bridger's daughter (Charlize Theron), a professional safecracker, plotting to steal the money back.

The revenge heist is the main focus of the film, and although the scene shifts to a location far from Italy—Los Angeles—a trio of Mini Coopers once again plays a key role in the plan's (and the film's) success. The remake downplays the humor of the original somewhat (though it does a much better job of integrating it into the story), but like those souped-up models of the Mini Coopers at the end, this slick and stylish updated version leaves the original in its dust.

The Sting (1973)

The Sting (directed by George Roy Hill, screenplay by David S. Ward) opens with the first few notes of Scott Joplin's jaunty ragtime piano classic, "The Entertainer," which promises that what follows will be fun. The first faces the viewer sees are those of Paul Newman and Robert Redford, whose reunion four years after their previous outing in *Butch Cassidy and the Sundance Kid* (also directed by Hill) ensures that what follows will indeed be enjoyable.

Set in Chicago in 1936, the film features grifters, gangsters, gamblers, con men, and crooked cops. The action begins with a successful scam pulled off by Johnny Hooker (Robert Redford) and his partner Luther which has tragic consequences: though they pocket $11,000, they learn that the cash they stole actually belonged to a violent New York gangster named Doyle Lonnegan (Robert Shaw). When Luther, who had planned to retire on his share of the loot, is murdered by Lonnegan's henchmen, Hooker teams up with a veteran con man named Henry Gondorff (Paul Newman) to avenge Luther's death by pulling off a once-in-a lifetime sting on Lonnegan.

Caper films often derive their humor from the bungling efforts of a bunch of amateurs who aren't up to the task of executing a complicated scam. The crew that Gondorff assembles is composed of the best con artists in the business. And their target isn't some anonymous bank but a murderous gangster who deserves what he gets. One of the film's many pleasures is sharing the enjoyment these pros get from planning and then carrying out their elaborate sting.

The film's humor emerges naturally out of character and situation. A good example is a scene that takes place on a train heading to Chicago. Using the cash his girlfriend has picked from Lonnegan's pocket, Gondorff buys his way into a high-stakes poker game. He pretends to be drunk, loudly brandishing an almost full bottle of gin, which the audience knows is largely filled with water. Lonnegan, upset at Gondorff's boorish behavior, insists that he put on a tie he provides. Gondorff later returns the favor by sneezing and then wiping his nose on the borrowed item. After Lonnegan secretly switches to a marked deck and deals himself an apparently unbeatable hand, it looks like Gondorff is headed for defeat. Gondorff, however, proves to be an even better cheater by somehow managing to give himself a winning hand that fleeces Lonnegan out of $15,000 and sets him up for the Big Con being planned for him.

The Sting is a sleek and stylish comic caper film that benefits from a smart script, outstanding performances by the entire cast, a melodious soundtrack by Marvin Hamlisch, and the on-screen charisma of Newman and Redford. Its many achievements were honored with seven Academy Awards, including those for Best Picture, Best Director, Best Screenplay, and Best Musical Score.

Bottle Rocket (1996)

Bottle Rocket (directed by Wes Anderson, screenplay by Anderson and Owen Wilson) started out as a thirteen-minute black-and-white film made four years earlier by University of Texas friends Anderson (who would later go on to direct such hits as *Rushmore* and *The Grand Budapest Hotel*) and Wilson. Dignan (Owen Wilson) recruits two buddies, Anthony (Luke Wilson, Owen's brother), and Tom (Robert Musgrave) to help him begin executing his ambitious 75-year plan for a series of heists he has carefully written out in his notebook. The plan is doomed from the start. Dignan's boyish enthusiasm is matched only by his sweet ineptness; Tom's sole qualification for the job is that he's the only one who owns a car. The three guys behave like delusional kids playing at being adult bad guys, which gives the film the kind of quirky comic charm that has become a trademark of Anderson's later films.

The trio prepares for the big score by purchasing a gun, getting some explosives, and taping bandages on their noses (when asked why they need to do this, Dignan replies, "Exactly"), then going out and robbing a bookstore. With a plastic sack of cash in hand, the three of them hit the road as fugitives, or as Dignan in his typically goofy manner puts it, "On the road from Johnny Law. It ain't no trip to Cleveland."

Eventually they get around to the big score. Dignan completes his gang with the addition of Kumar and Applejack, two members of the lawn-mowing crew he once worked with. Now armed with walkie-talkies, colorful nicknames (Birddog, Scarecrow, Jackknife) and dressed in identical yellow jumpsuits, the merry band of misfits heads off to break into a safe. Not surprisingly, everything goes wrong: the elevator breaks down, the workers in the warehouse where the safe is located unexpectedly return from lunch early, a smoke bomb sets off the fire alarm, Applejack is accidentally shot in the arm, and the doors of their escape van are locked. Worst of all, the safecracker can't figure out how to open the safe. So much for big dreams.

Like the cheap skyrocket that gives the movie its name, *Bottle Rocket* lacks the dazzle of such heist classics as *The Sting* or *Ocean's Eleven*. But its low-key, droll approach to the caper film successfully launched the careers of Wes Anderson and the Wilson brothers and in the two decades since its release it has become something of a cult classic.

Fargo (1996)

Fargo (written and directed by Joel and Ethan Coen) is a much darker comedy than their earlier film, *Raising Arizona*. Both movies involve kidnappings, but where *Raising Arizona* is a goofy slapstick comedy, *Fargo* is more violent and tragic. Unlike the earlier film where a baby twice falls off a moving car and is unharmed, innocent people die in the later film. The location changes from sunny Arizona to the bleak wintery landscape of Minnesota and the rollicking soundtrack that accompanied the action in *Raising Arizona* is replaced by more somber and ominous music. Despite the differences, however, the Coen brothers' trademark humor is still very much an integral part of the mix.

Fargo is a botched-caper movie. Jerry Lundegaard (William H. Macy) is the sales manager at a Minneapolis car dealership owned by his father-in-law. He has gotten himself into a big hole financially and comes up with a plan to raise cash by hiring a pair of guys to kidnap his wife and hold her for ransom, which her wealthy father will pay and which he will split with the kidnappers. Then things go very wrong. After his father-in-law agrees to a business proposition Jerry has made, his wife no longer needs to be kidnapped, but it's too late to call it off. And then one of the kidnappers shoots a policeman who has stopped their car over a minor license infraction, as well as a pair of innocent victims who happened to witness the shootings. The murders occur in Brainerd, Minnesota, whose police chief, a very pregnant Marge Gunderson (Frances McDormand), is called in to investigate.

Fargo is a film of contrasts. Instead of being shot in the dark tones of a noir, the violent action unfolds in a bright landscape of snowy white. Humor is also created in the contrast between the macabre and the mundane. The film is filled with details of everyday life that at first seem out of place in a grisly crime story. Some of this humor is visual: we watch as a very pregnant Marge wrapped in a bulky coat waddles around the gruesome murder scene along the highway, stopping momentarily to vomit not because of the bloody killings but due to morning sickness; shortly afterwards, we watch her heap piles of food on her plate at a lunch buffet.

Scenes like these emphasize the ordinary reality of life lived amidst the presence of the dead bodies.

As in *Raising Arizona*, much of the humor comes from the language. *Raising Arizona* used the disparity between the sunny language of the main character's narration and the action he described for comic effect. Here the humor is derived from the Minnesota language the characters speak. (Born and raised in the state, the Coen brothers know it very well). Marked by lilting Scandinavian inflections and peppered with homespun expressions like "Okey Dokey," "Oh, geez," "you betcha," "you're darned tootin'" and "for Pete's sake," the distinctive flavor of Minnesota speech isn't necessarily humorous but becomes so when employed as the quaint discourse in a bloody crime story.

Kidnapper Carl Showalter, played by Steve Buscemi with his trademark jittery irritability, is another major source of humor. A foul-mouthed compulsive talker with a hair-trigger temper, he doesn't handle frustration well. Little annoyances drive him to Yosemite Sam–like temper tantrums. When he can't get a signal on his television set, he lashes out insanely, hammering it with his fists while pleading, "Plug me into the ozone, baby" (56). A parking lot attendant who insists he is required to charge Carl, even though he drove in only long enough to steal a license plate from another car, unleashes another torrent of foul-mouthed abuse. Getting shot in the mouth doesn't stop his talking, just turns his steady stream of invective into garbled mush: e.g., "Jeshush Shrist…. Jeshush fuchem Shrist!" Seeing the poor fellow's sock-clad foot being fed into a wood chipper by his partner at the end of the film shouldn't be funny. But it is.

The film earned a Best Actress Academy Award for Frances McDormand and a Best Original Screenplay for the Coen brothers. In 2014, it also inspired an award-winning TV series that introduces new characters but uses the same atmospheric wintery setting, homespun Minnesota language, and quirkiness to capture the film's distinctive blend of dark comedy and gruesome violence.

Ocean's Eleven (2001)

Ocean's Eleven (directed by Steven Soderbergh, screenplay by Ted Griffin) is an entertaining remake of *Ocean's 11* (1960; directed by Lewis Milestone, screenplay by Harry Brown and Charles Lederer), which provided Frank Sinatra and his fellow Rat Pack members (Dean Martin, Peter Lawford, Sammy Davis, Jr., Joey Bishop, Angie Dickinson) ample opportunities to sing, joke, mug, and have fun while pulling off a New Year's Eve robbery of five Las Vegas casinos. While Dean Martin croons for the casino audience's listening pleasure, his partners pull off the heist effortlessly. Unfortunately, in classic best-laid-plans-go-awry fashion, the loot ends up in a coffin headed to the crematorium. But all is not lost, for some four decades later the film would inspire a successful trio of remakes.

Oceans Eleven boasts an even more celebrated cast of A-list movie stars (George Clooney, Brad Pitt, Matt Damon, Andy Garcia, Julia Roberts) and seasoned pros (Don Cheadle, Elliott Gould, Carl Reiner) who effortlessly deliver the comic goods. The heist is carried out with a mixture of ingenious scams and eye-popping maneuvers performed by a Chinese acrobat. The film hums along with plenty of laughs thanks to the clever byplay between the actors, whose easy charm animates the whole enterprise. Unlike *Ocean's 11*, which struggled too hard to be hip, the remake is permeated by what might be called "Clooney cool." These guys make stealing $150 million look like so much fun.

Soderbergh followed up the critical and popular success of *Ocean's Eleven* with a pair of sequels. *Ocean's Twelve* (2004) reunites the same cast, adds Catherine Zeta-Jones to the mix, and sends them all off to exotic locations in Europe in search of new places to rob. *Ocean's Thirteen* (2007) returns to Las Vegas and adds Al Pacino to the cast as the victim of their latest scam. There are still plenty of humorous moments amidst the criminal proceedings, but not surprisingly neither film fully captures the high-spirited magic of Soderbergh's first effort.

Cops

The police have been used for comic purposes in movies since 1912 when Mack Sennett began featuring a group of seven bumbling cops in a series of silent films he made for the Keystone Film Company. The Keystone Kops became famous for their frantic behavior in one crazy chase after another. Why are cops running around helter skelter in circles funny? Film historian Jeanine Basinger offers this theory:

> People hate cops. Even people who have never had anything to do with cops hate them. Of course, we count on them to keep order and to protect us when we need protecting, and we love them on television shows in which they have nerves of steel and hearts of gold, but in the abstract, as a nation, collectively we hate them. They are too much

like high school principals. We're very happy to see their pants fall down, and they
look good to us with pie on their faces [76].

And so for the next hundred years and more, cops racing around and bump-
ing into one another have become a staple in comic crime movies and, to
a lesser degree because their humor is largely visual, in some comic crime
novels.

A Shot in the Dark (1964)

A different kind of bumbling cop is French Police Inspector Jacques
Clouseau, first portrayed by Peter Sellers in *The Pink Panther* (1963). Clouseau would eventually appear in eleven films and be played by several
other actors including Alan Arkin, Roger Moore, and Steve Martin, and
was even featured in animated cartoons. But no one surpassed the comic
genius of Peter Sellers, and of the five films in which he appeared, none
showed him at his comic best better than *A Shot in the Dark* (1964; directed
by Blake Edwards, co-written by Edwards and William Peter Blatty).

Clouseau is supremely confident yet woefully incompetent. Usually
dressed in a trim trench coat and sporting a classy mustache, he's the very
picture of French dignity and authority; that is, until he moves and reveals
himself to be a clumsy buffoon who has never picked up an object he
couldn't drop or encountered a piece of furniture he didn't trip over. He
is equally bumbling in his police work, mistaking clues and reaching wrong
conclusions, all of which adds up to pure delight for the audience.

Sellers was a masterful slapstick actor and the funniest bits in his
films are visual—stumbling over objects, stepping on the feet of suspects
he has gathered together in a room, getting tangled up in a telephone cord,
opening a jar of cold cream to smell it, leaving a big dab of it on his nose,
etc. Dressing in a suit of iron for a costume party or investigating at a nud-
ist colony result in extended scenes of inspired clutziness. What heightens
the humor in each instance is Sellers's deadpan expression; like Buster
Keaton, he never cracks a smile while leaving a trail of mayhem behind
him.

Not all the humor is visual. Sellers speaks in French-accented English
with his own peculiar twists: he mangles big dramatic pronouncements—
"You killed him in a rit of fealous jage"—and his odd pronunciations—
"beumb" for "bomb," "beump" for "bump" and "meth" for "moth"—
heighten the comic confusion. His explanations for his clumsiness are
equally silly, whether he argues that, "Everything I do is carefully planned"

or shrugs off crushing a violin which he inadvertently walks over by saying, "When you've seen one Stradivarius, you've seen them all."

Some of the characters surrounding Clouseau also provide humor. His long-suffering boss, who dismisses his underling as an idiot, a nincompoop, and a lunatic, groans, "Give me ten men like Clouseau and I could destroy the world." He develops comic twitches and facial tics and eventually turns into a homicidal madman trying to rid the world of his menace. Clouseau also hires a karate expert named Cato to help him improve his martial arts skills by attacking him at unexpected times, which results in several hilarious encounters.

Crime in a Clouseau film is simply an excuse to launch the Inspector off on another bungled investigation. But thanks to the talents of Peter Sellers, crime-solving has never been so much fun.

Beverly Hills Cop (1984)

Casting a well-known comedian in a crime film might help ensure that the effort will be funny, but it doesn't guarantee the result will be a good movie. That's not the case with *Beverly Hills Cop* (directed by Martin Brest, screenplay by Daniel Petrie, Jr.), which unquestionably benefits from the comedic talents of Eddie Murphy. But the film has much more to offer than jokes as it effectively balances humor with a serious murder mystery while also incorporating elements ranging from buddy movies to Keystone Kop comedies.

Eddie Murphy plays Axel Foley, a brash undercover Detroit cop whose childhood friend is murdered outside Foley's apartment while on a visit to Detroit from L.A. where he worked as a security guard for a Beverly Hills art dealer. Foley takes some vacation time and heads to California to investigate his friend's murder. He soon runs into opposition from some murderous drug smugglers as well as the Beverly Hills police who aren't happy about a visiting cop working by his own rules in their town.

A street-smart cop with a cocky attitude and an irreverent sense of humor, Foley may bend the rules but he gets the job done. He's both funny and convincing whether he's posing as a government inspector to get access to a customs warehouse or as a gay hustler trying to gain admission into a private club to question the prominent Beverly Hills art dealer he suspects was involved in his friend's murder. He also has a playful sense of fun which is shown in how he deals with a pair of Beverly Hills cops who have been assigned to tail him. After distracting them by having sandwiches delivered to the parked car where they are watching the entrance to the hotel where he's staying, he disables their car by sticking a banana up its tailpipe. It stalls when they try to follow him, allowing him to safely drive away.

Murphy isn't the only source of humor in the film. Crusty veteran Beverly Hills cop John Taggert (John Ashton) and his wet-behind-the-ears partner Billy Rosewood (Judge Reinhold) generate some laughs out of their odd-couple pairing. They also contribute some slapstick humor as they perform a Laurel and Hardy imitation while trying to climb over a wall at a Beverly Hills estate. A half dozen of their fellow Beverly Hills cops do a Keystone Kop imitation by crashing their vehicles into one another during a wild car chase.

Beverly Hills Cop was the highest grossing film of 1984 and spawned a pair of sequels, both of which starred Eddie Murphy and also featured the return of Taggert and Rosewood. Though the films succeeded in cashing in on the popularity of the original, both fell short of re-capturing its adroit balance of crime, comedy, and cop story.

The Guard (2011)

Partnering a pair of mismatched cops—either a by-the-book cop with a maverick or a seasoned veteran with a wide-eyed rookie—has proven to be a reliable source of humor and a very lucrative formula for box-office success. A representative list of comic cop buddy films would begin with *48 Hrs.* (1984; Nick Nolte and Eddie Murphy) and include the following, many of which became franchises that spawned multiple sequels: *Lethal Weapon* (1987; Mel Gibson and Danny Glover); *Bad Boys* (1995; Will Smith and Martin Lawrence); *Rush Hour* (1998; Chris Tucker and Jackie Chan); *21 Jump Street* (2012; Channing Tatum and Jonah Hill); *The Other Guys* (2010; Will Farrell and Mark Wahlberg).

Variations on the two-man formula, which range from the mildly amusing to the embarrassing, have included the pairing of a cop and his mother (*Stop! or My Mom Will Shoot*; 1992: Sylvester Stallone and Estelle Getty), a cop and an eight-year-old boy (*Cop and a Half*; 1993: Burt Reynolds), a cop and a dog (*K-9*; 1989: James Belushi; *Turner and Hooch*; 1989; Tom Hanks; *Top Dog*; 1995; Chuck Norris), and a recent rarity, two women (*The Heat*; 2013: Sandra Bullock and Melissa McCarthy).

Most of these films are action-oriented with central characters created largely for laughs. Occasionally a filmmaker will tone down the noise and replace cartoon behavior with characters who talk and act like real people. One such film is *The Guard,* a darkly comic buddy cop film written and directed by John Michael McDonagh, brother of *In Bruges's* writer/director Martin, which became the most successful Irish independent film of all time. It stars Brendan Gleeson (who also starred in *In Bruges*) as a loutish Irish cop named Gerry Boyle who works in the west of Ireland. A major international drug-smuggling operation draws the attention of the FBI, which sends a strait-laced African American agent named Wendell Everett (Don Cheadle) to Ireland to lead the investigation.

The pairing of the mis-matched duo produces great comic dialogue similar to that between Gleeson and Colin Farrell in *In Bruges,* but with a decidedly racist twist. When Everett accuses Boyle of being racist for remarking, after being shown a photograph of a white suspect in the drug operation, that he thought only blacks were drug dealers, Boyle explains, "I'm Irish, racism is part of my culture." Boyle loves needling Everett, even when he compliments him on his well-dressed appearance: "Nice outfit. Do you juggle as well?" Gradually, however, we come to realize that there's much more to Boyle than his offensive persona, and the pair end up making an effective team. Along the way we are also treated to some wildly entertaining (and largely politically incorrect) banter between the two.

Detectives, Amateur and Private

Private detectives, both amateur and professional, have long been featured in movies. Many of Hollywood's most popular films have been serious stories about crime solvers: *The Maltese Falcon, The Big Sleep, Farewell, My Lovely, Kiss Me Deadly, Chinatown.* But there have also been several classic comic detective films as well, many of which have found humor by toying with the conventions of the more serious ones.

The Thin Man (1934)

The Thin Man (directed by W. S. Van Dyke; screenplay by Albert Hackett and Frances Goodrich) was the first of six films featuring husband and wife Nick and Nora Charles, characters originally created by Dashiell Hammett for a novel of the same name that also appeared in 1934. Nick (William Powell) is a retired private detective and Nora (Myrna Loy) a rich heiress; their witty back-and-forth banter soon became a trademark of the series (e.g., Nick, referring to a newspaper story about his encounter the previous night with an armed man, tells Nora, "I'm a hero. I was shot twice in the *Tribune*." "I read where you were shot five times in the tabloids," she says. "It's not true," he replies. "He didn't come anywhere near my tabloids"). Nick manages to solve crimes without having to do very much detective work, which leaves him and his wife plenty of free time for their favorite activity, drinking martinis.

Although Hammett also wrote original stories for two additional films, *After the Thin Man* (1936) and *Another Thin Man* (1939), the mystery elements take a definite back seat to the glamorous lifestyle and affectionate relationship of the sophisticated couple. Though he lived comfortably off the money he earned from the characters he created, Hammett later confessed that, "nobody ever invented a more insufferably smug pair of characters" than Nick and Nora Charles. "They can't take that away from me, even for $40,000" (Tuska 201).

The films became wildly popular largely because of their breezy comic tone. Roger Ebert singled out Powell's performance, noting that he "is to dialogue as Fred Astaire is to dance. His delivery is so droll and insinuating, so knowing and innocent at the same time, that it hardly matters what he's saying" ("Thin"). Eventually, however, the films devolved into little more than sophisticated situation comedies, with the married couple encountering comic situations involving either their dog Asta or son Nick Jr.: e.g., on one occasion Nick, whose liquid intake is normally limited to martinis, is forced to choke down a glass of milk in order to persuade little Nick to drink his. Myrna Loy herself even reportedly complained that what had once been a give-and-take camaraderie between Nick and Nora eventually degenerated into nothing more than a "sequence of gagging wisecracks" (Tuska 203).

Murder by Death (1976) and *The Cheap Detective* (1978)

In the late seventies, playwright Neil Simon and director Robert Moore collaborated on an entertaining pair of mystery spoofs. *Murder by Death* brings together five famous detectives to solve a murder at a country house owned by a rich man (Truman Capote) and overseen (ironically) by a blind butler (Alec Guinness). The movie has great fun with its comic versions of Charlie Chan (Peter Sellers), Hercule Poirot (James Coco),

Nick and Nora Charles (David Niven and Maggie Smith), Sam Spade (Peter Falk) and Miss Marple (Elsa Lanchester), though there's nothing particularly memorable about the dialogue or jokes.

More successful is *The Cheap Detective*, a comic spoof of *The Maltese Falcon* and *Casablanca* (with a clever nod or two in the direction of *Chinatown*). Peter Falk, reprising his Bogart imitation from the earlier film, plays San Francisco private eye Lou Peckinpaugh. Like Sam Spade, his partner is murdered, he becomes entangled with a duplicitous femme fatale, and he matches wits with a fat man named Jasper Blubber (John Houseman mimicking Sydney Greenstreet's Casper Guttman) and his sidekick Pepe Damascus (Dom DeLouise impersonating Peter Lorre's Joel Cairo). Lou also gets mixed up in a second case featuring another alluring woman (Louise Fletcher) modeled on Ingrid Bergman's character from *Casablanca*.

All the classic hard-boiled film elements are here: the moody noir cinematography; the jazzy soundtrack; the whiskey in the desk drawer, though this time not in a bottle but already conveniently poured into a glass; and Neil Simon's laugh-a-minute comic riffs on such familiar items as tough-talking cops, "You're gonna be giving the Golden Gate Bridge a new coat of paint ... with your tongue," and wisecracking banter, "She's a student at the Hail Mary, Hail Mary, Sister Therese Convent and Kennels." "Kennels? Isn't that for dogs?" "Well, I'm afraid none of the girls are very pretty."

Dead Men Don't Wear Plaid (1982)

Dead Men Don't Wear Plaid (directed by Carl Reiner, screenplay by Reiner, Steve Martin, and George Gipe) is both an affectionate homage to the classic private-eye noir films of the 1940s as well as a comic parody of many features of the genre. The film incorporates scenes from eighteen vintage films (including such crime classics as *The Glass Key*, *Double Indemnity*, *The Big Sleep*, and *The Postman Always Rings Twice*) into a story about private eye Rigby Reardon (Steve Martin). Reardon is hired by beautiful Juliet Forrest (Rachel Ward) to investigate the murder of her father. Filmed in black and white and featuring costumes by famed designer Edith Head and a score by Miklos Rosza, both of whom worked on many of the vintage films used, *Dead Man Don't Wear Plaid* faithfully recreates the look of the films it is honoring. Thanks to some editing wizardry, Steve Martin even gets to act on screen with Hollywood legends like Humphrey

Bogart, Fred MacMurray, James Cagney, Bette Davis, Ingrid Bergman, Ava Gardner and Lana Turner.

Much of the humor in the film comes from the way it revisits and updates scenes from the older movies, such as the famous one from *To Have and Have Not* where Lauren Bacall tells Humphrey Bogart all he has to do if he wants her is to whistle: "You know how to whistle, don't you? Just put your lips together and blow." In this updated (and sexier) version, Juliet Forrest tells Reardon, "If you need me just call. You know how to call, don't you. You just put your finger in the hole and make tiny little circles." Another familiar scene depicts the hero placing a pair of cigarettes in his mouth, lighting both with one match, and then giving one to the woman he's with. Here Rigby Reardon lights one cigarette, removes it, turns it around and puts the lighted end in his mouth. Then he lights the other end, removes the cigarette, breaks it in two, and gives one half to the woman.

The film also finds humor in silly ongoing jokes—every time Reardon gets shot, always in the same place in his arm, the lovely Juliet sucks the bullet out—funny lines—"I hadn't seen a body put together like that since I solved the case of The Murdered Girl with the Big Tits" and "My plan was to kiss her with every lip on my face"—and parodies of snappy dialogue—"Haven't I seen you somewhere before?" "Maybe, I've been somewhere before."

Who Framed Roger Rabbit (1988)

Another film that gets great comic mileage by combining a crime story with classic film characters of the past is *Who Framed Roger Rabbit* (directed by Robert Zemeckis, screenplay by Jeffrey Price and Robert Watts) In this instance, however, the old-time movie stars are cartoon characters like Donald Duck, Mickey Mouse, Bugs Bunny, Woody Woodpecker, even Betty Boop. Like *Dead Men Don't Wear Plaid*, *Who Framed Roger Rabbit* takes full advantage of film's visual magic to create a technical tour-de-force of eye-popping scenes that combine live action with animation.

Based on Gary K. Wolf's 1981 novel *Who Censored Roger Rabbit?*, the film was a creative collaboration between Disney Studios and Stephen Spielberg. Set in 1947, it features a private eye in a rumpled raincoat named Eddie Valiant (Bob Hoskins) who is hired by a movie mogul to follow the wife of one of his cartoon stars, Roger Rabbit, to determine if she has been unfaithful to him. The rabbit is devastated to learn that his wife, the voluptuous Jessica Rabbit (voiced with sultry flirtatiousness by Kathleen Turner) has been caught playing patty-cake with another man. When that man is later murdered, Roger Rabbit becomes the prime suspect, though Valiant suspects he's being framed. But why and by whom?

The movie magic is on full display once Valiant enters Toontown, where all the famous Hollywood cartoon characters reside. In the end, after several classic battles between human and cartoon characters, the evil criminal Judge Doom (Christopher Lloyd), the mastermind behind everything, is defeated and his scheme to demolish Toontown in order to make way for L.A.'s first freeway is thwarted. All ends well in classic fashion as Porky Pig delivers his famous send-off line, "T-T-T-T-That's all, folks!"

Kiss Kiss Bang Bang (2005)

Kiss Kiss Bang Bang (written and directed by Shane Black) features a two-bit burglar named Harry Lockhart (Robert Downey, Jr.) who ends up posing as a private eye in Los Angeles. The film might well have been alternatively titled *Wink Wink Nod Nod*, for it is full of sly spoofs and cheeky parodies of both pulp era crime fiction (the screenplay is based on a 1941 private-eye novel by Brett Halliday, and each chapter of the film bears the title of a Raymond Chandler book) and any number of classic crime genres. Its convoluted mystery plot is all but incomprehensible, but stellar comic performances, outrageous action, witty dialogue, and clever voice-over narration combine to turn it into one of the funniest among recent crime films.

The individual parts of the film are greater than the whole. Depicting how Harry ends up playing a private eye is one example. As he and his partner flee the site of a burglary they have botched, a woman on a fire escape begins shooting at them, wounding Harry and killing his partner. He manages to escape by bursting into a room where a movie producer and his assistant are casting a role for an upcoming movie. Thinking he's just another actor arriving for an audition, they hand him the script. He begins reading it in a monotone, but when the lines refer to a man whose partner was killed, he becomes so emotional that the producer is impressed by his style of method acting. Next stop, Hollywood.

It is here where Harry joins up with two partners in solving a murder mystery. He crosses paths with a woman named Harmony who has come to Hollywood with dreams of breaking into movies as well as hopes of finding the killer of her younger sister. Amazingly, she turns out to be the same young girl we saw in the opening scene of the movie who was being sawed in half by a young magician, who also just happens to be Harry. The third member of the trio is a homosexual private eye named Perry Shrike (Val Kilmer), widely known as Gay Perry, who is hired to give Harry lessons in how to act like a private eye for a possible film role.

This setup launches several scenes of screwball humor à la Quentin Tarantino. Harry accidentally loses a finger when a door is slammed on it, but manages to get it sewn back on. Later, a pair of tough guys attempt to force him to talk by cutting off that same finger. Then the severed finger is stolen by a dog, who playfully tantalizes Harry by displaying it sticking out of his teeth. Harry can't let the dog keep the finger because if the police find it they will be able to use it to identify him as the killer of a man he has just shot. The problem is solved when the dog helpfully swallows the digit.

The narration, a cross between the typical movie voice-over and a DVD commentary, is especially humorous. Harry admits to being a bad narrator for forgetting to mention important details and chastises himself for unnecessarily describing action that viewers can clearly see for themselves ("I hate it when the narrator does that"). At another point in the film he even warns Times Square audiences not to shout at the screen, and than adds this bit of helpful advice: "Stop picking at that, it'll just get worse." He also criticizes the ending of the film in which one of the characters miraculously survives. "Yeah, boo—hiss, I know—look I hate it too." But the studio wants to avoid a downer ending, so it gets its wish. "It's a dumb movie thing," Harry agrees, but adds, "What do you want me to do, lie about it?"

Sherlock (BBC, 2010–)

Sherlock Holmes has been subjected to every kind of adaptation imaginable. One of the best of them all is *Sherlock*, a BBC series of ninety-minute films about Arthur Conan Doyle's Great Detective that began airing in 2010. All the familiar elements are here: location (London, 221B Baker Street); characters (Mrs. Hudson, Professor Moriarty, Mycroft Holmes, Inspector Lestrade, Mary Morstan); Holmes's habits (violin playing, cocaine, shooting his gun at the wall when he's bored); even his pet phrases ("The game is on"). The one thing that is different is the time period, and that makes all the difference. Steven Moffat and Mark Gatiss, co-creators and writers of the series, have updated the stories to 21st-century London and the look and feel of the contemporary city adds to the series' appeal. But rather than making Holmes and Watson (played with great verve by Benedict Cumberbatch and Martin Freeman) Victorian anachronisms in the modern city, the creators have made the two of them very much at home in the digital age.

One reason for the films' enormous popularity is the way they appeal to two separate audiences: those who know very little about Holmes and Watson as well as those with an intimate knowledge of the original stories. Moffat and Gatiss have managed the tricky task of both "blow[ing] away the Victorian fog" of the Holmes stories ("Unlocking") while at the same time remaining so faithful to them that Moffat can proudly promise, "You'll never see a more obsessively authentic version of Sherlock Holmes than this one" ("Sherlock").

Holmes and Watson have become so familiar in our culture that they are even loved by those who have never read a single Conan Doyle story. For this audience the producers have created younger versions of the famous duo who are no longer Victorian gentlemen but very techno-savvy characters living in 21st-century London. The films take full advantage of all the modern cinematic wizardry, including sweeping cameras shots, speeded-up action, split-screen images, on-screen captions, text messages, all cleverly edited and punctuated by pulsating music. Film audiences raised on the kinetic energy of the Jason Bourne films will feel very much at home viewing this dashing duo of crime-solvers.

The films also use inventive cinematic techniques to illustrate how Sherlock's mind works. In keeping with their overall rapid pace, the films often dispense with Sherlock's virtuoso performances of his deductive brilliance; instead his thoughts are superimposed on the screen, allowing the viewer to immediately see his deductions. In one particularly ingenious sequence in "The Hounds of Baskerville," Sherlock retreats into his "mind palace" in an effort to solve the mystery of the legendary giant hound by shuffling through his memories, which then flash on the screen. Among them are shots of several dog breeds, including a picture of hound dog accompanied by a photograph of Elvis Presley.

Modern technology also plays a key role in transforming Sherlock from a simple genius in the art of deduction into what Stein and Busse term a "millennial technowizard" who knows how to use digital data quickly and instinctively in pursuit of the solution to a mystery (10). For example, instead of reporting back to Sherlock about what he has seen at a crime scene, John can Skype him so he can see the details for himself.

Sherlock even watches YouTube videos when he needs to learn how to do something like fold napkins.

A special treat, however, awaits those with a greater familiarity with Conan Doyle's stories, for the creators inventively play off the originals. For those in the know, hidden jokes abound. In this regard the films resemble novels like *Gulliver's Travels* and *Huckleberry Finn*, which can be enjoyed by young readers not sophisticated enough to grasp the more serious levels of satire and commentary their elders understand. The more familiarity one has with the Holmes canon, the more humorous these new versions are.

The humor begins with the updating of small details, some of which don't need to be changed at all: e.g., like his nineteenth-century counterpart, John was wounded while serving in Afghanistan. Other details are modified only slightly: Sherlock's comment to John, "I am lost without my Boswell," is changed to, "I'd be lost without my blogger," for instead of preparing written accounts of Sherlock's cases, John blogs about his friend's cases. Sherlock even has his own website entitled "The Science of Detection." (The series' creators have actually set up such web sites, which adds to the impression that the pair really exist. It is widely known that for years actual letters have been arriving regularly at 221B Baker Street addressed to Sherlock Holmes; viewers who might wish to believe Sherlock and John are real people can now actually read their writing on the web.)

Conan Doyle's villains are also given a fresh updating. Charles Augustus Milverton, the notorious blackmailer who buys incriminating information to use against others, becomes Charles Augustus Magnussen. Like Rupert Murdoch, he is the foreign-born owner of several London newspapers who secretly gathers information he then uses to gain control over the powerful. Ironically, Magnussen stores his information on hard copies rather than on computers because he knows how easily computers can be hacked, which might remind viewers that several high-level editors at Murdoch's newspapers were forced to resign after being accused of hacking the cellphones of politicians, celebrities, even the royal family in search of scandalous material.

There are also several running gags in the series. One involves the question of the nature of the personal relationship between Sherlock and John, bachelors who share the same flat. Whether or not they also share the same bedroom has been a subject of curiosity from the beginning. The creators of the show have great fun with the whole subject by repeatedly raising and then dismissing such speculation about their possible homosexual relationship. For example, at one point, Sherlock tells John to grab his hand as they prepare an escape. "Now people will definitely talk," says John.

Another gag involves the famous deerstalker hat, which has become a signifying feature of the Holmes identity, though it never actually appeared in Conan Doyle's stories. It was introduced in the Basil Rathbone films and quickly became a permanent part of the image. In *Sherlock*, Holmes grabs such a hat to avoid being identified as he slips past a gaggle of photographers, but then a picture of him in the hat soon goes viral. From then on, the hat he hoped would disguise his identity becomes his trademark.

The banter between Sherlock and John is another ongoing source of humor. Much of it, like that between Nero Wolfe and Archie Goodwin, reflects John's irritation at Sherlock's sometime overbearing attitude. Though Sherlock publicly praises John as "the bravest and kindest and wisest human being I have ever had the good fortune of knowing," he is also a master of the cruel putdown, saying to him at one point, "Dear God, what is it like in your funny little brains? Must be so boring." John later retaliates by telling Sherlock, "Nobody can fake being such an annoying dick all the time." In another episode when Sherlock asks John if he heard him when he told him to punch him in the face, John replies, "I always hear 'punch me in the face' when you're speaking."

"A Scandal in Belgravia," inspired by Conan Doyle's "A Scandal in Bohemia," is the best example of how the creators cleverly mix the old and the new. In the original story, Holmes is hired by the King of Bohemia to recover an incriminating photograph of him and the alluring Irene Adler. Holmes succeeds in gaining entry to her home by disguising himself as a clergyman who has been injured. Once inside, he has Watson toss a smoke bomb through a window to trigger an uproar he knows will cause Irene to instinctively look at the location where the photograph is hidden. But when he returns the following day, she and the photograph are gone. Holmes has been outfoxed by a woman whom he henceforth honors by always referring to her as "*the* woman."

In this episode it is the updated details that provide much of the humor. Sherlock's client is now a female member of the British royal family. Once again Sherlock disguises himself as a clergyman to gain entry to Irene's residence, but this time John causes the disturbance aimed at revealing the photograph's hidden location by holding a burning magazine underneath a smoke detector. And it is Irene Adler herself who uses the phrase "The Woman" in ads for her services as a dominatrix.

Her initial meeting with Sherlock is especially dramatic: she enters the room completely naked, which among other things frustrates any chance he might be able to deduce information about her by examining her clothing. But he outsmarts her by gaining entry to the locked safe where she stores the photographs, now contained on her smartphone, by correctly guessing the digital code—her measurements—which he has determined by gazing at her naked body. Later, she begins sending him text messages that are accompanied by the sound of a woman's sexual moans. The cat-and-mouse flirtatious game the two end up playing involves several clever twists and turns, culminating in Sherlock finally figuring out the four-letter code that unlocks her smartphone—SHER—which changes the display from "I Am ____Locked" to "I am SHERlocked."

The series even has fun with an updating of Sherlock's "death" in "The Reichenbach Fall." In this newer version, the scene switches from the Reichenbach Falls in Switzerland, where Holmes and Moriarty reportedly fell to their deaths, to the roof of St. Bartholomew's Hospital in London, where Sherlock appears to leap to the pavement below. (The producers even manage to work in a nod to the original story by having Moriarty hire an actor to play himself named Richard Brook, whose name resembles Reichenbach.) When Sherlock miraculously appears very much alive two years later, his explanation to John about the ruse is brief and to the point: "The short version, not dead."

Bibliography

Adams, Abby. "Living with a Mystery Writer." In *Murder Ink: The Mystery Reader's Companion*. Edited by Dilys Winn. New York: Workman, 1977: 76–78.

Ambrose, Terry. "Craig Johnson on the Latest Walt Longmire Mystery." terryambrose.com. 7 May 2015. Web. 18 Mar. 2016.

Aussenac, Dominique. "Retournement des morts." *Le Matricule des anges*. Aug.-Sept. 1999.

Bargainnier, Earl, ed. *Comic Crime*. Bowling Green, OH: Bowling Green State University Popular Press, 1987.

Baring-Gould, William. *Nero Wolfe of West 35th Street*. New York: Penguin, 1982.

Basinger, Jeanine. *Silent Stars*. New York: Alfred A. Knopf, 2000.

Bateman, Colin. *Belfast Confidential*. CB Creative Books, 2005. Kindle Edition.

_____. *The Day of the Jack Russell*. London: Headline, 2009.

_____. *Divorcing Jack*. CB Creative Books, 1995. Kindle Edition.

_____. *Dr. Yes*. CB Creative Books, 2010. Kindle Edition.

_____. *Driving Big Davie*. CB Creative Books, 2004. Kindle Edition.

_____. *The Horse with My Name*. London: Headline, 2002.

_____. *Mystery Man*. London: Headline, 2009.

_____. *Nine Inches*. CB Creative Books, 2011. Kindle Edition.

_____. *Of Wee Sweetie Mice and Men*. CB Creative Books, 1996. Kindle Edition.

_____. *Shooting Sean*. CB Creative Books, 2012. Kindle Edition.

_____. *Turbulent Priests*. CB Creative Books, 1999. Kindle Edition.

Bauer, Eric. "The Mouth and the Method." In *Quentin Tarantino: Interviews*. Rev. ed. Edited by Gerald Peary. Jackson: University Press of Mississippi, 2013: 12–17.

Belth, Alex. "The Professional: Donald E. Westlake." *The Stacks*. thestacks.deadspin.com. 14 May 2014. Web. 20 Aug. 2016.

Berger, Peter L. *Redeeming Laughter: The Comic Dimension of Human Experience*. New York: Walter de Gruyter, 1997.

Block, Lawrence. *The Burglar in the Closet*. New York: Dutton, 1995.

_____. *The Burglar in the Rye*. New York: Dutton, 1999.

_____. *The Burglar on the Prowl*. New York: William Morrow, 2004.

_____. *The Burglar Who Liked to Quote Kipling*. New York: Signet, 1997.

_____. *The Burglar Who Painted Like Mondrian*. New York: Signet, 1999.

_____. *The Burglar Who Studied Spinoza*. New York: Random House, 1980.

_____. *The Burglar Who Traded Ted Williams*. New York: Harper Torch, 2005.

_____. *Burglars Can't Be Choosers*. New York: Dutton, 1995.

Booth, William. "He Came from the Swamp." *Washington Post*. 4 Mar. 1992. Web. 23 Aug. 2016.

Breen, Jon L. *Hair of the Sleuthhound: Parodies of Mystery Fiction.* Metuchen, NJ: Scarecrow Press, 1982.

_____. "The Mystery of Craig Rice." *The Weekly Standard.* 27 May 2002. Web. 27 Sept. 2016.

Brett, Simon. *Cast, in Order of Disappearance.* In *Simon Brett: Four Complete Mysteries.* Avenel, NJ: Wings Books, 1993.

_____. *A Comedian Dies.* New York: Scribner, 1979.

_____. *Corporate Bodies.* New York: Maxwell Macmillan, 1992.

_____. *Dead Giveaway.* New York: Scribner, 1986.

_____. *Dead Room Farce.* New York: St. Martin's Press, 1998.

_____. *A Decent Interval.* Sutton, England: Créme de la crime, 2013.

_____. "The Origins of Charles Paris." In *The Fine Art of Murder.* Edited by Ed Gorman, Martin H. Greenberg, Larry Segriff with Jon L. Breen. New York: Carroll & Graf, 1993: 183–85.

_____. *Situation Tragedy.* New York: Scribner, 1981.

_____. *So Much Blood.* In *Simon Brett: Four Complete Mysteries.* Avenel, NJ: Wings Books, 1993.

_____. *Star Trap.* In *Simon Brett: Four Complete Mysteries.* Avenel, NJ: Wings Books, 1993.

_____. *What Bloody Man Is That?* Severn House Digital, 2012. Kindle Edition.

Browne, Ray B. "Christie Tea or Chandler Beer." *The Armchair Detective* 18:3 (Summer 1985): 262–66.

Bruce, Leo. *Case for Three Detectives.* Chicago: Chicago Review Press, 2005.

Bruen, Ken. *Ammunition.* New York: Minotaur, 2007.

_____. *Blitz.* New York: Minotaur, 2004.

_____. *Calibre.* New York: Minotaur, 2006.

_____. *The Devil.* London: Transworld, 2010.

_____. *The Guards.* New York: Minotaur, 2003.

_____. *Headstone.* New York: Mysterious Press, 2011.

_____. *The Killing of the Tinkers.* New York: Minotaur, 2004.

_____. *The Magdalen Martyrs.* New York: Minotaur, 2003.

_____. *The McDead.* In *The White Trilogy.* Boston: Kate's Mystery Books, 2003.

_____. *Priest.* New York: Minotaur, 2006.

_____. *Purgatory.* New York: Mysterious Press, 2013.

_____. *Sanctuary.* New York: Minotaur, 2009.

_____. *Vixen.* New York: Minotaur, 2005.

_____. *A White Arrest.* London: Do-Not-Press, 1998.

Brunet, Rob. "Rob Brunet Interviews Carl Hiaasen." *The Thrill Begins.* n.d. Web. 12 Nov. 2016.

Burke, Declan. "Why Colin Bateman Is a Mystery Man No More." *Dublin Herald.* 14 Nov. 2012. Web. 19 Oct. 2015.

Byrne, Jennifer. "Interview with Carl Hiaasen." *Foreign Correspondent.* abc.net.au. 16 May 2001. Web. 23 Aug. 2016.

Camilleri, Andrea. *Angelica's Smile.* Translated from *Il sorriso di Angelica* (2010) by Stephen Sartarelli. New York: Penguin, 2014.

_____. *Excursion to Tindari.* Translated from *La gita a Tindari* (2000) by Stephen Sartarelli. New York: Penguin, 2005.

_____. *The Paper Moon.* Translated from *La luna di carta* (2005) by Stephen Sartarelli. New York: Penguin, 2008.

_____. *The Potter's Field.* Translated from *Il campo del vasaio* (2008) by Stephen Sartarelli. New York: Penguin, 2011.

_____. *Rounding the Mark.* Translated from *Il giro di boa* (2003) by Stephen Sartarelli. New York: Penguin, 2006.

_____. *The Shape of Water.* Translated from *La forma dell' acqua* (1994) by Stephen Sartarelli. New York: Penguin, 2002.

_____. *The Smell of the Night.* Translated from *L'odore della notte* (2001) by Stephen Sartarelli. New York: Penguin, 2005.

_____. *The Snack Thief.* Translated from *Il ladro di merendine* (1996) by Stephen Sartarelli. New York: Penguin, 2004.

_____. *The Terra-Cotta Dog.* Translated from *Il cane di terracotta* (1996) by Stephen Sartarelli. New York: Penguin, 2003.

_____. *The Track of Sand.* Translated from *La pista di sabbia* (2007) by Stephen Sartarelli. New York: Penguin, 2010.

_____. *Treasure Hunt.* Translated from *La caccia al tesoro* (2010) by Stephen Sartarelli. New York: Penguin, 2013.

_____. *Voice of the Violin.* Translated from *La voce del violino* (1997) by Stephen Sartarelli. New York: Penguin, 2003.

Cannon, Mark. "A Comic Crime Writer." *Publishers Weekly.* 2 Feb. 2007. Web. 10 Aug. 2016.

Carpenter, Richard C. "Martha Grimes." In *St. James Guide to Crime & Mystery Writers,* 4th Edition. Edited by Jay P. Pederson. Detroit: St. James Press, 1996: 460–62.

Carr, David. "Leaving Out What Will Be Skipped." *New York Times.* 12 May 2005. Web. 5 June 2015.

Carr, John C. *The Craft of Crime: Conversations with Crime Writers.* Boston: Houghton Mifflin, 1983.

Carroll, Noel. *Humour: A Very Short Introduction.* Oxford: Oxford University Press, 2014.

Chandler, Raymond. *The Big Sleep.* New York: Ballantine, 1971.

_____. *Farewell, My Lovely.* New York: Vintage Crime, 1992.

_____. *The High Window.* New York: Ballantine, 1973.

_____. *The Little Sister.* New York: Ballantine, 1973.

_____. *The Long Goodbye.* New York: Ballantine, 1973.

_____. *Selected Letters of Raymond Chandler.* Edited by Frank MacShane. New York: Columbia University Press, 1981.

_____. *The Simple Art of Murder.* New York: Ballantine, 1977.

Christian, Ed, ed. *The Post-Colonial Detective.* London: Palgrave, 2001.

Coen, Ethan, and Joel Coen: *Collected Screenplays 1.* London: Faber and Faber, 2002.

_____. *Fargo.* London: Faber and Faber, 1996.

Collins, Max Allan. "Screwball Tragedy." Introduction to Jonathan Latimer. *Headed for a Hearse.* New York: International Polygonics, 1990.

Cousins, Norman. *Anatomy of an Illness as Perceived by the Patient.* New York: Norton, 1979.

Crispin, Edmund. *Buried for Pleasure.* New York: Garland, 1976.

_____. *Frequent Hearses.* New York: Penguin, 1982.

_____. *The Glimpses of the Moon.* New York: Walker and Company, 1978.

_____. *Holy Disorders.* London: Ipso Books, 2014. Kindle Edition.

_____. *Love Lies Bleeding.* London: Ipso Books, 2013. Kindle Edition.

_____. *The Moving Toyshop.* New York: Felony & Mayhem Press, 2011.

_____. *Swan Song.* London: Ipso Books, 2014. Kindle Edition.

Davis, Norbert. "Cry, Murder!" *Detective Fiction,* July 1944.

_____. *The Mouse in the Mountain.* New York: Grosset & Dunlap, 1943.

_____. *Oh, Murderer Mine.* New York: Handi-Books, 1943.

_____. *Sally's in the Alley.* New York: William Murray, 1943.

DeSilva, Bruce. "My Interview with Fellow Crime Novelist Timothy Hallinan." *Bruce DeSilva's Rogue Island.* 3 Apr. 2015. Web. 12 June 2015.

Dirda, Michael. "Edmund Crispin." In *Mystery & Suspense Writers: The Literature of Crime, Detection, and Espionage.* Vol. I. Edited by Robin W. Winks and Maureen Corrigan. New York: Scribner's, 1998: 251–58.

Dove, George N. *The Police Procedural.* Bowling Green, OH: Bowling Green University Popular Press, 1982.

Dunne, Michael, "The Comic Capers of Donald Westlake." In *Comic Crime*. Edited by Earl F. Bargainnier. Bowling Green, OH: Bowling Green State University Popular Press, 1987: 168–180.

Durant, John & Jonathan Miller, eds. *Laughing Matters: A Serious Look at Humour*. London: Longman, 1988.

Dwyer, Ciara. "Novelist: Colin Bateman." *Irish Independent*. 13 Apr. 2008. Web. 19 Oct. 2015.

Eagleton, Terry. *The Truth About the Irish*. Dublin: New Island Books. 1999.

Ebert, Roger. "The Ladykillers." rogerebert.com. 26 Mar. 2004. Web. 2 Apr. 2016.

_____. "The Thin Man." rogerebert.com. 22 Dec. 2002. Web. 11 June 2015.

Estleman, Loren D. *The Midnight Man*. New York: Pinnacle Books, 1984.

Evanovich, Janet. *Four to Score*. New York: St. Martin's Paperbacks, 1999.

_____. *High Five*. New York: St. Martin's Paperbacks, 2000.

_____. *Hot Six*. New York: St. Martin's Paperbacks, 2001.

_____. *One for the Money*. New York: HarperPaperbacks, 1995.

_____. *Seven Up*. New York: St. Martin's Paperbacks, 2002.

_____. *Three to Get Deadly*. New York: St. Martin's Paperbacks, 1998.

_____. *Two for the Dough*. New York: Pocket Books, 1996.

Fish, Robert L. *The Incredible Schlock Homes*. New York: Avon Books, 1976.

_____. *The Memoirs of Schlock Homes*. Indianapolis: Bobbs-Merrill, 1974.

Fogle, Sarah D. *Martha Grimes Walks into a Pub: Essays on a Writer with a Load of Mischief*. Jefferson, NC: McFarland, 2011.

Forbus, Jennifer. "The Faces of Brad Parks." *Jen's Book Thoughts*. 11 Dec. 2009. Web. 14 Oct. 2015.

Fowler, Christopher. *Bryant & May and the Bleeding Heart*. New York: Bantam, 2014.

_____. *Bryant & May and the Burning Man*. New York: Bantam, 2015.

_____. *Bryant & May Off the Rails*. New York: Bantam, 2010.

_____. *Bryant & May on the Loose*. New York: Bantam Paperbacks, 2010.

_____. *Full Dark House*. New York: Bantam, 2004.

_____. "Funny, How? Why Comedy Has a Place in Crime Fiction." *Mystery Fanfare*. 14 Dec. 2016. Web. 15 Dec. 2016.

_____. *The Invisible Code*. New York: Bantam, 2013.

_____. *The Memory of Blood*. New York: Bantam Paperbacks, 2013.

_____. *Ten Second Staircase*. New York: Bantam, 2006.

_____. *The Victoria Vanishes*. New York: Bantam, 2008.

Fraiberg, Allison. "Between the Laughter: Bridging Feminist Studies Through Women's Stand-Up Comedy." In *Look Who's Laughing: Gender and Comedy*. Edited by Gail Finney. Langhorne, PA: Gordon and Breach, 1994: 315–334.

France, Louise. "Murder, They Wrote." *The Observer*. guardian.co.uk. 12 June 2005. Web. 15 Dec. 2015.

Friedman, Kinky. *Armadillos & Old Lace*. New York: Simon & Schuster, 1994.

_____. *Frequent Flyer*. New York: Berkley Books, 1990.

_____. *God Bless John Wayne*. New York: Simon & Schuster, 1995.

_____. *The Mile High Club*. New York: Simon & Schuster, 2000.

_____. *The Prisoner of Vandam Street*. New York: Simon & Schuster, 2004.

_____. *Roadkill*. New York: Simon & Schuster, 1997.

_____. *Spanking Watson*. New York: Simon & Schuster, 1999.

_____. *Ten Little New Yorkers*. New York: Simon & Schuster, 2005.

Gee, Eva Tan. "Janet Evanovich." *Crime Time*. n.d. Web. 1 May 2016.

Godwin, Richard. "Chin Wag at the Slaughterhouse: Interview with Timothy Hallinan." *Welcome to the Slaughter House*. richardgodwin.net. 24 July 2011. Web. 21 July 2016.

Goudreau, Jenna. "Janet Evanovich Talks Bounty Hunters and Fifty Shades of Grey." *Forbes*. 26 June 2012. Web. 1 May 2016.

Goulart, Ron. "The Peppermint-Striped Goodbye." In *Boucher's Choicest*. Edited by Jeanne F. Bernkopf. New York: Dutton, 1969: 280–86.

Grafton, Sue. *"A" Is for Alibi.* New York: Signet, 1984.

_____. *"C" Is for Corpse.* New York: Henry Holt, 1986.

_____. *"D" Is for Deadbeat.* New York: Henry Holt, 1987.

_____. *"E" Is for Evidence.* New York: Bantam, 1989.

_____. *"F" Is for Fugitive.* New York: Henry Holt, 1989.

_____. *"G" Is for Gumshoe.* New York: Henry Holt, 1990.

_____. *"H" Is for Homicide.* New York: Henry Holt, 1991.

_____. *"J" Is for Judgment.* New York: Henry Holt, 1993.

_____. *"K" Is for Killer.* New York: Fawcett, 1995.

_____. *"L" Is for Lawless.* New York: Henry Holt, 1995.

_____. *"P" Is for Peril.* New York: Ballantine, 2002.

Grimes, Martha. *The Dirty Duck.* New York: Dell, 1990.

_____. *Help the Poor Struggler.* New York: Dell, 1986.

_____. *I Am the Only Running Footman.* New York: Dell, 1987.

_____. *Jerusalem Inn.* Boston: Little, Brown, 1984.

_____. *The Man with a Load of Mischief.* Boston: Little, Brown, 1981.

_____. *The Old Fox Deceiv'd.* Boston: Little, Brown, 1982.

_____. *Rainbow's End.* New York: Knopf, 1995.

Hall, Parnell. "Spenser's Code of Humor." In *In Pursuit of Spenser: Mystery Writers on Robert B. Parker and the Creation of an American Hero.* Edited by Otto Penzler. Dallas: BenBella Books, 2012. Kindle Edition.

Hallinan, Timothy. *Crashed.* New York: Soho Crime, 2012.

_____. *The Fame Thief.* New York: Soho Crime, 2013.

_____. *Herbie's Game.* New York: Soho Crime, 2014.

_____. *King Maybe.* New York: Soho Crime, 2016.

_____. *Little Elvises.* New York: Soho Crime, 2013.

Halpern, Daniel, ed. *Who's Writing This? Fifty-Five Writers on Humor, Courage, Self-Loathing, and the Creative Process.* New York: Harper Perennial, 2009. Kindle Edition.

Harrison, Bernice. "Dark Heart of Galway." *The Irish Times.* 18 Feb. 2006. Web. 27 Aug. 2016.

Henley, Jon. "True Crime." *The Guardian.* 18 Nov. 2004. Web. 12 Dec. 2015.

Herbert, Rosemary. *The Fatal Art of Entertainment: Interviews with Mystery Writers.* New York: G. K. Hall, 1994.

Hess, Joan. *Madness in Maggody.* New York: St. Martin's Press, 1991.

_____. *Maggody and the Moonbeams.* New York: Simon & Schuster, 2001.

_____. *Martians in Maggody.* New York: Dutton, 1994.

_____. *Miracles in Maggody.* New York: Dutton, 1995.

_____. *Misery Loves Maggody.* New York: Pocket Books, 1998.

_____. *Mortal Remains in Maggody.* MysteriousPress.com/Open Road, 2016. Kindle Edition.

_____. *Much Ado in Maggody.* New York: St. Martin's Press, 1989.

Hiaasen, Carl. *Native Tongue.* New York: Knopf, 1991.

_____. *Razor Girl.* New York: Knopf, 2016.

_____. *Skin Tight.* New York: Fawcett, 1990.

_____. *Skinny Dip.* New York: Knopf, 2004.

_____. *Star Island.* New York: Knopf, 2010.

_____. *Stormy Weather.* New York: Knopf, 1993.

_____. *Tourist Season.* New York: Warner, 1987.

High, Chris. "Interview with Joseph Wambaugh 2007." *Chris High.* chrishigh.com. 21 Nov. 2015. Web. 12 Mar. 2016.

Jacobson, Howard. "Howard Jacobson on Taking Comic Novels Seriously." *The Guardian.* 9 Oct. 2010. Web. 12 Feb. 2016.

James, Pamela. "Three to Get Deadly: An Interview with Janet Evanovich." *The Armchair Detective* 30:1 (Winter 1997): 50–52.

Johnson, Craig. *Another Man's Moccasins*. New York: Penguin, 2009.

_____. *As the Crow Flies*. New York: Penguin, 2013.

_____. *The Cold Dish*. New York: Viking, 2005.

_____. *The Dark Horse*. New York: Viking, 2009.

_____. *Death Without Company*. New York: Penguin, 2007.

_____. *Hell Is Empty*. New York: Penguin, 2012.

_____. *Junkyard Dogs*. New York: Viking, 2010.

_____. *Kindness Goes Unpunished*. New York: Viking, 2007.

_____. *A Serpent's Tooth*. New York: Viking, 2013.

_____. *Wait for Signs*. New York: Viking, 2014.

Jordan, Jon. "Colin Bateman." In *Interrogations: Author Interviews*. Lutz, FL: Down and Out Books, 2012. Kindle Edition.

Kellaway, Kate. "You Have to Make Sure Things Don't Go to Your Head." *The Guardian*. theguardian.com. 6 Mar. 2005. Web. 5 June 2016.

Kerridge, Jake. "Fred Vargas: 'I Write My Novels in Three Weeks Flat.'" *The Telegraph*. 6 Mar. 2013. Web. 21 Dec. 2015.

Latimer, Jonathan. *The Dead Don't Care*. New York: International Polygonics, 1991.

_____. *Headed for a Hearse*. New York: International Polygonics, 1990.

_____. *The Lady in the Morgue*. New York: International Polygonics, 1988.

_____. *Murder in the Madhouse*. New York: Triangle Books, 1940.

_____. *Red Gardenias*. New York: International Polygonics, 1991.

Leonard, Elmore. *Bandits*. New York: Warner, 1988.

_____. *Freaky Deaky*. New York: Arbor House, 1988.

_____. *Get Shorty*. New York: Delacorte, 1990.

_____. *Glitz*. New York: Arbor House, 1985.

_____. "Making It Up as I Go Along." *AARP Magazine*. July/August, 2009: 28–31.

_____. *Mr. Paradise*. New York: Morrow, 2004.

_____. *Pagan Babies*. New York: Delacorte, 2000.

_____. *Split Images*. New York: Arbor House, 1981.

_____. *Stick*. New York: Arbor House, 1983.

_____. *Tishomingo Blues*. New York: Morrow, 2002.

Levin, Harry. *Playboys and Killjoys: An Essay on the Theory and Practice of Comedy*. New York: Oxford University Press, 1987.

Lewis, Paul. *Comic Effects: Interdisciplinary Approaches to Humor in Literature*. New York: State University of New York Press, 1989.

Luhr, William G. *The Coen Brothers' Fargo*. New York: Cambridge University Press, 2004.

Lutz, Lisa. *Curse of the Spellmans*. New York: Simon & Schuster Paperbacks, 2009.

_____. "5 Favorite Comics." *Crimespree Magazine*. 19 July 2013. Web. 12 Jan. 2016.

_____. *The Last Word*. New York: Simon & Schuster, 2013.

_____. *Revenge of the Spellmans*. New York: Simon & Schuster Paperbacks, 2012.

_____. *The Spellman Files*. New York: Simon & Schuster, 2007.

_____. *The Spellmans Strike Again*. New York: Simon & Schuster Paperbacks, 2011.

_____. *Trail of the Spellmans*. New York: Simon & Schuster, 2012.

Marks, Steven. *Who Was That Lady? Craig Rice: The Queen of Screwball Mystery*. Delphi Books, 2010. Kindle Edition.

Marshall, William. *Far Away Man*. New York: Rinehart, 1984.

_____. *The Hatchet Man*. New York: Rinehart, 1976.

_____. *Nightmare Syndrome*. New York: Mysterious Press, 1997.

_____. *Sci Fi*. New York: Rinehart, 1981.

_____. *Skulduggery*. New York: Owl Books, 1984.

_____. *Yellowthread Street*. New York: Mysterious Press, 1988.

Mathew, David. "London in the Blood: An Interview with Christopher Fowler." *SF Site*. 2000. Web. 4 Apr. 2016.

McBain, Ed. *Ax*. New York: Signet, 1974.

_____. *Eight Black Horses.* New York: Arbor House, 1985.

_____. "The 87th Precinct." In The *Great Detectives.* Edited by Otto Penzler. New York: Penguin, 1978: 87–97.

_____. *Fat Ollie's Book.* New York: Simon & Schuster, 2002.

_____. *Fuzz.* New York: Signet, 1968.

_____. *Hail, Hail, the Gang's All Here!* New York: Signet, 1972.

_____. *Hark!* New York: Simon & Schuster, 2004.

_____. *Heat.* New York: Ballantine, 1983.

_____. *Jigsaw.* New York: Signet, 1970.

_____. *Killer's Payoff.* New York: Signet, 1974.

_____. *The Last Dance.* New York: Simon & Schuster, 1999.

_____. *So Long as You Both Shall Live.* New York: Signet, 1977.

McCall Smith, Alexander. "Author Talk." *Bookreporter.* April 2004. Web. 9 June 2016.

_____. *The Full Cupboard of Life.* New York: Pantheon, 2003.

_____. *In the Company of Cheerful Ladies.* New York: Anchor Books, 2006.

_____. *The Miracle at Speedy Motors.* New York: Pantheon, 2008.

_____. *Morality for Beautiful Girls.* New York: Anchor Books, 2002.

_____. *The No. 1 Ladies' Detective Agency.* New York: Anchor Books, 2002.

_____. *Tears of the Giraffe.* New York: Anchor Books, 2002.

McGrath, Charles. "'The Hot Kid': The Old Master." *New York Times.* 8 May 2005. Web. 5 June 2015.

Mertz, Stephen. "Captain Shaw's Hard-Boiled Boys." *The Armchair Detective* 12:3 (Summer 1979): 264–65.

Montgomery, Scott. "MysteryPeople Q&A with Craig Johnson." mysterypeople.wordpress.com. 9 May 2012. Web. 18 Mar 2016.

Moore, Clayton. "In the Company of the Cheerful Author: An Interview with Alexander McCall Smith." *Bookslut.* Oct. 2005. Web. 6 June 2016.

Morreall, John. *Humor Works.* Amherst, MA: HRD Press, 1997.

_____, ed. *The Philosophy of Laughter and Humor.* Albany: State University of New York Press, 1987.

Morreall, John, and Robert Mankoff. *Comic Relief: A Comprehensive Philosophy of Humor.* Malden, MA: Wiley Blackwell, 2009.

Nayar, Parvathi. "Life and Times of a Serial Novelist." *The Hindu: Literary Review.* 4 June 2006. Web. 5 June 2016.

Neubauer, Erica Ruth. "The Writer Should Be Invisible." *Los Angeles Review of Books.* 25 July 2014. Web. 12 June 2015.

Oring, Elliott. *Engaging Humor.* Urbana: University of Illinois Press, 2003.

O'Shannon, Dan. *What Are You Laughing At? A Comprehensive Guide to the Comedic Event.* New York: Continuum, 2012.

Padilla, Stephanie. "Interview with Craig Johnson." *New Mystery Reader.* May 2007. Web. 18 March 2016.

Palmer, Jerry. *Taking Humor Seriously.* London: Routledge, 1994.

Parker, Robert B. *A Catskill Eagle.* New York: Dell, 1985.

_____. *Early Autumn.* New York: Delacorte, 1981.

_____. *God Save the Child.* New York: Berkley, 1974.

_____. *The Godwulf Manuscript.* New York: Berkley, 1975.

_____. *The Judas Goat.* Boston: Houghton Mifflin, 1978.

_____. *Looking for Rachel Wallace.* New York: Delacorte, 1980.

_____. *Mortal Stakes.* Boston: Houghton Mifflin, 1975.

_____. *Paper Doll.* New York: Putnam, 1993.

_____. *Playmates.* New York: Berkley, 1990.

_____. *Promised Land.* Boston: Houghton Mifflin, 1976.

_____. *Small Vices.* New York: Putnam, 1997.

_____. *Stardust.* New York: Berkley, 1991.

Peary, Gerald. *Quentin Tarantino: Interviews*. Revised and Updated. Jackson: University Press of Mississippi, 2013.

Pederson, Jay P. *St. James Guide to Crime & Mystery Writers*, 4th Edition. Detroit: St. James Press, 1996.

"A Penguin Reader's Guide to *Another Man's Moccasins*." *Another Man's Moccasins*. New York: Penguin, 2009: 1–8.

"A Penguin Reader's Guide to *Death Without Company*." *Death Without Company*. New York: Penguin, 2007: 1–8.

"A Penguin Reader's Guide to *Hell Is Empty*." *Hell Is Empty*. New York: Penguin, 2012: 1–8.

Perelman, S. J. *The Most of S. J. Perelman*. New York: Simon & Schuster, 1958.

Pettengell, Michael. "Kinky Friedman." In *St. James Guide to Crime & Mystery Writers*, 4th Edition. Edited by Jay P. Pederson. Detroit: St. James Press, 1996: 387–88.

Porter, Dennis. *The Pursuit of Crime: Art and Ideology in Detective Fiction*. New Haven: Yale University Press, 1981.

Preiss, Byron, ed. *Raymond Chandler's Philip Marlowe: A Centennial Celebration*. New York: Knopf, 1988.

Pronzini, Bill. *Gun in Cheek: A Study of "Alternative" Crime Fiction*. New York: Mysterious Press, 1982.

_____. *Son of Gun in Cheek*. New York: Mysterious Press, 1987.

Rehder, Ben. "Ben Rehder—Author." benrehder.wordpress.com. n.d. Web. 10 April 2016.

_____. *Bone Dry*. New York: St. Martin's, 2003.

_____. *Buck Fever*. New York: St. Martin's, 2002.

_____. *Flat Crazy*. New York: St. Martin's, 2005.

_____. *Guilt Trip*. New York: St. Martin's, 2005.

_____. *Gun Shy*. New York: St. Martin's, 2007.

_____. *Hog Heaven*. New York: Amazon Digital Services, 2014. Kindle Edition.

_____. *Holy Moly*. New York: St. Martin's, 2008.

Reisz, Matthew J. "Fred Vargas: Digging Up the Past." *The Independent*. 10 Feb. 2006. Web. 21 Dec 2015.

Rentilly, J. "Interview #1: The Interrogation." lisalutz.com. n.d. Web. 12 July 2015.

Rice, Craig. *The Big Midget Murders*. St. Swithin Press, 2012. Kindle Edition.

_____. "Don't Go Near." Wonder eBooks, 2009. Kindle edition.

_____. *Eight Faces at Three*. Rue Morgue Press, 2011.

_____. *The Fourth Postman*. New York: Simon & Schuster, 1948.

_____. *Lucky Stiff*. Amazon Digital Services, 2016. Kindle edition.

_____. "Murder Makes Merry." In *The Art of the Mystery Story*. Edited by Howard Haycraft. New York: Carroll & Graf, 1983: 238–244.

_____. *My Kingdom for a Hearse*. New York: Bantam, 1986.

Rosh. "Interview with Christopher Fowler." *Rosh ETC*. roshetc.com. 1 April 2015. Web. 29 June 2016.

Ross, Jean W. "Interview with William Marshall." In *Contemporary Authors*, Vol. 133. Edited by Susan M. Trosky. Detroit: Gale Research, 1991: 256–59.

Roth, Philip. *Reading Myself and Others*. New York: Farrar, Straus and Giroux, 1975.

Rozovsky, Peter. "Fred Vargas: The Detectives Beyond Borders Interview, Part II." *Detectives Beyond Borders*. 14 June 2003. Web. 10 Dec. 2015.

Ruttan, Sandra. "In Conversation with Ken Bruen." *Spinetingler Magazine*, Spring 2007. Web. 1 Aug. 2015.

Sartarelli, Stephen. "Notes from the Purer Linguistic Sphere of Translation." Preface to Emanuela Gutkowski. *Does the Night Smell the Same in Italy and in English Speaking Countries? An Essay on Translation; Camilleri in English*. Enna: Ilion Books, 2009.

Schaffer, Rachel. "Armed (With Wit) and Dangerous: Sue Grafton's Sense of Black Humor." *The Armchair Detective* 30:3 (Summer 1997): 316–22.

Schickel, Richard. *Woody Allen: A Life in Film*. New York: Ivan R. Dee, 2003.

Schier, Norma. *The Anagram Detectives*. New York: Mysterious Press, 1979.

"Sherlock Uncovered." *Sherlock: Season 2.* DVD.

Silet, Charles L. P. *Talking Murder: Interviews with 20 Mystery Writers.* Princeton: Ontario Review Press, 1999.

Spencer, Ross H. *The Reggis Arms Caper.* New York: Avon, 1979.

Stasio, Marilyn. "Crime." *New York Times Book Review.* 12 June 1994. Web. 1 Aug. 2015.

Stein, Louisa Ellen and Kristina Busse. *Sherlock and Transmedia Fandom: Essays on the BBC Series.* Jefferson, NC: McFarland, 2012.

Stephenson, Mimosa. "Humor, Murder, and the Ludicrous in Human Behavior." In *Martha Grimes Walks into a Pub: Essays on a Writer with a Load of Mischief.* Edited by Sarah D. Fogle. Jefferson, NC: McFarland, 2011: 114–136.

Stott, Andrew. *Comedy.* New York: Routledge, 2005.

Stout, Rex. *All Aces: A Nero Wolfe Omnibus.* New York: Viking, 1958.

_____. *Champagne for One.* New York: Bantam, 1996.

_____. *The Golden Spiders.* New York: Bantam, 2008.

_____. *Homicide Trinity: A Nero Wolfe Threesome.* New York: Viking, 1962.

_____. *Prisoner's Base.* New York: Bantam, 1992.

_____. *The Red Box.* In *The Nero Wolfe Omnibus.* Cleveland: World Publishing, 1944.

_____. *The Second Confession.* New York: Bantam, 1995.

_____. *Some Buried Caesar.* New York: Bantam, 2008.

_____. *Three at Wolfe's Door: A Nero Wolfe Threesome.* New York: Viking, 1960.

_____. *Three Doors to Death: A Nero Wolfe Threesome.* New York: Viking, 1950.

Tanner, Stephen L. "The Function of Simile in Raymond Chandler's Novels." In *The Critical Response to Raymond Chandler.* Edited by J. K. Van Dover. Westport, CT: Greenwood, 1995: 167–175.

Thompson, Kirsten Moana. *Crime Films: Investigating the Scene.* London: Wallflower, 2007.

Thompson, Neal. "Amazon Asks: Timothy Hallinan, Author of *Herbie's Game.*" *Amazon Book Review.* omnivoracious.com. 6 Aug. 2014. Web. 18 June 2015.

Trachtenberg, Jeffrey A. "LAPD Blue." *Wall Street Journal.* 27 Nov. 2006. Web. 16 Dec. 2015.

Tuska, Jon. *The Detective in Hollywood.* Garden City, NY: Doubleday, 1978.

"Unlocking Sherlock." *Sherlock: Season 1.* DVD.

Vargas, Fred. *The Chalk Circle Man.* Translated from *L'Homme aux cercles bleus* (1996) by Sian Reynolds. New York: Penguin, 2009.

_____. *Have Mercy on Us All.* Translated from *Pars vite et reviens tard* (2001) by David Bellos. New York: Simon & Schuster, 2005.

_____. *Seeking Whom He May Devour.* Translated from *L'Homme à l'envers* (1999) by David Bellos. New York: Simon & Schuster, 2006.

_____. *This Night's Foul Work.* Translated from *Dans les bois éternals* (2006) by Sian Reynolds. New York: Penguin, 2008.

_____. *The Three Evangelists.* Translated from *Debout les morts* (1995) by Sian Reynolds. London: Vintage, 2006.

_____. *Wash This Blood Clean from My Hand.* Translated from *Sous les vents de Neptune* (2004) by Sian Reynolds. New York: Penguin, 2007.

Wambaugh, Joseph. *The Black Marble.* New York: Delacorte, 1978.

_____. *The Choirboys.* New York: Delacorte, 1975.

_____. *The Delta Star.* New York: Bantam 1984.

_____. *The Glitter Dome.* New York: Bantam, 1982.

_____. *Hollywood Station.* New York: Little Brown, 2010.

Weems, Scott. *Ha! The Science of When We Laugh and Why.* New York: Basic Books, 2014.

Weinman, Sarah. "The Idiosyncratic Interview: Alexander McCall Smith." *Confessions of an Idiosyncratic Mind.* sarahweinman.com. 20 Oct. 2004. Web. 6 June 2016.

Westlake, Donald E. *Bad News.* New York: Grand Central Publishing, 2001.

_____. *The Bank Shot.* New York: Mysterious Press, 1989.

_____. *Dancing Aztecs.* New York: M. Evans & Co, 1976.

_____. *Don't Ask.* New York: Mysterious Press, 1993.

_____. *Drowned Hopes.* New York: Mysterious Press, 1990.

_____. *The Getaway Car: A Donald E. Westlake Miscellany.* Edited by Levi Stahl. Chicago: University of Chicago Press, 2014.

_____. *Good Behavior.* New York: TOR, 1988.

_____. *Help, I Am Being Held Prisoner.* New York: Ballantine Books, 1974.

_____. *Jimmy the Kid.* New York: Mysterious Press, 1989.

_____. *Nobody's Perfect.* New York: M. Evans & Co, 1977.

_____. *Who Stole Sassi Manoon?* New York: Random House, 1969.

_____. *Why Me?* New York: MysteriousPress.com/Open Road, 2011. Kindle Edition.

White, E. B. and Katherine S. White, eds. *A Subtreasury of American Humor.* New York: Coward-McCann, 1941.

Zafon, Carlos Ruiz. "Christopher Fowler, a Very Personal Demon." *The Barcelona Review,* 1998. Web. 9 April 2016.

Index